MAKING THE DIFFERENCE?

The Irish Labour Party 1912–2012

THE EDITORS

Paul Daly is a graduate of University College Dublin and holds a Masters degree in Political Communication from Dublin City University. He formerly worked in the Labour Party Press Office. In November 2008 his book *Creating Ireland* – a history of Irish parliamentary debates – was published. He currently manages his own communications consultancy in Dublin and lectures part-time in Dublin City University.

Rónán O'Brien joined the Labour Party in 1989 while studying history and politics at University College Dublin. He was Chef de Cabinet to Ruairi Quinn TD as leader of the Labour Party between 1997 and 2002. He has a particular interest in early twentieth-century Irish history and has contributed a number of articles on this era to 'An Irishman's Diary' in *The Irish Times*.

Paul Rouse, formerly of Prime Time in RTÉ, has written extensively on Irish history and on the GAA. He teaches history at UCD and is co-author of *Handling Change – A History of the Irish Bank Officials' Association* with Mark Duncan. He co-authored *The GAA – A People's History* (2009) and *The GAA – County by County* (2011) with Mark Duncan and Mike Cronin.

MAKING THE DIFFERENCE?

The Irish Labour Party 1912–2012

Edited by
PAUL DALY, RÓNÁN O'BRIEN & PAUL ROUSE

The Collins Press

FIRST PUBLISHED IN 2012 BY
The Collins Press
West Link Park
Doughcloyne
Wilton
Cork

British Library Cataloguing in Publication Data

Making the difference? : the Irish Labour Party, 1912-2012.
1. Labour Party (Ireland)—History. 2. Political parties—
Ireland History—20th century. 3. Political parties—
Ireland—History—21st century. 4. Ireland—Politics and
government—1922- 5. Ireland—Politics and government—
1910-1921.
I. Daly, Paul, 1971- II. O'Brien, Ronan. III. Rouse, Paul.
324.2'41707-dc23
ISBN-13: 9781848891425

Typesetting by The Collins Press
Typeset in Bembo

Cover image: A 1990s Labour Party poster designed by Brian Dennington.

CONTENTS

ABBREVIATIONS

AC	Administrative Council
ANV	Alliance for a No Vote
CCCA	Cork City & County Archives
CPGB	Communist Party of Great Britain
DL	Democratic Left
ECB	European Central Bank
EEC	European Economic Community
FIDAC	International Federation of Ex-Servicemen
GPB	General Prisons Board
ICTU	Irish Congress of Trade Unions
ILLA	Irish Land and Labour Association
ILO	International Labour Organisation
ILP	Irish Labour Party
IMF	International Monetary Fund
IRB	Irish Republican Brotherhood
ITGWU	Irish Transport and General Workers' Union
ITUC	Irish Trades Union Congress
ITUC&LP	Irish Trades Union Congress & Labour Party
ITWU	Irish Textile Workers' Union
IWFL	Irish Women's Franchise League
IWLM	Irish Women's Liberation Movement
IWWU	Irish Women's Workers' Union
LCLL	Liaison Committee of the Labour Left
LWNC	Labour Women's National Council
MEP	Member of the European Parliament
NAI	National Archives of Ireland
NDC	National Development Corporation
NLI	National Library of Ireland
PDs	Progressive Democrats

PLP	Parliamentary Labour Party
SDLP	Social Democratic Labour Party
SEA	Single European Act
SFIO	French Section of the Workers' International (Section Française de l'Internationale Ouvrière)
SIPTU	Services Industrial Professional and Technical Union
SLP	Socialist Labour Party
SPD	Social Democratic Party (Sozialdemokratische Partei Deutschlands)
TNA	The (British) National Archives
TOAI	Textile Operatives Association of Ireland
TUC	Trades Union Congress
UCD	University College Dublin
UCDA	University College Dublin Archives
USNA	United States National Archives
WSPU	Women's Social and Political Union

ACKNOWLEDGEMENTS

IT HAS BEEN a pleasure to put this book together and in the process we incurred many debts of gratitude. First and foremost we are greatly indebted to the authors of the various chapters. That people should so willingly have given up their free time to contribute without (material) reward to this project is greatly appreciated. As the centenary of the foundation of the Labour Party loomed ever larger, the response to tightening deadlines was marked with diligence and forbearance. We thank all who contributed for their scholarship and we hope they are pleased with the final result.

All at The Collins Press were supportive of this project from the outset. In the tradition of these things, we sought to try their patience as often as possible. It is a credit to their team that this book was published in such short order and to such a high standard.

The original discussions on the ideas that led to his book were initiated by Mark Garrett, Chef de Cabinet to the Labour Party leader. Thanks are due to Eamon Gilmore, in particular, for his contribution and to others, including Colm O'Reardon and David Leach, who offered encouragement and comment along the way. Tom Butler, Angus Laverty and Pat Magner generously took the time to read and comment on the text, as did Eoin Kinsella of UCD.

Finally – and on a personal note – huge thanks to Nuala Egan; Cáit, Éilis and Joe Rouse; Eileen Reilly and Áine O'Brien.

Paul Daly, Rónán O'Brien and Paul Rouse

INTRODUCTION

AFFORDING A TITLE to a collection of essays as diverse as those gathered here is no easy task. After some soul searching, the editors settled on *Making the Difference?* This title is derived from the party's 1997 election slogan 'Making The Vital Difference' – the election following what was arguably the party's most successful period in government and the occasion of one of its greatest electoral setbacks. Such has been the Labour Party's first hundred years.

'Making the difference?' also encapsulates an important aspect of what it means to have been a member of the Labour Party at any stage during the past ten decades. To join the Labour Party is, in itself, an act of difference. While criticism of the party's successes and failures abound, and are certainly included in this volume, the Labour Party's intent has always been to change Ireland. At its best the party has argued for the Ireland that might be, rather than accept an Ireland as it is or romanticise a mythic Ireland of the past. For that reason alone, many of Labour's successes – the liberalisation of society, for instance – have been achieved both outside and inside government.

Underpinning the party's first century has been a desire to make a difference through an idea – or more properly a set of ideas – which has evolved over time. At their core these ideas imagined Ireland as a society defined by equality, justice and tolerance. It is the nobility of these ideas, and the vision which flows from them, that has attracted generations of Irish people to the Labour Party and has brought such people to toil in its service, often without reward and often, too, in the face of cynicism and criticism. It is why the party survived in arid times.

This book does not, of course, offer a detailed narrative account of the events than happened in and around the Labour Party over the course of its first hundred years. Indeed, a perusal of the chapter themes may point to some notable absences, such as the party's relationship with the trade unions or its seminal achievements in the sphere of education. There are also many contributors who, perhaps, should have been included: Labour has never wanted for writers.

However, the aim of this book is to look at aspects of the history of the party from a host of different perspectives. The result is a spectrum of opinions from historians, political scientists, journalists, elected representatives and party members. Whether the project lives up to its ambition is for the reader to judge. While proud of its past and at times frustrated at how its contribution is often written out of history, the party did not want to perpetrate an 'official' history – bland and sanitised as they inevitably come.

The origins of this volume come from within the Labour Party itself. Indeed, the idea of a diverse collection of essays to mark the party's centenary originated from within the party leader's office. However, it evolved into an 'unauthorised' project, compiled without input or direction from the party, precisely because this degree of editorial independence was necessary to ensure the contribution of as talented and broad a collection of voices as came on board. That the Labour Party should welcome such an acute and, at times, critical analysis of its past is a tribute to its long-standing and occasionally problematic respect for diversity of opinion.

Inevitably, there are opinions expressed in the chapters that follow with which many people – both inside and outside the Labour Party – will disagree. More than that, some of these opinions will, most likely, infuriate, frustrate and displease. It would not be the Labour Party, if that were not the case. Fergus Finlay, who has been an advisor to two party leaders, Dick Spring and Pat Rabbitte, tells a story of the party membership's capacity for self-criticism. It goes something like this:

> Upon reading criticism of the party in national newspapers, members of Fianna Fáil would likely as not burn editions of the paper at cumainn meetings and demand the resignation of the editor. Fine Gael members faced with a similar dilemma would write long and worthy letters to the paper defending their party. Labour members, however, would move immediately to table motions of no confidence in the party leader!

One of the central theses of Irish political life has been that the Labour Party has not risen to the heights of other social democratic parties across Europe, so much so that former General Secretary Brendan Halligan countered that to survive at all in the climate in which the party had to operate was a success in itself. The former opinion is, in part, based on a starry-eyed view of the success of parties far away – take the unflattering first forty years of the British Labour Party as a case in point – and on definitions of political achievement that equate progress solely with electoral success.

Perhaps Brendan Halligan's hurdle is a low one, but this series of essays does set out the difficult environment in which the party had to develop and which it has largely overcome. Only in recent years, for example, has Labour's role in ensuring parliamentary democracy during the early years of the state received credit. The achievement of 'success', too, is a more difficult one for a party that sets its goal as the transformation of society rather than short-term electoral victory. Indeed, many of the failings of the Labour Party – sometimes too timid, sometimes too acquiescent, sometimes too short-sighted – are wider failings of Irish society.

But Labour, too, can also claim to have contributed to many of Ireland's successes. To put the scale of Ireland's progress over the past hundred years in context, when the Party was founded in 1912, Ireland was part of the United Kingdom, isolated on the periphery of Europe, with an economy dominated by agriculture and a society dominated by subservience to a controlling and authoritarian religion. The story of the last hundred years has been the transformation of those features of Irish life; this is a process to which the Labour Party and its members have contributed in large measure.

In short, Ireland in 2012 is a fairer, more inclusive and tolerant society. The Labour Party's role in bringing about this change is as great, if not greater, than most. As Eamon Gilmore points out in his epilogue, which looks forward to the next hundred years, there is much still to do.

The problems that confront this country now may at times resemble, in magnitude at least, the economic, social and political problems that confronted a generation a century ago. Then as now, there was a body of Irish people who believed that politics was not just about victory or defeat, personal advancement or party decline. They believed that politics is about a set of ideas – equality, justice and tolerance. These ideas are still the common thread that binds together the Irish Labour Party, and they are ideas that will have a central place in the Ireland of the twenty-first century.

1. A Various and Contentious Country: Ireland in 1912

William Murphy

In 1912 it seemed obvious to many that Ireland was a country in the throes of significant change. Streets, meeting rooms, workplaces, newspaper offices, homes, theatres, indeed individuals, were animated with the energy of sometimes contending, sometimes complementary, social, cultural and political movements. In a frequently cited speech of 1913, W. B. Yeats argued that there 'is a moment in the history of every nation when it is plastic, when it is like wax, when it is ready to hold for generations the shape that is given it. Ireland is plastic now and will be for a few years to come ...'[1] The decision taken by the Irish Trades Union Congress at Clonmel on 28 May 1912 'that the independent representation of Labour upon all public boards' should be among its objectives, a decision that signalled the birth of the Labour Party,[2] was a product of that energy and the prevailing sense of possibility. It was a declaration by the trade union movement – or more accurately by some within that movement – that they intended to influence the shape of Irish society using district council room, city hall and, most importantly, the anticipated Home Rule parliament. Others in this book will concentrate on the direct circumstances of the foundation of the Labour Party. The purpose of this essay is to give that decision some context by offering a short, inevitably partial, introduction to that apparently plastic place, Ireland in 1912.

I

In December 1912 the Ulster Literary Theatre staged a play by Gerald

4

MacNamara called *Thompson in Tír-na-nÓg*. It told the story of Andy Thompson, a loyal Orangeman, who is blown into Tír-na-nÓg when his rifle explodes during a re-creation of the Battle of the Boyne. There he meets the heroes of Irish myth and a comedy of mutual incomprehension ensues. The play was a warning against the dangers of a contemporary politics bolstered by 'essentialist' and 'nostalgic' versions of history.[3] Just such a politics seemed to be tightening its grip on Ireland in response to the most widely expected, and widely feared, development of 1912: the introduction of the third Home Rule Bill, which provided for limited self-government for Ireland. The legislative path to Home Rule had opened when the Parliament Act, which limited the powers of the House of Lords, received royal assent on 18 August 1911. In the early months of 1912, the Liberal government and their Irish Party allies discussed the detail of the Home Rule Bill and it was introduced on 11 April. Nationalist public opinion seems to have been marked by complacency in the months prior to the opening of parliamentary debate. The *Cork Examiner* expressed this in the confident assertion that 'History repeats itself; and despite the threats of the Ascendancy class, Home Rule is as certain as Church disestablishment, land reform and franchise extension'.[4] The Irish Party attempted to generate, and put on display, widespread nationalist enthusiasm through a mass Home Rule demonstration in Dublin on 31 March and a Home Rule convention on 23 April. Despite these events, historians have noted the continued lack of dynamism that marked popular support for Home Rule during 1912.[5]

In contrast, unionist apprehension was rapidly transformed into action. The primary organisational vehicle for unionist resistance was a network of Unionist Clubs that swelled from 164 in December 1911 to 316 in August 1912. By May, some of these clubs had begun to drill and to establish associated rifle clubs. So too had some Orange Lodges.[6] In June, an amendment to the Home Rule Bill, proposing the exclusion of counties Antrim, Armagh, Londonderry and Down, was defeated after an acrimonious debate, but the opponents of the Bill continued to ratchet up the pressure. Andrew Bonar Law, leader of the Conservative Party, told an anti-Home Rule demonstration at Blenheim Palace that the Bill was the product of 'a corrupt Parliamentary bargain' and that Ulster unionists 'would be justified in resisting by all means in their power, including force'. He continued, 'under the present conditions I can imagine no length of resistance to which Ulster will go in which I shall not be ready to support them'.[7] The intimidating mobilisation of unionist resistance reached a popular crescendo with Ulster Day, on 28 September, when well over 200,000 men signed Ulster's Solemn League and Covenant in which they pledged to use 'all means that may be found necessary to defeat the present conspiracy to set up a Home Rule parliament in Ireland'. A similar number of women signed a declaration associating themselves with 'the men of Ulster'.

Wild rumour, millennialist prediction and spurious allegation had become commonplace. One of the more unusual outcomes of this was a court case heard in Edinburgh in March 1912 when Robert Browne, the Catholic Bishop of Cloyne, and six of his diocesan priests sued the *Dundee Courier* for libel. They sought £2,000 in damages for the bishop and £500 for each priest because in an article published on 1 August 1911, under the headline 'Sinister Sidelights on Home Rule', the *Courier* alleged that they had used their influence with Catholic businessmen and traders in the town of Queenstown (Cobh), County Cork, to secure the dismissal of all Protestant employees. It further alleged that when one trader refused to comply they had ruined his business. Browne travelled to Edinburgh to give evidence on his own behalf, bringing with him various Irish Party MPs, a collection of the respectable citizens of Queenstown (both Catholic and Protestant) and an assortment of well-disposed Protestants from Limerick, Cork and Dublin to testify on his behalf. Browne and the priests won the case: he was awarded £200 and each priest £50.[8]

That summer, the heightened tension expressed itself in violence on the streets. On 29 June 1912, a Sunday school outing from Whitehouse Presbyterian Church in Belfast was attacked at Castledawson, County Derry, by a group of (allegedly drunken) members of the Ancient Order of Hibernians. The Hibernians were returning from a Home Rule meeting at Maghera when, apparently, one of their number took offence at a Union Jack carried by the Sunday school children as they 'processed' through the town, sparking a violent confrontation.[9] In Belfast, fuelled by accounts of Castledawson, July was marked by serious sectarian rioting and the expulsion of thousands of shipyard workers, mostly Catholics. News of this provoked some in southern counties to campaign for a boycott of Belfast manufacturers.[10] When, a few weeks into the new football season on 14 September, Belfast Celtic and Linfield met at Celtic Park, a full scale riot saw over fifty people admitted to hospital, some with gunshot wounds.[11] Despite this atmosphere nationalists and unionists continued to cooperate in matters of mutual interest. When the English Board of Agriculture introduced regulations to restrict the import of Irish cattle, following an outbreak of foot-and-mouth in Ireland in the summer of 1912, unionists and nationalists combined in condemnation.[12]

Matt Kelly and James McConnel have explored the manner in which Fenian sentiment found expression and, indeed, former Fenians found a place on the benches of Redmond's Parnellite party of the 1890s and the reunited Irish Party of the first decade of the twentieth century.[13] This 'domestication' of Fenianism was not, however, complete or secure. In the vituperative and increasingly polarised atmosphere of 1912, Home Rule – an attempt to forge a constitutional framework that rendered Irish nationalism compatible with the link to Britain and the Empire – was increasingly vulnerable to simpler, more extreme, perhaps more coherent ideologies. In 1912, the primary threat seemed to come from irredentist unionism. Manifestations of Irish nationalism that were more radical than the Irish Party remained, on the face of it, marginal and organisationally weak, but the longer Home Rule was deferred and the more bellicose unionism became, the more fertile the ground for more radical expressions of Irish nationalism. As Michael Wheatley has demonstrated, many of the Irish Party's own supporters continued to be less comfortable with the idea of Empire and the language of compromise than John Redmond and some of his allies within the leadership had become.[14] In the same month as the introduction of the Home Rule Bill, the Abbey Theatre staged the premiere of *Patriots* by Lennox Robinson. The play told the story of a Fenian, James Nugent, who returns to his home town after nearly two decades in prison for a 'political murder'. Nugent finds a public that is willing to celebrate him for his prison suffering but has little interest in his efforts to promote a re-invigorated radical separatism. This seemed an accurate enough assessment of the contemporary political scene on Robinson's part, although critics noted that the Abbey audience seemed not only to sympathise with the fictional Fenian, but to approve of his uncompromising rhetoric.[15]

Non-fictional Fenians were busily reorganising the Irish Republican Brotherhood (IRB). In the early months of 1912 and after a bitter struggle, a faction centred on Tom Clarke and consisting of a young, energetic and militant cohort that included Seán MacDermott, Denis McCullough, Bulmer Hobson and Patrick McCartan seized control of the IRB's supreme council and of its newspaper, *Irish Freedom*. Matt Kelly, again, has offered an interesting analysis of this group's thinking as reflected in the pages of *Irish Freedom*: it was then edited by Hobson. Just as the prospect of Home Rule prompted some in the labour movement to advocate the establishment of a political party, so too the newly dominant faction within the IRB began to consider a republican party which would engage in electoral politics under a Home Rule dispensation. The aim of this party, they suggested, should be to expose Home Rule and its creators as imperialist sell-outs. If, on the other hand, Home Rule failed, *Irish Freedom* insisted 'our work will be destructive and will be an attack all along the line on every English institution in Ireland'.[16] Simultaneously, in the summer of 1912, *Irish Freedom* began to promote the establishment of Freedom Clubs by those who shared the paper's ideals. It is possible that Hobson imagined these clubs would provide a foundation for the mooted post-Home Rule republican party. Within months, clubs were formed in Belfast, Dublin, Sligo, Galway and Maryborough, County Laois.[17]

That Hobson should contemplate a new political party was, perhaps, not that surprising. In 1905, along with McCullough, he had established the Dungannon Clubs. These had later combined with other groups, including Arthur Griffith's National Council, to form Sinn Féin. Hobson and McCullough left Sinn Féin in 1910 and had since concentrated their energies on the IRB; however, they had no objection in principle to separatists' participation in electoral politics. Having been a growing, if small, organisation between 1907 and 1909, Sinn Féin then began to decline. By 1912 it seemed to be nearing extinction.[18] At the municipal elections of January 1912, Seán T. O'Kelly did take a seat on Dublin Corporation on a Sinn Féin ticket (for the Inns Quay ward) but the party did not muster a candidate, never mind a victory, in any of the nineteen other wards they could have contested in the city.[19] In contrast, labour had a good election in Dublin as five of the seven candidates for the corporation, behind whom the *Irish Worker* threw its weight, won. Elsewhere, there were occasional labour victories, including in Sligo, Waterford and Drogheda. Jim Larkin was among labour's victors in Dublin, although he would be removed from the seat within months, on the grounds that he was a convicted felon of recent vintage.[20]

The year 1912 also saw the election of a woman to Dublin Corporation for the first time. Although she was not an official 'labour' candidate, Sarah Cecilia Harrison's victory was celebrated by the *Irish Worker*.[21] The better relief of the unemployed had been a major plank of Harrison's campaign in the South City Ward and, once in office, she embarked upon a crusade challenging the operation of the Distress Committee of Dublin Corporation. That body, which had been established in 1906 under the terms of the Unemployed Workmen's Act of 1905, was a mechanism for keeping a register of the city's unemployed and offering relief. Harrison alleged that it was operating corruptly and inefficiently, and succeeded in forcing a public inquiry which met in August and September 1912.[22] Although the inquiry rejected many of Harrison's charges, her campaign highlighted the plight of the unemployed at a time of 'chronic unemployment, particularly among building workers and general labourers', following an apparent collapse in the city's building industry from around 1906.[23]

Harrison, like Dr Mary Strangman who became the first woman elected to Waterford Corporation in January 1912,[24] was a campaigner for female suffrage. Although women could vote at, and contest, local government elections by 1912, they were still denied the parliamentary franchise. The emergence in Britain in 1903 of the Women's Social and Political Union (WSPU) marked the beginning of a militant campaign for female suffrage which involved, among other tactics, the breaking of windows in public buildings, politicians' homes and shops. These actions led to the imprisonment of suffragettes (as the militants were known) and, beginning in 1909, these women embarked upon a campaign of hunger strike, demanding treatment as political prisoners.[25] Initially, Irish suffragism did not respond to this development, remaining comparatively moderate. Even after the establishment of the avowedly militant Irish Women's Franchise League (IWFL) in November 1908, Irish suffragists refrained from militant acts on Irish soil.

In 1912, however, this changed dramatically when, on the morning of 13 June, eight women threw stones through the windows of various government offices in Dublin and were arrested.[26] The women acted then because they were angered at the contribution of Irish Party MPs to the recent defeat of the Conciliation Bill, a bill that provided for a limited female parliamentary franchise, and because of the Irish Party's failure to insist that the female franchise should be included in the Home Rule Bill.[27] From May 1912, with the establishment of the *Irish Citizen*, they also had a weekly paper with which to put their case to the public. The IWFL women were soon joined in Mountjoy by three members of the WSPU. They had followed Prime Minister Herbert Asquith to Ireland – he was on a visit to Dublin to speak at a Home Rule event on 18 July – and succeeded in throwing a hatchet at him and Redmond before attempting to set the Theatre Royal ablaze.[28] The suffragette prisoners would garner some public sympathy when, in August, they embarked upon the first 'political' hunger strike in Ireland during the twentieth century,[29] but in the immediate aftermath of the attack on Asquith and Redmond Irish public opinion was demonstratively anti-suffragette. Suspected suffragists were attacked in the streets and Francis Sheehy-Skeffington reported to his wife, Hanna, who was in Mountjoy, that when they organised a rally at the Phoenix Park, on 28 July, an 'enormous and entirely hostile crowd' gathered and engaged in 'organised & continuous howling ... Even I, standing behind the bench close by the speakers, could not hear a word they said.' Among the speakers at the meeting was James Connolly. He insisted 'that free speech was involved, and that this crowd might be turned on labour meetings any time'. Sheehy-Skeffington contrasted this with Jim Larkin's failure to offer support.[30] At Trade Union Congress in May, however, Larkin, with Connolly, had proposed a motion calling for full adult suffrage. When a delegate of the bookbinders' union had objected, warning that female suffrage would end peaceful 'home life' and see 'the destruction of the nobility of character for which their women were prized' his comments were rebutted by Connolly and Mary Galway, general secretary of the Textile Operatives Association of Ireland (TOAI). The motion was carried.[31]

At that Congress, Galway and Connolly were more often at odds. During the previous autumn a dispute had arisen between them when Connolly organised female linen workers in Belfast into a new union called the Irish Textile Workers' Union (ITWU), beginning with a group at the York Street mill. Galway regarded Connolly as 'an adventurer' encroaching upon her territory and sought redress, first, at the Belfast Trades Council, and later at Congress in 1912. In turn, Connolly and others accused Galway and the TOAI of failing to cater for many mill workers.[32] The 1912 Congress also saw the affiliation of the Irish Women's Workers' Union (IWWU) represented by its general secretary Delia Larkin. Like the ITWU, the IWWU was established in autumn 1911 and it too aroused suspicion among existing trade unions, fearing the loss of members to the new 'catch-all' organisation.[33]

II

The IWWU's one big brother, the Irish Transport and General Workers' Union (ITGWU), was busy getting bigger in 1912. In 1911, and again in 1913, the growth of syndicalist militancy was evident in a series of bitter strikes. In comparison, 1912 was quiet, as if the 'Labour movement was pausing to catch its second wind'.[34] The concern that the apparent rise of socialist and syndicalist ideas prompted in some quarters is evident, however, in 1912. In January, in the *Irish Ecclesiastical Record*, John MacCaffrey ended his review of the year just gone with the warning that 'Ireland has a labour problem of its own which requires solution, and is likely also soon to have a Socialist group of its own compensating themselves for the smallness of their numbers by the extreme violence of their theories'.[35] Several Catholic bishops used their Lenten pastorals to warn against 'the mania for organising strikes'[36] and the most popular Irish novelist of the era, Canon P. A. Sheehan, responded with the publication of *Miriam Lucas*, a preposterously plotted tale in which striking was portrayed as a misguided tactic that played into the hands of the employer while workers' grievances were constructed as largely imagined, inculcated by false leaders spreading false ideologies.[37] Soon there was talk among Catholics, influenced by ideas of Catholic action, of establishing a Leo Social Guild 'which seeks to form study circles of workmen and students of all classes for the understanding and application of Catholic principles to social evils'.[38]

But it was the alleged combined danger posed by modern literature and the British press that really generated action among Catholic conservatives in 1912. The final months of 1911 had seen a campaign in Limerick city against newsagents who sold certain English Sunday newspapers and the establishment of the Dublin Vigilance Committee with the purpose of protecting people of that city from the 'insidious attempts of modern journalism to corrupt them'.[39] For obvious reasons, the *Freeman's Journal* and the *Irish Independent* gave a good deal of publicity to this movement and, on 4 January 1912, the Executive Council of the Dublin Vigilance Committee wrote to the *Irish Independent*, claiming that 187 newsagents in Dublin had signed undertakings not to sell 'objectionable newspapers'.[40] Further vigilance committees were founded in that year, encouraged by the Catholic hierarchy in their Lenten pastorals.[41] On 1 July the Lord Mayor of Dublin, Lorcan Sherlock, hosted a large meeting at the Mansion House to encourage the movement. The Lord Lieutenant, Lord Aberdeen, addressed the meeting and messages of support from the Pope and Cardinal Logue were read: Logue informed the attendees that 'no protest can be too strong and no vigilance can be too great to protect our people from the plague of dangerous and unclean publications'.[42]

Beginning in February 1912, the *Catholic Bulletin*, which was influential in its promotion of a particular brand of extreme Catholic nationalism, began to publish a regular item entitled 'Notices of Books Approved as Suitable for Libraries', dividing these books into three categories:

Class A – Books written by *Catholics* for *Catholic* youth, with a *direct* religious or moral tendency.

Class B – Books written by *Catholics* to interest youthful readers, with no *direct* religious or moral aim. Books of 'Historical' or 'Adventure' class, written in a healthy *Catholic* tone, with little or nothing of a sentimental character about them.

Class C – Books of the 'Historical' or 'Adventure' class, written by non-Catholics, but with no anti-Catholic bias or sectarian opinions of any kind; books of a negative character as regards religion, inculcating merely natural virtues of manliness, courage, honesty, truth; written in a healthy style, with no sentimentalism unless introduced in a harmless, passing way.[43]

James Joyce's final, futile efforts during the summer of 1912 to persuade George Roberts at Maunsel & Co. to proceed with the publication of *Dubliners* were almost certainly hampered by the atmosphere generated by this campaign against 'pernicious' literature.[44] The *Catholic Bulletin's* concern to influence the stock of libraries, in particular, was a response to the opening of a wave of libraries during the preceding decade. These libraries were established at local initiative and many were funded by the Scottish-born, American industrialist and philanthropist Andrew Carnegie. In 1912, such libraries opened at Cabinteely, Garristown and Kingstown (Dún Laoghaire) in Dublin while district councils in west Limerick announced their intention to open Carnegie-supported libraries at Athea, Broadford, Cloncagh and Feenagh.[45] These institutions did not always prosper, but (however temporarily) the access to books they provided transformed the lives of ordinary people in many small towns, villages and suburbs.

In this period, Irish cities and towns also witnessed the emergence and rapid proliferation of cinemas. James Joyce was manager of the first stationary cinema in Ireland, the Volta Electric Theatre, when it opened on Mary Street, Dublin, in December 1909. As with many early cinemas, that building had been converted from a previous use. In the case of the Volta, the building had been the premises of a builder and ironmonger. The first purpose-built cinema, the Phoenix Picture Palace, was officially opened on 3 December 1912 on Ellis Quay, Dublin. The 'spacious auditorium' seated 730 patrons.[46] By 1916, 149 cinemas and halls were listed as 'showing motion pictures'.[47] If popular culture was in the process of profound transformation under the influence of technological innovation, then the changing face of popular culture was, in turn, recorded using new technologies. The Munster hurling final of 1912 between Cork and Tipperary at Dungarvan was filmed by 'cinematograph operators', the film to be shown in America.[48] Mark Duncan has noted that in these years the somewhat older technology of photography recorded the emergence of county colours within the GAA. Throughout 1912 the *Gaelic Athlete*, a newspaper which was established in that year to promote Gaelic games, mounted a campaign, urging all county boards to switch from the practice of fielding the county team in the colours of their champion club and instead to decide upon county patterns that would remain in place, year in year out. The great Kilkenny team that dominated hurling in that era won the 1909 All-Ireland in the colours of Tullaroan, but they wore new 'Kilkenny' jerseys in winning three-in-a-row between 1911 and 1913. Quickly, this became standard practice.[49] Modern grounds and improved transportation were keys to the growing crowds in attendance at sporting fixtures. According to Neal Garnham, when Shelbourne Football Club opened a new ground in 1912 the fact that it was 'just a penny tram fare' from the centre of Dublin was considered a considerable advantage.[50]

Although sport, and the Gaelic Athletic Association in particular, prospered in rural Ireland, urbanisation was a key to the development of modern sport in this era, and Ireland, as with much of Europe, was an increasingly urban society. According to Cormac Ó Grada, between the Great Famine and the outbreak of the First World War the proportion of Ireland's population living in towns or cities with populations of 2,000 people or more increased from one-seventh to one-third.[51] The extent to which the Irish urbanised in the sixty years prior to 1912 is even more striking when those who had migrated from rural Ireland to the great cities of the USA's east coast and the industrial centres of Britain are taken into account. In 1912, more than 29,000 men and women emigrated: there had been only two years since 1851 when the figure leaving was lower.[52] In Ireland, Belfast had grown with a singular rapidity: its population in 1851 was 97,784, rising to 386,947 in 1911.[53] By then, Harland & Wolff and Workman Clark, the biggest shipbuilding firms in Belfast, were producing over 150,000 tons between them annually.[54] Infamously, of course, 1912 was the year in which the most famous product of Belfast's shipyards, the *Titanic*, sank on its maiden voyage.

In comparison, Dublin's growth had been sluggish, so much so that 'the deposed capital', as Mary E. Daly called it, was outstripped in population terms by Belfast; Dublin grew from 246,465 in 1851 to 304,802 in 1911. The populations of Cork and Limerick actually contracted during the period, although these declines were smaller than those evident in Galway city and, more importantly, rural Ireland.[55] Increased suburbanisation was a common trend in these cities. Even in Limerick, with its declining population, the city's footprint increased as a significant proportion of the middle classes moved to new suburbs.[56] Many poorer city dwellers, however, continued to live in city centre slums. In Belfast in 1901 as few as 1 per cent of families lived in one-room tenements, but in Cork the figure was 11 per cent and in Dublin it was a staggering 36 per cent.[57] In 1911, the number of families in Dublin living in the poorest category of housing, fourth class accommodation, was 20,564.[58] This contributed to Dublin's failure to match the improvement in mortality experienced by equivalent British cities during the late nineteenth and early twentieth centuries. In 1905 Dublin had a death rate per thousand of 22.3 whereas for Liverpool the figure was 19.6, for Birmingham it was 16.2 and for London it was 15.6.[59]

The contribution of tuberculosis to this figure began to receive greater attention in the first decade of the twentieth century. Campaigns aimed at preventing 'the contamination of public and private spaces by the human tuberculosis sufferer' were mounted by the National Association for the Prevention of Tuberculosis and Consumption (branches of which were established in Dublin and Belfast in 1899) and the Women's National Health Association, founded by Lady Aberdeen in 1907.[60] The isolation of sufferers in sanatoria was forwarded as the most effective answer to the problem and 1912 saw the opening of Peamount Sanatorium in south county Dublin. Sanatoria had opened at Whiteabbey, just outside Belfast, in 1906, Buttevant, County Cork, in 1910 and at Crooksling, also in south county Dublin, in 1911, while others would open at Armagh, Dungannon, Cloonanhan, Roscrea, and Monaghan before 1920.[61] The foundation of these specialist institutions was facilitated by legislation introduced by the Liberal government in 1908 and 1911. That government was in the process of rapidly transforming the relationship between the state and the citizen by instituting a wide-ranging programme of welfare reform. Most famously, in 1908 they introduced old-age pensions for those over seventy and in 1911 a system of unemployment and health insurance.[62] The government had underestimated the extraordinary impact in Ireland of the introduction of old-age pensions; by March 1912, 205,317 Irish people were in receipt of such pensions, constituting 21.8 per cent of all those receiving pensions in the United Kingdom.[63] The National Insurance Act of 1911 was not delivered through the establishment of a vast state bureaucracy, but by cooperation between the state and a network of 'approved societies'. By 1912, around 675,000 Irish people were members of such societies, the biggest of which was the Ancient Order of Hibernians.[64]

Alongside these emergent, modern systems of welfare and health existed older practices and attitudes. On 7 December a jury at the Munster Assizes acquitted Thomas Burke, a Clare farmer and 'bone-setter', of manslaughter. He was prosecuted when a man named John Sullivan, whom he had treated, died of complications from a leg injury. A doctor gave evidence that Burke was guilty of 'gross negligence' and this had caused Sullivan's death, but Burke claimed that although he had in this instance made a mistake he was experienced at setting fractures. Burke's acquittal suggests that for many bone-setting was still regarded as a legitimate practice while the judge certainly influenced the jury when he commented that 'Clare farmers look twice at a halfpenny before they would spend it, and they are slow to give money to a doctor, a lawyer, or their priests'.[65]

The farmers of Clare may have been careful with their money, but the living standards of farmers in rural Ireland had increased significantly since the Great Famine as a consequence of changed fertility and inheritance patterns, consistent emigration and reforms in land distribution and ownership facilitated by a series of Land Acts introduced from the 1880s. This transfer of land had accelerated greatly following the Wyndham Land Act of 1903; according to Diarmaid Ferriter, 3 per cent of rural dwellers were owner occupiers in 1870, by 1906 this figure was 29.2 per cent, and by 1916 it had increased again to 63.9 per cent.[66] In the years 1911–12 and 1912–13 alone a combined total of over 1.5 million acres was purchased by tenants.[67] Eventually, this created a conservative rural polity of small farmers, but during the process it generated huge potential for unrest and radical activity among those rural dwellers (well over a third in 1912) who remained tenants or landless labourers. This was evidenced in the Ranch War of 1904–08, in the large-scale land agitations that took place during 1917–18, and again during the Civil War.[68]

It was also evidenced in the enormous growth of the ITGWU in rural Ireland and a wave of strikes for better pay among agricultural labourers, particularly in the years 1917–19.[69] By 1911, David Fitzpatrick has argued, the Irish agricultural labourer was a member of a much reduced and deeply discontented class, earning 'much less than his English counterpart and absurdly less than his relatives employed in foreign cities'.[70] Unlike his Dublin counterpart, however, the accommodation available to agricultural labourers was improving rapidly at this point as a consequence of the Labourers' (Ireland) Act, 1906, which provided significant funding for the construction of labourers' cottages. In 1912 alone, 39,241 such cottages were constructed, most of these in Munster and Leinster.[71]

In late August 1912, the press reported daily on the consequences of a particularly wet and cold summer. In various parts of the country, houses were flooded, a little boy was swept away by the Tolka River in Dublin, sporting fixtures were disrupted, bogs were on the move, crops were in danger, and food prices were on the increase.[72] This is a reminder of the truth of a point made by L. P. Curtis, Jr, when concluding an article 'Ireland in 1914' in *A New History of Ireland VI*. He noted that many Irish men and women 'had much on their minds' other than the great political struggles of the day or 'the search for their "true" cultural identity'.[73] The texture of everyday Irish lives consisted of a rich weave of changing social and economic realities, vibrant and contested popular cultures, a political circumstance in a state of flux, and, of course, a few constants. 'The newspapers were right.' The rain was 'general all over Ireland. It was falling on every part of the dark central plain, on the treeless hills, falling softly upon the Bog of Allen and, farther westward into the dark mutinous Shannon waves.' It was falling 'upon all the living and the dead',[74] but in 1912 there was no archetypal Irish place or Irishman or Irishwoman.

2. A Divided House: The Irish Trades Union Congress and the Origins of the Irish Labour Party

Rónán O'Brien

When the representatives of Ireland came to meet in the old historic building in Dublin (College Green) were the workers to be the only class that was not to be represented? – James Connolly[1]

THE LABOUR PARTY takes great pride in its establishment at the 1912 meeting of the Irish Trades Union Congress (ITUC) at Clonmel, County Tipperary. It places the centenary of the party's establishment firmly within the series of centenaries that mark the second decade of the twentieth century as the most politically exciting decade in Ireland's history. Yet the motion passed in Clonmel was not to establish a 'Labour Party' in name, but to determine that 'the independent representation of labour upon all public boards be and is hereby included among the objectives of this Congress'.[2] The decision taken that day marks as much an end to a process of debate within the Congress as it does the beginning of the modern political party that exists today.

As Michael Laffan points out elsewhere in this series of essays the opening years of the party's existence were more faltering than dynamic. The party's place in the national story of this decade is marked as much by the actions of its individual originators, Connolly and Larkin in particular, as by the party as an entity in itself. Allowing for that, the constructive role played by Labour between 1918 and 1921 now gets a better hearing than heretofore. However, not even the most partisan of commentators could claim the new entity hit the ground running in 1912.

The decision to establish an Irish labour party reflects the Ireland of its time. In 1912 the ITUC was by no means a republican body – or even entirely a nationalist one. It reflected the full gamut of Irish political opinion of its time. Its cleavages were between nationalist and unionist, nationalist and advanced nationalist, artisan and general trade unions and old and new trade unionism. As the quote at the start of this chapter from James Connolly illustrates, it was the imminence of Home Rule that drove the immediate decision to establish an 'Irish Labour Party'. The nature of the party to be established represented as much Connolly's compromise with his times as his vision of a future.

It is said that winners write history and the story of the Irish Labour Party is no exception. In 2012, the Labour Party commemorates the centenary of the victory of one faction within the ITUC – that is, the faction that supported the establishment of an independent labour party in Ireland. Before 1912, however, not only were there several other factions, but the faction that supported the establishment of an independent labour party in Ireland was clearly not the dominant one. Indeed, up until 1911 the ITUC was passing motions urging member unions to affiliate with the British Labour Party. The issue of labour representation dominated Congress proceedings for a full decade prior to its final determination at Clonmel. It was, according to political scientist Brian Farrell, the 'hardy annual'[3] of the Congress, and the eventual establishment of an Irish labour party was by no means the inevitable outcome of deliberations.

I

The ITUC was born in 1894 out of frustration at the treatment of Irish issues at the British Trades Union Congress. This frustration was shared by both nationalists and unionists alike. Part of the ITUC's founding *raison d'être* in 1894 was that a purely Irish body would be able to bring greater influence to bear on parliamentarians. The Congress resolved that 'we are convinced that the resolutions adopted and the reforms demanded thereat will commend the serious attention of the Parliamentary representatives of the country, irrespective of party'.[4] A Parliamentary Committee was established to ensure it did just that and its report to Congress became the meat and drink of the Congress' debates in the years that followed. There was no immediate talk, however, of independent labour representation through the establishment of a political party.

The first significant addressing of the issue came in the presidential address of Richard Wortley of the Belfast Trades Council in 1898, which was undoubtedly influenced by the local government reforms of that year which established county councils and urban/rural district councils. While the President did not call for the establishment of a labour party by the Congress, he did argue that the best way to achieve their aims was 'by united action at the polling booths'.[5]

The 1898 reforms reframed the matter of political representation: the Congress of 1899 held in Londonderry brought a debate about the multiplicity of Labour candidates in Drogheda and the importance of official labour representation. The debate illustrates the extent to which labour political and electoral activism in Ireland long precedes the formal establishment of the Congress-supported Party. The following year – 1900 – the Belfast socialist William Walker advanced the argument somewhat further with a motion calling on 'elected representatives of Labour to observe the urgent necessity of abstaining from publicly supporting the nominees of any political party unless such nominee has been approved of by the local trades council, or trades union, where no trades council exists'.[6] Here, twelve years before the formal establishment of the Labour Party is the kernel of its idea. The Walker motion was defeated, and so too was an amendment from IRB member and future Sinn Féin councillor, P. T. Daly, calling for Labour Electoral Associations to be established across Ireland.

Change was coming, however, and a motion similar to Walker's was actually passed by Congress in 1901, when it was held in Sligo. Another like-minded motion at the 1902 Congress in Cork gave rise to a further amendment from Daly. In this amendment, Daly sought to instruct the Parliamentary Committee that 'in order the better to give effect to this resolution the Parliamentary Committee be and is hereby instructed to take all necessary steps to formulate a scheme for the creation of a pledge-bound labour party, controlled by, and answerable to the Irish Trades Union Congress'.[7] Interestingly, the amendment, though defeated, was supported by William Walker. This debate marks the first occasion in which ITUC considered the founding of an explicitly Irish labour party.

The debate continued year after year. In 1903 at Newry, County Down, came the passing of the first motion recommending that Irish trade unions affiliate with the British Labour Representation Committee (founded in 1900, this was the precursor to the establishment of the British Labour Party in 1906). The motion introduced at Newry recommended joining the British Labour Representation Committee 'to promote the independent labour representation in Ireland'.[8] This is the position that became synonymous with William Walker and suggests that Congress was moving towards the idea of independent labour representation more speedily than towards the idea of independent *Irish* labour representation. While neither position held sway, a variant of this 1903 motion was passed at successive ITUC conferences until 1911.

The position of William Walker is critical. In his presidential address to Congress in 1904, Walker stated the case for independent labour representation in a trenchant fashion: 'The housing of the working classes, amendments to the Workmen's Compensation Act, amendments to the Factories Acts, the fixing of standard hours of employment, the improving of the condition of the rural labourer, and the many other necessary improvements can only be sympathetically grasped by a strong and vigorous Labour Party ... and if we can find a platform common to the workers, then we can dominate the electoral machine and the dominating of the electoral machine means the obtaining of every advantage that the worker requires, but it also entails that the worker separate himself from his old political associations.'[9]

Walker went on to advocate political action as potentially more effective than that of direct industrial struggle: 'Trades Union funds can be devoted to no better purpose than the improvement of the social condition of the members. Surely it is a saner and wiser policy to spend £1,000 in the return of a member to the House of Commons than it is to spend ten times that amount on a strike, which is often not successful, and even if successful entails upon the members participating in such strike great privations.'[10]

Given his later involvement with the British Labour Party and his subsequent dispute with James Connolly, William Walker has been afforded practically no role in the story of the establishment of the Irish Labour Party. His sympathies undoubtedly lay with the promotion of labour political representation and, had he not been a political unionist, perhaps the Irish Labour Party would have been established earlier than it was. Walker, though, no more than the adherents of the Irish Parliamentary Party (Irish Party) within Congress and those of an independent Irish Labour Party, remained captured by his 'old' political associations.

The reality was that Congress was split three ways on the issue of political representation until 1912 and, while each of the three factions had views in common with one of the other factions, the differences between them were insurmountable. In broad terms these groups were firstly a northern-dominated grouping that supported independent labour representation but within a United Kingdom context by way of affiliation to the British Labour Party. A second grouping believed that the Irish Party fulfilled the needs of the Irish trade union movement, leaving it unnecessary to establish independent labour representation. The third and final group were the ultimate victors; they supported the establishment of an independent Irish Labour Party. The debate between these groups ebbed and flowed until finally resolved in 1912.

II

In 1911 arguments over the establishment of labour representation in Ireland became the subject of an infamous exchange between James Connolly and William Walker in the Scottish socialist magazine *Forward*. Walker had unsuccessfully stood as a Labour parliamentary candidate in Belfast on three occasions and had also run for parliament in Scotland. The dispute serves to illustrate how intractable the difficulties caused by differing national affiliations were, even among avowed socialists. While it ostensibly centred on the competing merits of Connolly's Socialist Party of Ireland and the UK-based Independent Labour Party, it became a dispute about the basis on which labour in Ireland should organise – independently or as part of a wider United Kingdom framework.

Walker argued that the true socialist and internationalist basis for organisation would be alongside their UK colleagues. Connolly argued that such internationalism was bogus. He pointed out that the debate of Congress motions urging affiliation to the British Labour Party had had no effect outside Belfast: 'We want an Irish Labour Party because the Irish Trade Unions have not, as a whole, affiliated with the British Labour Party. Has any Trades Council outside of Belfast affiliated with it in actual practice? Where is there a branch of the Labour Party, or a Labour Representation Committee affiliated with England, south of Belfast? The vast mass of the Trade Unionists of Ireland look upon the Labour Party as essentially British, and even when they are members of an amalgamated Union nationally affiliated to the Party, they in Ireland refuse to take steps to embody that theoretical affiliation in actual Irish Practice.'[11]

The divisions between the two men and the factions they represented ultimately proved to be unbridgeable. Despite achieving high office within the British Labour Party Walker retired from political activity in 1912 to work in the administration of the new national insurance system.

Ideas around nationality also informed the existence of an Irish Party faction within the ITUC. Later, the decision not to contest the 1918 General Election is associated with the reported de Valera dictum that Labour must wait. But, by then, Labour had already been waiting. Continued support given by trade unionists to the Irish Party before 1912 undoubtedly delayed the establishment of an Irish labour party. This was at least partly because the leadership of the Irish Party had long claimed that it was the party of labour. Indeed, the first nationalist to make this claim was arguably Charles Stewart Parnell, although the point was made more forthrightly by John Redmond who asserted that 'labour and nationality must march together'.[12] Indeed, the Irish Party's dominance in the early 1900s reflected its ability to adapt to the changing strands in Irish life, albeit with the purpose of maintaining unity around the demand for Home Rule. The party's attitude to labour issues can be seen in this light.

In 1900, for example, the rules of the newly united Irish Parliamentary Party vehicle, the United Irish League, allowed for representation at its conventions by delegates from the Irish Land and Labour Association (ILLA) and for other possible trade unionists on a constituency basis.[13] The ILLA was one of a number of labour-minded groups acting under the umbrella of the nationalist movement, which had been affiliated to Congress in its earlier years. Under the influence of Michael Davitt, the Irish Party had elected labour nationalists like Michael Austin, Edward Crean, William Field and Davitt himself, as early as 1892. In 1896 the ITUC had passed a motion recommending that a branch of the ILLA be formed 'in every parish throughout Ireland'.[14]

The first president of the Dublin Trades Council, J. P. Nanetti, elected in 1886, was subsequently elected to Parliament as an Irish Party MP in 1900 and thereafter operated as a link between the Irish Party and the ITUC, facilitating meetings between the Parliamentary Committee and Redmond on more than one occasion. Motions at ITUC Annual Conferences congratulating the Irish Party were not unknown and a source of some discomfort to the Belfast delegations. At the Congress in 1903 the point was made that correspondence to Conservative MPs from Congress was not even being responded to – 'a matter which the northern members of Congress might look to'.[15]

J. P. Nanetti put the case for Labour allowing the status quo to remain:

> 'Where was the necessity of setting up new parties? The platform on which he was proud to stand was broad enough for any workingman. They could make the Parliamentary Party do everything they wished

... They were purely labour as well as Nationalist and he as a worker could not be with them on the platform that day were it not that he was a Nationalist as well (hear, hear). He could not be a Member of Parliament were he a purely labour candidate, and he challenged contradiction when he said that not a single constituency in Ireland would return a man on the labour question purely.'[16]

In the judgement of F. S. L. Lyons this did not count for much and he described the claims of those like Nanetti as 'trying the credulity'[17] of Congress.

Yet, while the reality is that the Irish Party has been associated with failure to intervene in the travails of the Labour movement in 1913, it was previously regarded as moderately progressive by many. The links, for example, between British radicals and the Irish Party, which went back to the land war, were still alive and well in the 1900s. Reporting to the Independent Labour Party in 1901 following completion of his first term in parliament, Keir Hardie said of the Irish Party that: 'The outstanding feature in this parliament was the way in which it was dominated by the Irish Party. A considerable number of the representatives from Ireland were men who, by training and instinct, were in the closest sympathy with the claims and aspirations of the workers, and they had been given many proofs of the fact that their sympathies in this direction were not bounded by the Irish sea. The truest representatives of Democratic feeling in the house of commons were the Irish Parliamentary Party, a fact which the workers of Britain would do well to recognise.'[18]

The links between the Irish Party and the nascent British Labour Party went so far as the issuing of a manifesto by the United Irish League of Great Britain in advance of the 1906 general election calling for the support of the Irish in Britain for Labour candidates, in addition to established Liberal Home Rulers. The manifesto stated: 'The Irish National Party have always been steady and consistent supporters of the claims of labour, while the Labour members who have succeeded in getting into the House have always been courageous and steady supporters of the Irish National Demand.'[19] Prominent Irish Party figures, including both Redmonds, even appeared on Labour Party platforms.

In his seminal work on the history of the Labour movement in the nineteenth century, J. W. Boyle offers a reason why this might be the case: 'The members of the Irish parliamentary party were socially much closer to trade unionists than were the MPs of the two main political parties, and dependent to a greater extent on popular support. The small number of labour members in the House of Commons before 1906, and the growing attention paid by the Irish Party to trade union demands, helped to extend the period of dependence of Irish trade unionists on nationalist members.'[20] Indeed, the Irish Trades Union Congress used to report regularly on how Irish MPs had acceded to its representation on labour issues. The party's record between 1906 and 1912, in alliance with a radical Liberal administration, was a good one. On issues like the Old-Age Pensions Act and on legislation on the Taff Vale judgement, the Irish Party acted as a staunch advocate of both this progressive change and Ireland's entitlement to its just share of it. Connolly, however, rightly castigated the party for its role in opting Ireland out of the National Insurance legislation of 1911–13.

The modern Labour movement later chose to ignore this element of its history. The activities of labour-minded men, however moderate, like Nanetti, are afforded no roles in Labour's story. Does this contribute to a perception that the Labour movement had not been embodied in the national struggle and arrived baby-fresh onto the planet in 1912? Even a figure like Michael Davitt is only now emerging into Labour Party narratives as a Labour figure despite his support for industrial workers and the British Labour movement. In the minds of many trade unionists of the time, as opposed to socialists, the struggle for the land in the late nineteenth century stands as a precursor of the later labour struggles. The generosity of one pre-independence nationalist Labour figure writing in 1921, Captain D. D. Sheehan, to Labour, which he indicated would take 'its place on the stage or larger happenings and events and is likely to play a part in the moulding of Ireland that will arise when the old vicious systems and forms are shattered for evermore'[21] has hardly been reciprocated.

III

Ultimately, the debate between rival factions was overtaken by time and political events that were independent of Congress. It was clear that the strength of the Irish Labour Party faction was growing and did so in particular following the establishment of the Irish Transport and General Workers' Union. This can be seen in the reaction of James Larkin. While Larkin was prepared in 1907 to acquiesce to the annual Walker motion – on the basis that Home Rule would inevitably 'follow as the night the day'[22] and the labour party to be established would be an Irish Labour Party in effect – by 1910 he was much more assertive. Larkin proposed in that year:

'That in the opinion of this Congress the time has arrived for the formation of an Independent Labour Party in Ireland, and that the Parliamentary Committee be hereby instructed to convene a conference in Dublin on or before 15th August, 1910, comprising representatives of all trades councils, labour associations and other bodies interested for the purpose of drafting a constitution and to take such action as will ensure the starting of such Labour Party.'[23]

In 1911, a similar motion from Thomas Murphy was defeated by three votes by a Walker Amendment restating the by now traditional position of recommending affiliation to the British Labour Party. At that stage, though, the writing was on the wall. The two inconclusive general elections in 1910 which afforded John Redmond the balance of power in the House of Commons between Liberals and Unionists, followed by the passing of the Parliament Act of 1911, created the sense that Home Rule was inevitable. And it was this sense that Connolly exploited the following year – 1912 – to ensure the passage of the motion to establish an independent labour party and that 'the years in which they would be waiting for Home Rule should synchronise with the preparation of labour for Home Rule'.[24]

Indeed, the motion moved by Connolly in Clonmel in 1912 which is regarded as the founding motion of the Irish Labour Party is devoid of rhetoric and matter of fact in nature: 'That the independent representation of Labour upon all public boards be, and is hereby, included amongst the objects of this Congress; that one day at least be hereafter set apart at our annual gathering for the discussion of all questions pertaining thereto; that the affiliated bodies be asked to levy their members 1s per annum for the necessary expenses, and that the Parliamentary Committee be instructed to take all possible action to give effect politically to the resolution.'[25]

IV

Nonetheless, despite the practical bent of Connolly's motion, the new party hardly got off to a spectacular start. As Brendan Behan would have had it, the first item on the party agenda was a split. In so far as the party itself could not sunder because it did not exist, the principals to the founding motion before the Irish Trades Union Congress in 1912 were soon at loggerheads with both William O'Brien[26] and James Connolly frustrated by the attitude taken to their joint initiative by James Larkin, as Chairman of Congress' Parliamentary Committee.

Following a dispute at the Parliamentary Committee meeting in August

1912, Larkin refused to have anything to do with a Connolly proposal to have a meeting to launch the new initiative at the Antient Concert Rooms in September. When William O'Brien proceeded to organise the meeting, Larkin attended and disrupted the proceedings. It was not until the 1913 Congress reaffirmed the decision taken at Clonmel that serious work began to put in place the beginnings of a party structure, to be agreed at the 1914 Congress.

Unsurprisingly, some historians of the party have questioned the appropriateness of fixing the founding year of the party in 1912. In his book, *The Irish Labour Party in Transition 1957–82*, Michael Gallagher argued that: 'The ILP was founded by the Irish Trades Union Congress (ITUC), but the year of its foundation is a matter for debate. The party itself commemorates 1912, when the ITUC, meeting in Clonmel, passed a motion to the effect that it establish its own party. Little, if any, action ensued, so a slightly stronger case could be made for 1914, when the ITUC added "and Labour Party" to its name.'[27] Barry Desmond, the Labour Minister of the 1980s, described the 1912 foundation date as being of 'popular political history' and it was not until the 1914 Congress that a formal structure and programme was launched.[28]

To confuse the picture even further 1912 also saw the establishment of the Independent Labour Party of Ireland – an amalgamation between the Socialist Party, the latest manifestation of Connolly's Irish Republican Socialist Party, and southern branches of the UK-based Independent Labour Party – in which O'Brien and Connolly were both involved. Indeed, it was about this time that the Dublin Trades Council-sponsored labour candidates for Dublin Corporation began to be called the Dublin Labour Party, bringing the full total of Labour parties established within a short period of time to three!

However, while the establishment of the party may not have led to an immediate flurry of activity it did not sit totally dormant either. Public meetings, however problematic, were held. The party's story may legitimately be considered to begin in 1912. If anything, there is also a valid case to be made that the party's lineage is even older. The phrase 'the Labour Party' had already come to be used as a general description of elected Labour candidates since the first local government elections in 1899. While Thomas Farren may have been the first official Labour Party parliamentary candidate in 1915 when he contested the College Green Division against a Home Rule candidate, he was certainly not the first candidate to be tagged as a Labour candidate. William Walker had contested parliamentary elections in Belfast under the broad Labour banner as early as 1905.[29] The term was even used to describe Nationalist MPs like Nanetti and the group of Labour councillors elected in 1899[30] whose performance was later to incur Connolly's wrath. Labour, as a term in Ireland depicting working men seeking election on their own issues, clearly predates the foundation of the Irish Labour Party.

It is clear that the problematic relationship between Labour and 'the National Question' predates the establishment of the party. On the question of independent labour representation, the more radical wing in the south was in agreement with the northern faction within Congress but, as the dispute between Connolly and Walker illustrates, they were simply unable to find common ground on the national basis for organisation. This dilemma dogged Congress and Labour long after the decision at Clonmel. Famously, in the aftermath of the Easter Rising, Congress paid tribute both to the dead of the Rising and of the Western Front. At a time when the national divide was polarising north and south, Congress, seeking to maintain its unity between both factions, was not in a position to take a leadership role one way or the other.

The debate at Congress about political representation was ultimately settled by the perceived imminence of a Home Rule Parliament. It is probably true that the emergence of the new trade unionism under the leadership of Connolly and Larkin, with the organisational support of William O'Brien, would probably have also represented a decisive shift in the debate anyway. Yet the passing of the Parliament Act in 1911 and the introduction of the Home Rule Bill in 1912 fundamentally altered the dynamic of the Congress debate up to that point. If there was to be an Irish parliament, Irish Labour uniquely needed to be represented in it.

This begs the question of how Labour might have fared had Home Rule been implemented. For a start, it might not have been denied the services of James Connolly, its foremost thinker. Nor is it conceivable that Labour would have stood aside in the first election under Home Rule. Whether John Redmond would have been able to hold the allegiance of his labour-minded supporters is a moot point – we will never know. The reality is that far from rising above the national differences in Irish life, the Labour movement reflected the polarity itself.

V

It has always been a bone of contention on the Left as to whether the Labour Party has been sufficiently socialist, or indeed socialist at all. And while the party came to adopt a more avowedly socialist position in 1918, the truth is that the party's socialism was not a key issue for its founding fathers regardless of their own personal views. The establishment of the Labour Party in Great Britain in the previous decade had brought together all strands of left-wing groupings including the trade unions, the cooperative movement and intellectual movements like the Fabians. By contrast, the ITUC and Labour Party was to be simply that – an extension of the trade union movement. Under its rules, drawn up principally by William O'Brien, Tom Johnson and the Parliamentary Committee for the 1914 Congress, membership of the party was confined to affiliated trade unions and trades councils. The purpose was to ensure that control of elected representatives remained firmly in the hands of the trade unions, an issue which had proven problematic since the first Labour candidates were elected to local authorities in 1899.

The significance of Congress' disappointment at the performance of candidates elected under a broad Labour banner in 1899 cannot be underestimated in maintaining this position after 1912. From that point on, and this is reflected in the early discussions of pledge-bound parties, the importance of controlling their candidates and elected representatives became a critical element of Congress' approach to the issue of political representation. In his seminal book *Labour in Irish Politics*, Arthur Mitchell noted:

> 'The Irish movement ... voted for strict controls over Labour candidates. They had to be approved by the congress executive, and pledged to support the constitution and pronouncements of the congress. Candidates were to remain members of their unions if elected to office and were barred from supporting other parties. The numerous precautions and controls put into the constitution at this time stem from the unhappy days at the turn of the century when many labour representatives failed to remain faithful to the labour organisations which first sponsored them. The political side of the labour movement had also been plagued by "friends of labour" and unofficial labour candidates who proved to be unreliable advocates of the workers' interests.'[31]

Niamh Puirséil and others have suggested that Connolly was intent on establishing a labourist party to maximise its appeal to workers. Hence, in 1914, it was the Belfast delegates, consistent with their sense of affiliation to the British movement, who argued for wider access to party membership than was then allowed for. Mitchell puts it this way: 'The difficulties of combining the industrial and political activities of the labour movement in one organisation were becoming apparent. If all "progressive" forces were allowed inside such organisation, the trade unions feared that control over industrial questions might pass into the hands of non-trade unionists. If non-trade union bodies were kept out, the political side would lose the help of many intellectuals, reform-minded individuals and campaign workers.'[32]

As Connolly himself put it, 'the Irish Labour members would be responsible to the workers just as their leaders in the industrial fight were responsible'.[33] William O'Brien's biographer records that as far back as 1907 O'Brien noted that Labour's 'representatives should understand clearly that they are simply the servants of the organisation – not its masters'.[34] Understandably the debate at Congress had always been about the movement establishing its own political wing although given what prevailed it should also be noted that Larkin's motion of 1910 was more broadly defined, allowing for participation of 'other interested bodies'.[35] Socialists in the party, such as Connolly, Larkin and O'Brien, were free to pursue their socialism elsewhere and did in the Independent Labour Party of Ireland – a position, incidentally, for which they would be subject to disciplinary proceedings in the modern Labour Party!

This initial decision about the party's make-up lasted until 1930, when participation in the party was eventually opened up to all and sundry, and the Labour Party itself given an independent life. (The Irish Trades Union Congress and Labour Party had become the Irish Labour Party and Trade Union Congress in 1919.) Speaking in 1929 moving a motion to establish a commission to consider the links between the ITUC and the party, Congress President L. J. Duffy was forced to concede, 'Up to the present the trade unions have formed the party base, but in a country where the large mass of the people are independent land-owners, or owners of small business, it is inconceivable that a political party based exclusively on the trade unions can achieve an independent political majority in the State.'[36] The decision to separate the two wings of the movement in 1930 proved to be so uncontroversial that the principle itself barely merited debate at the special conference held in February. President T. J. O'Connell summed it up in the phrase 'our ranks must be as comprehensive as our policies'[37].

VI

How does the Labour Party of 2012 mirror that founded in 1912? On the face of it, there are myriad differences. In 2002 Pat Rabbitte was the first leader of the Labour Party elected following a ballot of individual members. The party takes great pride in its democratic structures and this innovative method of electing a party leader. Today, individual election candidates are also selected on a one-member one-vote system. By contrast, the Labour Party founded at Clonmel 100 years ago did not even allow for individual party members. It was a trade union party. As we have seen, the umbilical cord between the party and the unions was broken formally in 1930 and has diminished in significance ever since, although it remains an important link in the hearts and minds of many Labour members. Nevertheless, while the British Labour Party may have been more pluralist at its foundation, the union link has remained arguably more critical to it than its Irish counterpart. No Irish Labour leader in recent years has been perceived as being as dependent on the trade unions for his elevation to leadership as that of Ed Miliband in the UK.

But, if the relationship with unions has changed, there is continuity too. In her history of the Labour Party, Niamh Puirséil deals with the hostility afforded to Labour from its opponents, particularly those on the Left, who 'castigate it for its lack of radicalism'.[38] She defends the party from the charge by pointing out Labour's consistent ability to get more votes than its left-wing detractors. Ultimately, if the modern Labour Party is a moderate left-of-centre inclusive party so, too, was its founding entity. Puirséil argues convincingly that Connolly wanted Labour to be embodied by its mass appeal rather than its socialist purity.[39] After all, that is why he was in the Socialist Party and the Independent Labour Party in Ireland, while simultaneously pursuing the establishment of the Congress party.

Puirséil points out too that the party became, to a degree, (or made itself) the prisoner of Connolly's (and, to a lesser extent, Larkin's) magnificent personas and through its constant referral to their legacy always left itself open to the charge that it did not live up to that legacy – their legacy always being what Labour's opponents defined it as at any point in time. This argument too strikes a chord. Labour has been slow to play up other important figures in its history. Tom Johnson and William O'Brien are cases in point. It is the latter's development of the ITGWU in rural Ireland following Connolly's death and Larkin's departure that formed the bedrock of Labour support nationwide, even up to this day.

The party's obsession with Connolly and Larkin and their variant of trade unionism, while understandable, limits Labour's historical perspective. Another way of looking at things is that it could be argued that Labour's roots go back to the establishment of labour-affiliated organisations within the constitutional national movement, even the Land League itself, as well as the Irish Citizen Army. Indeed, the idea of embracing labour-minded figures like Michael Davitt, clearly a labour man, as Labour's own is only a recent innovation. Tom Johnson once said that Labour's strength outside the urban areas was attributable in part to the role played by organisations like the ILLA.[40] Labour is not the only political party to have its contemporary politics compared with its perceived radical past. It is a charge levelled at the British Labour Party just as frequently. What the debate about the establishment of the Labour Party suggests is that the party has always been a broad church, even more so than other Irish political parties.

3. In the Shadow of the National Question

Michael Laffan

In April 1912 the British Prime Minister, H. H. Asquith, introduced the Third Home Rule Bill in the House of Commons. Its aim was to establish a subordinate parliament in Dublin that would have power 'to make laws for the peace, order, and good government of Ireland'. Its terms provoked hope, disappointment and even derision. A hostile *Irish Times* sneered that the bill 'gives us none of the heroic possibilities of self-government. It is a mean, suspicious, nation-killing measure'.[1]

Some weeks later, on 28 May, James Connolly proposed to the Irish Trades Union Congress in Clonmel that it should include among its objectives 'the independent representation of Labour upon all public boards'. His motion was criticised as being premature and divisive, but it was approved by 49 votes to 18.[2] This marked the beginning of the Irish Labour Party, although for a long time it would remain more an aspiration than an organisation.

The timing was not a coincidence. For years the Irish Labour movement had ignored the example of its counterparts elsewhere and had refrained from creating a national political party. There were good reasons for this caution. The powerful Catholic Church regarded socialism with suspicion and fear, thereby making it difficult and often pointless for radicals to advocate a restructuring of society. Ireland was an agricultural country with only a small industrial base, and most of its factory workers lived in 'Protestant' Belfast – which was effectively part of the British and not the Irish economy. In consequence many Irish trade unionists were unionists not simply in terms of defending workers' interests against employers, but also in terms of their political loyalties. They inclined towards either the Ulster Unionists or the British Labour Party. To form a nationwide Irish Labour Party would antagonise the 'Ulster' half of the trade union membership, a large majority of which loathed the prospect of Home Rule and which wanted to maintain the union with Britain unchanged.

Yet a political party that avoided the issue would ignore or challenge the predominant mood of the country, and many trade unionists who sought a degree of autonomy or independence from Britain also wanted to establish closer links with the Home Rule movement. The creation of an Irish Labour Party was passionately opposed by Home Rule politicians – who viewed any such distraction from their principal objective as irresponsible self-indulgence, almost a form of treason. One feature shared by both moderate and radical Irish nationalists was their conviction that unity against Britain must be maintained until their political aims had been attained; only then could Ireland afford the luxury of class conflict. In these circumstances it was safer for the Irish Left to postpone forming a political wing and to concentrate on developing the trade union movement. In the years after 1908 Jim Larkin's Transport Workers' Union organised the unskilled workers, who had been neglected until then.

James Connolly's Socialist Party of Ireland and the Independent Labour Party in Belfast were among numerous small radical groups that attempted to survive in this hostile environment, but most of them achieved little and soon disappeared. Attempts were made to win representation at local level, and although Connolly failed to be elected to Dublin Corporation some of his colleagues proved more successful. Labour gained seats on several corporations in January 1912. It was more ambitious in North Belfast, where it ran candidates for parliament on four occasions in little more than four years, but after an initial advance it stalled and declined.

In 1911 the House of Lords lost its power to veto government measures; crucially, it could no longer block Home Rule. The government depended for its survival on the votes of Irish nationalists, so when Asquith introduced his bill the following year they felt that it was only a matter of time before they would secure their objective. There had already been speculation about Labour representation in the proposed Irish parliament.[3] Connolly now felt able to exploit the new favourable circumstances and to propose the formation of an Irish Labour Party, quite separate from its British counterpart, which would seek election to the new assembly.

But from the beginning he encountered apathy and opposition within the trade union movement, and a month later he inquired what was being done to implement the Clonmel resolution. He felt that if the Congress'

Parliamentary Committee (which had been instructed to implement the decision) would simply 'meet the statutory number of times, and arrange for the usual deputations, and make no effort to rise up to the level of the new situation it would have been better had we been defeated'. All trades bodies should have been asked to implement the resolution, and public meetings should have been held. He was convinced that while energetic measures would arouse the working class, 'without such action we will die amid the jeers of the reactionaries'.[4] But Larkin, who chaired the Parliamentary Committee, resigned from this office and refused to play a role in shaping the new party. He had supported its formation but his principal concern remained industrial agitation, and this priority was reinforced when he was legally debarred from membership of Dublin Corporation on the grounds that he was a convicted felon.[5] He maintained his surly attitude, and William O'Brien, the president of the Dublin Trades Council, feared that without Larkin's involvement their appeal would fall flat. The following year he reported sadly that the Irish Labour Party was 'doing only poorly', while the Home Rule party's organisation flourished.[6]

Home Rulers attacked the plans for a Labour Party as divisive, many elements in the trade union movement kept their distance, and Connolly feared that Larkin's impact might be fatal; 'our friend Jim ... will pull us all down with him in his fall. He does not seem to want a democratic Labour movement; he seems to want a Larkinite movement only ... He must rule, or will not work, and in this present stage of the Labour movement he has us at his mercy. And he knows it, and is using his power unscrupulously, I regret to say'.[7] Larkin was a charismatic figure, and it was said of him that although his career was 'strewn with the wreckage of lost strikes, law suits, and personal in-fighting, he is remembered not for this disunity, or even for his considerable practical achievements, but revered in legend'.[8] His active encouragement might have helped to launch the new party, and any impression of indifference undermined it.

Resolutions were passed endorsing the Clonmel decision but nothing further was done, and the trade union movement was soon distracted by other matters: the lockout of 1913–14, the formation of the Citizen Army, the radicalisation of Irish nationalism that followed the Ulster unionists' armed opposition to Home Rule, the outbreak of the First World War, and the Easter Rising. Labour ran six candidates for Dublin Corporation in 1913 and gained two seats but lost one.[9] 'Larkinism' provoked the hostility of the Home Rule party. John Dillon, its deputy leader, remarked in October 1913 that his main anxiety was the labour conflict in Dublin; in comparison, the

Ulster question appeared dim and distant, of minor importance. Shortly afterwards his party's newspaper declared that 'this campaign for the exploitation of the position of the unemployed in Dublin is motivated by anti-Christian as well as anti-Catholic sentiment ... doctrines repugnant to all Christian feeling are being expounded'.[10] The Church and the party joined forces against the Dublin workers in 1913–14, reflecting not only a common enemy but also the common geographical and cultural conditioning of their members.[11]

A year later, at the height of the lockout, the Dublin municipal elections were seen as a test of public opinion on the conflict between employers and workers. Labour put forward eleven candidates in the Dublin Corporation elections, of whom only two were elected, while Unionists won three seats and Home Rulers twenty-five.[12] Both friends and foes saw the result as proof that the electorate had repudiated 'Larkinism'. One of the city's leading trade unionists referred to the 'Dublin Labour Party', as if it had no connection with a national movement.[13] This was quite understandable, and by June 1914 the Irish Trades Union Congress was still engaged in formulating a scheme for establishing a Labour Party.[14]

The outbreak of the First World War further divided the Irish Left, with some elements supporting the British war effort, others taking a pacifist stand, while a third group made plans for a revolution.

Despite heavy defeats in the municipal elections of January 1915,[15] Labour decided to contest a by-election in the Dublin constituency of College Green some months later. It did so in an almost casual manner, and only days before the poll Thomas Farren, the general secretary of the Transport Workers' Union, was chosen as its candidate. He and his supporters were vilified, they were associated with riot, bloodshed and misery, and his opponent warned against the dangers of 'Anarchy and Syndicalism combined with pro-German intrigue'.[16] The Home Rule candidate won by 2,455 votes to 1,816. After the election Farren protested at insinuations in leaflets and in the press that the faith of Catholic children would not be safe in his hands. He claimed that he had not raised the question of religion during the campaign, but now he felt able to flaunt his credentials – with the boast that for twenty-two years he had been member of a men's confraternity in Dublin and was currently its secretary.[17] Labour candidates were obliged to defend themselves constantly against charges of impiety, or worse.

This campaign was significant. Not only was it the first parliamentary seat contested by the Irish Labour Party, but it was also the last occasion until the general election of 1922 that it would fight at national level –

as distinct from seeking representation in local government. The party remained for years an appendage of the trade unions, and this was illustrated by the sequence of words in the movement's official title; not until 1919 did the words 'Labour Party' feature before rather than after 'Trade(s) Union Congress'.

The formation of the Citizen Army in 1913 was an omen of the militarisation that was to come. Connolly, who had been the principal inspiration for the creation of the party, soon drifted away from politics and embraced a policy of revolution – to the dismay not only of those Belfast trade unionists who were also Ulster unionists, but also of many moderates in the south. Despite his earlier hopes of a workers' insurrection, in the event he committed himself to a conspiratorial rising without social content.[18]

The suppression of the Easter Rising, the destruction of the Transport Workers' Union headquarters in Liberty Hall, and the violent deaths of several leading figures in the Labour movement, all provoked a retreat by the Irish Left. It moved back from politics and rebellion, and returned to the task of expanding its trade union base. Symbolically, the Trades Union Congress that met a few months after the rebellion 'looked both ways', paying tribute to Connolly and others killed in and after the Rising as well as to the many others 'who have laid down their lives in another field, also for what they believed to be the Cause of Liberty and Democracy and for Love of their Country'.[19] Connolly's drift towards radical nationalism had been halted – with the consequence that as the Rising grew retrospectively more popular Labour was unable to benefit from its participation.

Trade union membership expanded rapidly during the second half of the war and its immediate aftermath, deflecting energies that might otherwise have been devoted to building up a political party. In particular, the Transport Workers' Union spread across the country, and between 1916 and 1920 its membership rose from 5,000 to 120,000.[20]

By contrast the Labour Party remained immobile, and it watched from the wings as its once-dominant opponent, the Home Rule party, was overcome by Sinn Féin. (Until the change in nationalist public opinion after the Rising this party had been no more active or successful than Labour, and it too contested only one by-election in its first decade.) The struggle between Home Rulers and Sinn Féiners polarised opinion around political and constitutional issues, around Ireland's relationship with Britain and the demand for a republic. Many people felt that Labour's concern with social and economic questions was a luxury, a matter of secondary importance; and as had been the case before the war, Labour seemed marginal to the principal struggle of the day. It was Sinn Féin and the Irish Volunteers who led the fight against conscription, while Labour and the Home Rulers acted as auxiliaries.

But Labour roused itself as the war neared its end and as it became clear that parliament would soon be dissolved. In late September 1918 the national executive decided unanimously to contest the forthcoming election and it directed trades councils to decide whether they would run candidates in their constituencies.[21] The party drafted a radical, socialist manifesto whose aims included securing workers' democratic management and control of all industries and services. But it admitted that the predominant issue before the electorate, 'the national question', was not of its own choosing, and it sought a compromise between the Sinn Féin and Home Rule positions: its MPs would abstain from Westminster, while reserving the right to alter this policy if circumstances changed. Neither Sinn Féin nor the Home Rule party was satisfied, and once again Labour risked being torn in two. An editorial in the *Freeman's Journal* cited William O'Brien's incautious linking of Bolshevism with the struggle for Irish freedom, and it complained that Bolshevik propaganda had been pursued steadily under cover of a movement for the organisation of unskilled labour. On the other side, Sinn Féin claimed 'there is no disguising the fact that the rank and file of Labour are now in no mood to have the interests of Ireland, a nation, submerged by any class interest'.[22]

Sinn Féin's leadership was prepared to make concessions and to hand over a few seats to Labour, provided that its candidates would pledge themselves to abstention from Westminster, but party members proved less accommodating; the relevant constituency branches refused to stand aside. In the pre-war years many trade unionists had been prepared to prioritise nationalist objectives by voting for Home Rule, and now most of them could be expected to support Sinn Féin. They were not prepared to follow through their union membership to the point of rallying around the Labour Party. William O'Brien tried to drum up support for the idea of running candidates and he envisaged contesting at least four seats,[23] but the results of inquiries he carried out were disappointing and it was clear that the outcome of any contest would be an embarrassment.

At a special conference Labour decided to abstain, and it did so by an overwhelming margin of four to one. Johnson argued implausibly that a wartime election had been expected, but since it would now take place in peacetime the circumstances were quite different. One delegate criticised the decision as a somersault, but another believed that the working classes were not sufficiently educated to justify running candidates, while a third revealed the real reason behind the change of policy: 'he had heard organised bodies of Labour down south stating that they would vote Sinn Féin against any man'.[24] This decision was welcomed by Sinn Féin, which had feared the impact of Labour candidates, and it was correspondingly deplored by Home Rulers, who had hoped that a split vote between Sinn Féin and Labour might enable them to save a few of their seats.

The consequences of this abstention have sometimes been seen as fatal to the Irish Left. At the first general election that was conducted under near-universal suffrage (women did not yet have the vote on equal terms with men), when political loyalties might have been consolidated, Labour had no voice and gave its supporters no chance to vote for a Left-wing candidate. The exception was Belfast where, as had been the case before the war, the local Labour organisation differed from the rest of the country.

The victorious Sinn Féin party made a 'thank you' gesture towards its passive Labour ally, and in cooperation with the Labour Party leader Tom Johnson it drafted a 'Democratic Programme'. This made a few gestures towards the interests of the working class and towards socialist ideals, but they were little more than window-dressing. *The Irish Times* might claim that the programme's 'astonishing vagueness allowed it to be associated with any one of a hundred brands of modern Socialism, or with them all',[25] but it had nonetheless been purged of its radical elements. Sinn Féin removed provocative statements such as 'wherever the land, the mineral deposits and other forms of productive wealth are wrongfully used, or with-held from use to the detriment of the Republic, there the Nation shall resume possession without compensation'. It even deleted what might have seemed relatively harmless aspirations, such as 'the Irish Republic shall always count wealth and property by the measure of health and happiness of its citizens'.[26] The new Republic might be Gaelic but it would not be socialist.

Soon Ireland slid downward into a new round of violence as small numbers of Irish Volunteers engaged in an increasingly vicious conflict with Crown forces. Once more Labour was overshadowed by its trade union partner. One-day general strikes were called against the threat of conscription in 1918 and to demand the release of hunger strikers in 1920. In April 1919 much of Limerick City was controlled by a 'Soviet', and even though this protest was supported by Johnson and the Labour Party it was controlled by trade unionists rather than by politicians. Other soviets flourished briefly, but in contrast to their Russian model they were democratic and bloodless. Only with economic difficulties and rising unemployment from late 1920 onwards did the trade union tide recede.

It was in the midst of these conflicts that Labour scored a remarkable success, proving that its abstention from the 1918 general election had not necessarily doomed it to irrelevance. Long-postponed local elections were held in 1920, in urban areas in January and for county councils and other rural authorities in June. Labour faced difficulties in its selection of candidates, it had to cope with independent trade unionists who competed with official party nominees, and its focus on national politics varied from one constituency to another. In some areas the Labour Party programme and its class analysis predominated, while elsewhere they were subsumed into a broad argument for independence.[27] But the results were dramatic. Little more than a year after the sweeping Sinn Féin victory of December 1918, in which it won 70 per cent of the parliamentary seats, the party secured a mere 27 per cent of the first preference votes in Irish towns and cities – while Labour, the former 'absentee', secured a respectable 18 per cent. It became by far the largest opposition party in Dublin Corporation.

Its performance in the summer was predictably less impressive; Labour was poorly organised in rural areas, Sinn Féin and the Volunteers were able to use greater pressure and intimidation, and the 9:1 ratio of seats won by the two parties was very different from the pattern of the urban elections. The *Watchword of Labour* concluded that these successes were 'satisfactory to a degree', but that Labour representatives on county and district councils would have to combine boldness and daring with circumspection. The aftermath was disillusioning, and months later the paper complained that Labour had abandoned many of its own interests in the elections with the aim of securing unity, but that it had been 'scurvily repaid by the Sinn Féin majority in some of the councils'.[28]

The British decision to partition Ireland cut off the industrial heartland from most of the country and thereby provided a further blow to the trade union movement. New elections were called for the two new 'Home Rule' parliaments that would be created under the Government of Ireland Act. Following its pattern of 1918 the Labour Party stood aside, although it objected that it had not been given 'at least a semblance of representation'.[29] The War of Independence was reaching its bloody climax, and Labour leaders felt that they should not do anything that might imply a divided front against the British. Nothing had changed since they were pressurised to facilitate the Home Rule cause before 1914, and then the demand for full independence after 1916. However it was pointed out at the Labour conference in August 1921 that only after the results had been announced was it revealed that the successful candidates now comprised the new, second Dáil; if voters had been informed that the election was more than a demonstration of political allegiance, and that those elected were to form a new legislative authority, in some cases a different choice might have been made. Labour's marginal role was confirmed by de Valera's speech to the conference. He praised the movement for its restraint in making no special claims and expressed his confidence of its future support if the fight against Britain were to continue. He offered nothing in return.[30] One verdict on Labour's stand in 1918 and 1921 was that 'without extracting any concessions from Sinn Féin, they committed themselves to an arid and ambiguous neutrality'.[31]

The truce of July 1921 was followed by negotiations in London, a treaty, and a split that ended in civil war. In all of these the Labour movement was no more than an observer, and during the treaty debates *The Voice of Labour* pointed out that the Dáil represented the people, its members were their 'chosen spokesmen', and it alone had the responsibility of coming to a decision on the treaty. The Labour movement should maintain its unity and refrain from taking sides.[32] In subsequent months republicans resorted to violence and intimidation, but the Labour movement remained democratic; there would be no attempt to follow the example of the Bolsheviks in Petrograd or the Spartakists in Berlin. The party's national executive opposed any group 'who seek to impose their will upon the people by virtue of their armaments alone'.[33]

In January 1922 unions and trades councils were urged to prepare for an election, but because the movement had concentrated almost entirely on industrial activity it had 'practically no electoral machinery in the political field either nationally or locally'. Labour would have to decide either to fight or to follow the precedent of 1918 and abstain. Two weeks later the executive urged that since an election was imminent local machines should be built up, manned and informed. They should check the electoral register, raise money, canvass, and distribute propaganda. And above all, members were warned not to attach themselves to either of the rival Sinn Féin electoral machines.[34]

At the party's special conference in February the executive urged that Labour could no longer afford to be relegated to the background; several members regretted that it had stood aside in 1918, and one delegate warned that the hackneyed phrase 'the time is not yet opportune for labour to enter the political field' would be repeated in the future. 'They could all remain united if they continued doing nothing.' But it was also argued that workers did not have the time to think of politics, and that by entering the political field they would split the movement from top to bottom. One member forecast that history would record 'labour also ran', and yet he favoured abstention. Ultimately the conference decided that Labour should take part in the election that would be held between six and eight weeks later, but a counterproposal, that the party should abstain, was defeated by a surprisingly narrow margin: 115 votes to 82.[35] Such lack of enthusiasm boded ill for Labour's prospects.

Fortunately for the party, the postponement of the elections until June gave it more time to prepare. Another bonus was provided by the Collins–de Valera pact, which declared that the treaty should not be an issue in the election; in these circumstances Labour's policies could less easily be branded as irrelevant to the main issues of the day. The fact that the system of proportional representation was to be used (as in the 1920 local elections) would also help dilute the impact and centrality of the treaty split. Yet despite these favourable circumstances Labour was still unready when the campaign finally began in May; towards the end of that month *The Voice of Labour* noted that the party had no election machinery and that most of its candidates had opened their campaign only in the course of the previous week.[36] These candidates were moderate in their demands and they were careful not to advocate a social revolution. They all supported the treaty, if with varying degrees of enthusiasm or resignation – although one of them later refused to sign the oath of fidelity to the king and take his seat in the new Dáil.

Republicans pressurised non-Sinn Féin candidates to withdraw, but they did so less forcefully in the case of Labour than of farmers and independents. After four withdrawals eighteen of its candidates ran for election, and as in the past some of them had to cope with smears and denigration. Traditional arguments were revived, and the republican leader Austin Stack told an audience that 'it would be time enough for the various class interests to get representation when they had completely driven the English out of Ireland'.[37] The results were astonishing. Seventeen Labour candidates were elected, the eighteenth was defeated only narrowly, and the party won 21.4 per cent of the first preference vote (an achievement it never matched in any of the following twenty-eight general elections). Voting patterns revealed that if it had run more candidates it would have won more seats. On the other hand party discipline was tight, and whenever possible second preferences were transferred overwhelmingly to other Labour candidates. The party topped the poll in five of the fourteen constituencies it contested – Carlow-Kilkenny, Cork City, Leix-Offaly, Louth-Meath and Wexford. In the cities of Dublin and Cork the three Labour candidates secured fractionally more votes than the seven republicans.[38]

In many respects this outcome was deceptive or even misleading. For months Ireland had been drifting towards civil war as a result of disputes between rival factions within the Sinn Féin party and the army. Labour bore no share of blame for the crisis, and it was the principal beneficiary of a widespread anger at those who were held responsible. In particular the electorate wished to punish the republicans, and their performance was appropriately disastrous; in those constituencies where contests took place over half of their candidates were defeated. Labour was the main party opposed to the rival Sinn Féin factions and it received many 'borrowed' votes that might have gone to other candidates (such as Home Rulers) if the republicans had permitted them to run. It performed particularly well where it provided the only opposition to Sinn Féin candidates, whether pro- or anti-Treaty.

The public revulsion against nationalist candidates in June 1922 would not be repeated. Labour's efforts to prevent the war, and then to mitigate and end it, were all unsuccessful,[39] and the war brought to a sudden end the relatively benign conditions of June 1922, when many nationalist politicians had urged voters not to prioritise the principal 'national' issue of the day. The Civil War polarised Irish voters along political or constitutional lines once more, and not along class lines as advocated by Labour. In the 1923 General Election, when every Dáil seat was contested, the Labour vote crashed, its share of first preference votes was halved, and only fourteen of its forty-four candidates were elected.

Back in 1912, the plan to form a Labour Party and to contest elections provoked apathy and even hostility within the ranks of the trade union movement. It also encountered ferocious opposition from those who prioritised 'the national question' and were determined that disagreements over social and class interests would not provide a distraction from political objectives. That pattern persisted until 1922, and the apparent escape represented by that year's election results was no more than a false dawn. Irish normality would soon be restored, and the Labour Party would soon be relegated to the margins where it had languished throughout its first difficult and inglorious decade.

4. Labour and Dáil Éireann, 1922–32[1]

Ciara Meehan

Labour had a remote relationship with Dáil Éireann before the establishment of the Irish Free State. The party had left the field open for Sinn Féin in the interest of national solidarity at the 1918 General Election, after which Sinn Féin MPs rejected their seats in the House of Commons, opting instead to establish Dáil Éireann. The party had stood aside again in 1921, but soon was questioning the advisability of remaining outside the Dáil. Self-imposed absence clearly frustrated members. On 10 January 1922 a deputation was received from the Irish Trade Union Congress & Labour Party (ITUC&LP). Tom Johnson, as secretary of the group, addressed the Dáil and, though not stating it explicitly, signalled Labour's ultimate intent to re-enter the fray. The party, he reminded those deputies present, had refrained from electoral contest in the interests of national solidarity, but had grown concerned that in the struggle, social problems had been neglected. Reference was made to 130,000 unemployed workers who had shown their solidarity with the nation, but whose patience was being exhausted.[2] Although declaring it the government's responsibility to address the situation, Johnson was evidently implying that Labour was prepared give a voice to the disaffected.

When the 1922 election was called in the aftermath of the establishment of the Irish Free State, Éamon de Valera appealed to Labour to stand aside once more.[3] The logic was that ongoing divisions over the treaty needed to be resolved. Labour leader Tom Johnson responded that if a firm, united front should be shown, it should take the form of a freely elected parliament,[4] while leading party member John O'Farrell argued that the time had arrived for a new organisation to 'come into the counsels of the nation'.[5] During the election campaign in 1922, a number of disturbances and cases of intimidation of candidates occurred; four of Labour's twenty-two candidates bowed to pressure and withdrew. Overall, though, the presence of Labour nominees tended to provoke less bitterness than that of farmers and independents because they did not inspire class resentment, nor could they easily be identified as agents of British rule.[6] Of the eighteen candidates who did stand, seventeen were successful. Among them was Richard Corish who had been elected on the Sinn Féin ticket in 1921, but who resigned to contest the seat for Labour in 1922.[7] The unsuccessful, eighteenth candidate, O'Farrell, was denied a seat by a margin of only thirteen votes. Overall, Labour, with a 21 per cent share of the vote, performed best of the 'others' outside of Sinn Féin.

The party entered Dáil Éireann under the leadership of Tom Johnson, with Cathal O'Shannon and later T. J. O'Connell as his deputy. Johnson had been instrumental in the establishment of the Irish Labour Party in 1912 and served as the secretary of the ITUC&LP from 1918. His upbringing in working class Liverpool drove his desire to reform the lives of the poor and unemployed.[8] He was a hard-working deputy, remembered by one colleague for being the first to arrive and the last to leave at the end of the day.[9] It was, of course, Johnson who had drafted the Democratic Programme for social and economic change, adopted at the inaugural meeting of Dáil Éireann on 21 January 1919. Although some of the radical elements survived, the finished product was stripped of much of the socialist content found in Johnson's original draft.[10] The great question now was what impact the Labour Party would make on Dáil Éireann from the summer of 1922 in the third Dáil.

I

The third Dáil, which opened in September 1922, had a lifespan of just less than one year; by August 1923, conditions appeared favourable for the government and a snap election was called. Much of the legislation which was passed during that year was inevitably concerned with state building and stability. Labour was equally concerned with socio-economic development. The party's resolve was admired from the government benches by Liam de Róiste, a disaffected Cumann na nGaedheal deputy from Cork. He observed it to be the most 'compact bloc' with a definite programme and confidence in what it wanted to achieve.[11] Labour's commitment to the principles of the Democratic Programme was evident from the debate on the new constitution. While unsuccessfully offering amendments to several of the articles, the party was particularly vocal on article 10. T. J. O'Connell argued that 'fundamental rights' should be expanded to clearly include food, clothing, shelter and education, while Johnson contended that the ideas enshrined in the Democratic Programme ought to be embodied in the new constitution also.[12] Unlike the Democratic Programme, Labour had no input into the drafting of the 1922 Constitution, which had been undertaken by the provisional government. Its content, contrary to the efforts of Michael Collins who had attempted to satisfy the republicans but was blocked from doing so by the British, were in accordance with the terms of the Treaty.

Labour also espoused a self-sufficiency or protectionist agenda. Dealing with the unemployment problem, Johnson expressed the view that the country could 'feed, clothe, house and make comfortable' its citizens 'out of its own soil, out of its own resources'.[13] He repeatedly advocated using domestic resources to reduce unemployment. Although reconstruction after the independence struggle and Civil War placed a significant financial strain on the state's coffers, he saw in it the potential to create opportunities. For example, he argued that remaking and reconditioning roads after damage caused by military vehicles would create jobs.[14] He also argued against the hiring of non-Irish workers on government contracts if suitable staff were available locally. On one occasion he cited the case of a contract held by the Clonmel-based coach-builders, Messrs O'Gorman Brothers who, in addition to hiring workers from different parts of the Free State, had also brought staff in from London. This was despite the fact, Johnson argued, that there were idle men in the area who had once been in the service of the company.[15]

The Labour Party was presented with a further opportunity to advance its agenda in 1923 with the holding of a new general election in August that year. Held in the aftermath of the Civil War, the political climate augured well for those who supported the Treaty. After the 1922 Pact election, *The Irish Times* had declared that the party had 'arrived', and saw in the results Labour's emergence as a 'definite political force'.[16] But the success of the 1922 election was not to be sustained. Despite more than doubling its number of candidates for the 1923 election, the Labour Party secured less than half the vote achieved the previous year and won only fourteen seats. However, as Richard Sinnott has pointed out, to compare subsequent elections with 1922 is perhaps unfair. Labour's share of the vote in 1922 was bolstered, not just by the labourer/farmer vote that would become the core of its support, but also by the fact that in several of the constituencies, it was the only alternative to the Sinn Féin panels, about which some voters were resentful or unsure.[17]

Labour's performance in 1923 was also hampered by internal disunion caused by Jim Larkin, general secretary of the ITGWU, who returned from America in April that year.[18] Shortly before his return, the ITGWU had resolved to devolve Larkin's powers to a five-man group and was thus opposed to him returning to his old position. Much had been done to build up the ITGWU and its finances in his absence. Larkin's reaction was one of hostility, which extended also to the Labour Party on account of its close relationship with the ITGWU. The result, as Niamh Puirséil has noted, was that 'in one fell swoop, Larkin detached so many of the workers who might otherwise have formed the backbone of Labour organisation in Dublin at precisely the time it needed to establish its roots'.[19]

Fourteen Labour candidates were elected to the fourth Dáil at the 1923 election, and those TDs continued to adhere to the themes which the party had raised before the 1923 election. With the loss of William O'Brien and Cathal O'Shannon at that election, Johnson continued to work demanding hours, compensating for the loss of his two active colleagues. This ultimately took its toll and in the summer of 1925 he tendered his resignation as leader of the Labour Party in Dáil Éireann. His offer was not accepted, however, and the party recommended instead that he take a holiday.[20] Johnson's exasperation was underlined by his party's frustrating experience in the fourth Dáil. Such was the size of the government's majority, an opposition party of fourteen deputies could have little direct impact. What Labour could do, however, was act as a check on the government, exposing mistakes or areas it considered problematic or neglected. As the life of that Dáil progressed, disillusionment with the government grew as it made difficult and unpopular decisions, and sometimes acted without due consideration of electoral implications. Certain decisions were necessary in light of the strained economic climate, but others, such as open attack in the Dáil by J. J. Walsh, Minister for Posts and Telegraphs, on civil servants in his own department, were reckless.

Labour was particularly critical of controversial legislation that was perceived to affect citizens' welfare. Strenuous opposition, for example, was offered to the 1923 budget framed by the Minister for Finance, Ernest Blythe, which reduced the old-age pension by one shilling and also relieved income tax by the same amount – a fact caustically observed by Labour's Daniel Morrissey to be a 'remarkable coincidence'. His colleague William O'Brien accused the Minister of having produced a 'rich man's budget'.[21] The party was equally critical of the reduction in teachers' salaries. In addition to acting as a check on the government, Labour also offered constructive opposition. As well as moving amendments, the party (unsuccessfully) introduced fresh legislation. Among its proposals were a national housing authority to deal with shortages and a Railways Bill, which favoured nationalisation.

II

Given the legislative agenda of the fourth Dáil, which was dissolved on 20 May 1927, Labour sought to have the June general election fought on economic and social issues. Johnson told one audience that a strong Labour Party was necessary to ensure that a focus on economic issues was maintained in the house.[22] In advance of the election, Kevin O'Higgins, the Minister for Justice, admitted that 'some of the most useful [government] deputies in the Dáil will have a hard fight to get back'.[23] An array of unpopular decisions introduced during its last term of government resulted in Cumann na nGaedheal receiving a severe drubbing.[24] Labour was the principal beneficiary. The results were encouraging given that the party, according to its own report, had gone into the campaign considerably handicapped for funds and without its election machine established in all constituencies.[25] Senator O'Farrell subsequently expressed the view that, with continued organisation, there was 'every reason to hope for the return to power of a Labour government at the next general election'.[26] However, June 1927 did not foreshadow a growth in the party's strength.

The summer months of 1927 were to be turbulent ones for the Free State. On 10 July Kevin O'Higgins was assassinated. His death had the potential to cause a realignment of those parties active in Leinster House. Johnson – taking the view that with '[Desmond] FitzGerald and [J. M.] O'Sullivan ill, [W.T.] Cosgrave, [Patrick] McGilligan, [Patrick] Hogan worn out, the ministry was very weak without O'Higgins' – offered support from the opposition benches.[27] The proposal was declined. Any prospect of cross-party unity was subsequently blown apart by the introduction of a Public Safety Bill and two bills designed to amend the electoral laws and Constitution. The Public Safety Bill provided for military courts with the power to enforce the death penalty for treason, murder or the unlawful possession of a firearm. Random searches of persons were also introduced and any individual found to be in possession of documents relating to illegal associations were to be arrested and such documents taken as proof of membership, unless proved contrary. Labour firmly rejected the introduction of what O'Farrell deemed to be 'repressive legislation, unequalled even in the worst days of foreign rule'.[28]

Labour also voiced opposition on economic grounds, conscious of the fact that suggestions of political instability could affect the terms of a new national loan. In its organ, *The Irishman*, the party expressed the view that 'this mad outrage may spell ruin to our tourist traffic this year, render much more difficult the flotation of a National Loan, and effectively deter the investment of capital in new industrial enterprises'.[29] Such concerns were echoed in the pages of various regional newspapers,[30] while *The Irish Times* asserted that the legislation would have to be reconciled with 'economic progress and the upkeep of the nation's credit'.[31] Labour's concerns were not without foundation; the Free State loan dropped by 5 per cent on the Dublin stock exchange the day after O'Higgins's murder.[32]

The government's in-built majority ensured safe passage for the contentious legislation, the enactment of which transformed the Dáil by forcing Fianna Fáil to confront its approach to parliamentary politics. De Valera, acknowledging that Sinn Féin was a spent political force and keen to influence the direction of Irish politics, had founded the party in 1926. However, like Sinn Féin, the party initially subscribed to the policy of abstention from the national parliament because of the contentious oath, which republicans interpreted as an expression of allegiance to the British crown. Fianna Fáil sought to have the oath removed by collecting signatures for a petition, but found that the new legislation undermined this strategy. The Constitution (Amendment No. 6) Bill made the initiative to remove the oath by petition the exclusive privilege of attending members of the Oireachtas. Under the Electoral Amendment (No. 2) Bill, candidates, when nominated to stand, had to agree that if elected they would take the oath. Those candidates who failed to fulfil this requirement within two months of being elected would automatically lose their seats. Fianna Fáil's Gerald Boland admitted to Johnson that the party 'would be wiped out unless they entered the Dáil'.[33]

By reinterpreting the oath as an 'empty formula', de Valera allowed his deputies to take their seats. Prior to Fianna Fáil's announcement, there had been much speculation that the party was preparing to enter the Dáil. The party had corresponded with Labour in advance of its decision; the move was welcomed by Labour, which saw participation as paving the way for political and economic change.[34] Naturally it claimed its share of the credit, 'proud' that it assisted in securing an end to 'the futile and dangerous abstention policy of one-third of the elected representatives'.[35]

The Dáil was immediately transformed, reducing Cumann na nGaedheal's artificial majority to a much more slender reality, and the prospect of the Labour Party being involved in government became more real. On 16 August Johnson, seconded by his party colleague Hugh Colohan, moved that 'that the Executive Council has ceased to retain the support of the majority in Dáil Éireann'.[36] W. T. Cosgrave, president of the Executive Council, interpreted the motion as an opportunistic grab for power, but the Labour contributors repeatedly emphasised that they had been motivated by economic concerns. The combined voting strength of Labour, Fianna Fáil and the National League, together with some independents, was such that the conspiring parties, the newspapers and even Cumann na nGaedheal predicted the government's defeat. So confident was Johnson that he did not deem it necessary to recall T. J. O'Connell from a teachers' conference he was attending abroad. Moreover, he contacted the Mayo South TD offering the education portfolio in the new government.[37]

Labour later revealed that it had anticipated, allowing for defections, the government would be brought down by two or three votes.[38] From the party's reports and notes by its members it is clear that Labour had expected certain independents to vote with them, and that a pledge of support might even have been made. Unsurprisingly, it would also seem that independents had been canvassed by government elements to reject the motion.[39] Enniskerry had played host to a political tryst of the Labour leaders on 13 August 1927 and the configuration of the next cabinet was the subject for discussion. Torn-up drafts were carelessly discarded in a bin, where they were discovered and pieced back together by the editor of *The Irish Times*. In what amounted to an incredible scoop, the paper printed the proposed cabinet in its entirety the following day. Among those given portfolios were independent deputies Bryan Cooper and John O'Hanlon, appointments designed to entice support.

Several meetings had taken place between key Labour and Fianna Fáil personnel.[40] A lack of cohesion in the arguments put forward by the opposition parties during the debate would suggest that no joint strategy had been agreed, or rather, that they reflected the individuality of the parties' interests and concerns. The situation was further complicated by the existence of another significant political party: the National League. Formed in 1926 by Thomas O'Donnell and John Redmond's son, William, the party was a short-lived entity and was wound up in 1931. During its existence, it attempted to appeal to supporters of the old Irish Parliamentary Party and was largely critical of the government, taking the lead, for example, on the rights of town tenants and opposition to Kevin O'Higgins' 1927 Intoxicating Liquor Act.

On both 12 and 15 August, Johnson told de Valera that he 'thought Labour would not form part of a coalition with de Valera as head'. At the first meeting he suggested, however, that he 'could satisfy the National League and form a Labour-National League coalition'.[41] The Saturday before the motion, de Valera announced that Fianna Fáil would not form a government but would support Labour. O'Brien 'pressed de Valera that they ought to form a government, but he said they would not'.[42]

If Labour was unsure about a de Valera-led coalition, the National League was utterly opposed to any involvement by Fianna Fáil. Correspondence between the party's leader William Redmond and Tom Johnson revealed a 'good deal of uneasiness'. Members were concerned that the new coalition should not place 'Labour in the saddle or Fianna Fáil in effective control and pulling the strings'.[43] Reassured by Johnson, the National League resolved to support the motion.[44] The stability of the new government, if the opposition had been successful, was questionable. The intention was that a Labour–National League coalition would be formed, with support offered by Fianna Fáil from the opposition benches. During the five-hour debate, Johnson affirmed that 'we are going to maintain the Treaty and the Constitution',[45] while Redmond confirmed that his party was 'absolutely wedded to the fundamentals of the Anglo–Irish settlement'.[46] This was in obvious contrast to de Valera who had a clear agenda of dismantling the Treaty.

The motion of no confidence was originally declared carried when first put to the chamber, causing Patrick McGilligan to challenge a division from the government benches, which left the house evenly divided. The National League's John Jinks, who had been seated behind his leader during the debate, left the Dáil before the vote, making the implications of O'Connell's approved absence glaringly apparent. The casting vote fell to the Ceann Comhairle who, in accordance with procedure, voted in favour of the government. Patrick Belton and Daniel Corkery, the only two independents who supported the motion, were not those intended for cabinet by the Labour Party. In contrast, John O'Hanlon not only voted with the government, but also asserted that 'I am an Irishman, and I cannot possibly give my vote to put at the head of this state an Englishman'. His views were echoed by fellow independent Jasper Wolfe who explained that he did not believe that the Free State was 'so bereft of intelligence' that they could not have an 'Ireland governed by Irishmen'.[47] Essentially, the Labour leader's nationality became an explicit factor in the debate.[48]

Although the government had survived the motion of no confidence, it was in a precarious position. When Cumann na nGaedheal triumphed in two by-elections held in the aftermath – considered by observers to be the people's motion of confidence – Cosgrave took the opportunity to call an early election. In a detailed statement issued to the press, he justified the decision based on the events of the summer, the country's need for stability and responsible governance, and the government's need for a 'margin of safety'.[49] Labour reacted strongly, and Daniel Morrissey described Cosgrave's actions as those of a dictator.[50] When, after the debate on the no confidence motion had been concluded, Cosgrave adjourned the House until October, doing so on the premise that if the government party candidates were defeated at the by-elections, the Dáil would reconvene within one week. Labour argued that 'this was an implied undertaking that if the two seats were won by government supporters, the Dáil would reassemble ... on 11 October'.[51] Nonetheless, the Governor General granted Cosgrave's request for a dissolution, and the Irish voters prepared themselves for a second election that year.

The events of the summer were the dominant theme on the hustings for the September 1927 general election. Cumann na nGaedheal recovered ground, and Fianna Fáil performed handsomely in its first election since entering the Dáil. For Labour, June 1927 (like 1922) was a false dawn. Its share of the vote slipped significantly and the most notable casualty among the party's losses was its leader, who was seen by some as having made a grab for power. 'Tom Johnson let the workers down / to dress himself in president's gown', wrote one (probably Cumann na nGaedheal) supporter.[52] Although the leader of the National League did not suffer a similar fate, his personal vote plummeted and, with the exception of James Coburn, the remainder of Redmond's party was wiped out. A significant portion of those voters who had supported the two parties as constitutional alternatives to Cumann na nGaedheal in June clearly resented the alliance with Fianna Fáil. Labour, however, chose to interpret the result as the consequence of a campaign hampered by a lack of funds, imperfect organisation and the distraction of a medley of abstract issues with no relevance to the affairs of the voters' everyday lives.[53]

III

After the September 1927 election, Fianna Fáil displaced Labour as the main opposition party. During this time, the separation of the ITUC&LP occurred.

As discussed elsewhere in this volume, the Labour Party was created as the political arm of ITUC, but union support was not sufficient to sustain the parliamentary party. As the defeat of Tom Johnson in a constituency with a strong union presence proved, votes were not materialising.[54] As the 1920s progressed, a parting of the two groups seemed inevitable; this was approved at a conference on 28 February 1930.

In the Dáil Labour returned to its familiar themes, and also moved closer to Fianna Fáil as the conservatism of the Cumann na nGaedheal government grew. The first session in 1927 had scarcely opened when Daniel Morrissey moved 'that the measures hitherto adopted by the government for the relief of unemployment are insufficient and ought to be extended immediately'.[55] But perhaps the biggest issue that arose during the seventh Dáil, on which Labour could have been expected to take the lead, was the question of land annuities (payments made to the British exchequer). Certainly, the party made representations on behalf of those who were struggling to meet the cost of those annuities. Archie Cassidy, the Labour TD for Donegal, outlined the harsh reality of the situation. He told the chamber that 'the small farmers are in a state of poverty, and many of them are unable to provide three meals a day for their families, much less pay their land annuities'.[56] But despite such appeals, Labour did not actively engage with the anti-annuities movement. Although the campaign against annuities did not originate with Fianna Fáil, it was appropriated by the party, which ran an emotional campaign based on grievances that dated back to the confiscation of land during the plantations. Eamon Cooney, for example, evoked history when he argued that annuities were being paid to 'the descendants of Cromwellian planters'.[57] In allowing Fianna Fáil to become the dominant voice on the matter, Labour arguably missed a real opportunity to secure support among small farmers, thus broadening the scope of the party's appeal. The matter also serves as an excellent example of how Fianna Fáil eroded Labour's support base during the seventh Dáil. With policies similar to Fianna Fáil's, but lacking a structure or support base to match that party's, Labour found itself outmanoeuvred by de Valera's party. Sections of the electorate, previously reluctant to support an abstentionist party and who may have consequently cast their vote for Labour as an alternative to the government, now turned to Fianna Fáil.

The importance of the annuities question to voters was emphasised during the February 1932 general election at which it was one of the dominant themes. Accounting for almost 17 per cent of Fianna Fáil's election statement,[58] the party made it the priority concern. In an election fought within the context of a global economic recession, voters looked to the political parties for signals as to how they would guide the country out of depression. Cumann na nGaedheal defaulted on offering any clear vision for the future, taking refuge instead in the security of its past achievements. William Norton argued that the government had no settled policy 'but appeared to drift helplessly before every economic wind that blew in other countries'.[59] In response to the growing unemployment problem, the government party pointed out that America faced similar challenges.[60] Norton dryly observed that 'it was an insult to their intelligence to say they ought to be hungry because there was hunger in China or America'.[61] Labour's judgement of the government's attitude towards the workers and the poor was expressed in the single line: 'the present ministry has failed'.[62] In contrast, Labour returned to the themes of the Democratic Programme, and promised to promote industries and agriculture, to make adequate provisions for the aged and disabled, and organise the employment of every willing man.

Despite its promises, only seven candidates were elected, five of whom had been returned continuously since 1923. Their election was as much the product of a personal vote as it was a show of support for Labour.[63] The party once more lost its leader following O'Connell's defeat in Mayo South. His successor, William Norton, proved to be the party's longest-serving leader. Notwithstanding the dismal result, Labour played a key role in the formation of the next government. For the first time since the foundation of the state, Cumann na nGaedheal did not sit on the government benches. However, de Valera was short of an overall majority and it was with the support of Labour's seven deputies that he formed the first Fianna Fáil government.

On the dissolution of the third Dáil, Johnson had spoken about building-up the idea of parliamentary institutions.[64] Labour's role until 1927 as the main opposition to a government it could not influence was unenviable, but it is, perhaps, the party's most important legacy from that era. The role that Labour played helped ensure that the parliament functioned properly, thus contributing to the creation of political normality and democratic stability at a time when the new state was being formed. Labour had stood aside in the national interest before independence; conversely it was for that very reason that the party participated in the political system after 1922.

5. Forging a Better World: Socialists and International Politics in the Early Twentieth Century

William Mulligan

SINCE THE LATE eighteenth century (at the latest) radicals in European politics recognised that domestic political, social and economic reform required an international system, in which states were free from the omnipresent threat of military invasion. Terms such as 'the balance of power' and 'the primacy of foreign policy' were viewed as rhetorical ploys to prevent domestic political reform, to promote militarism, and to expand the coercive powers of the state. 'A gigantic system of outdoor relief for the aristocracy' was how John Bright condemned the international system and its attendant diplomatic institutions in the nineteenth century. European socialists inherited many of the nineteenth century radical ideas about foreign policy. Far from ignoring the foreign policy context, socialists were amongst the most profound thinkers about the changing international system. Arbitration, minority rights, disarmament, free trade, labour regulations and international law and institutions were amongst the themes of a new vision of international politics that would promote harmony and enable great powers and small states to exist in harmony. Once peace was secured within the international system, it would enable states to devote resources to solving pressing political and social problems at home.

The success or failure of socialist movements in Europe in the first half of the twentieth century were as dependent on international political developments as they were on their organisation and the domestic social and political structures. The two world wars made clear to ordinary citizens the fundamental importance of foreign policy. While the concept of the cultures of war has become well established in scholarly debates, this chapter will suggest that socialists were at the forefront of thriving, but unstable, cultures of peace. The First World War, perhaps paradoxically, provided socialists with opportunities to enter government and promote reforms. The mobilisation for war generated new visions of a more peaceful and just domestic and international order, from which socialists tried to profit after 1918. Their attempts to create a robust culture of peace in the 1920s were undone by the Great Depression and the rise of Nazism. Exile and execution were the worst of the fates to befall many European socialists in the 1930s, but their vision had a persistent attraction and logic, so the post-Second World War settlement, in western Europe, represented the triumph of many of the socialist ideas at the core of the cultures of peace in the first half of the twentieth century – welfare states, regulated capitalism, international institutions, and human rights.

The international context, therefore, provided opportunities, challenges, and threats to socialist movements around Europe and this applies in the Irish context too. Socialists in Ireland made a distinctive contribution to European debates on the international system in the first quarter of the twentieth century and it is worth bearing in mind two points. First, many Irish nationalists shared the views of European socialists on the international system. A small Irish state needed an international system that favoured great power restraint, international law and institutions, minority rights, and disarmament. There were some differences on international commerce and trade, where European socialists favoured free trade that would lower food prices and ensure thriving export industries – with the additional bonus that trade was supposed to strengthen the bonds of peace. Nationalists, on the other hand, tended to a degree of self-sufficiency. In other words, it was difficult for Irish socialists to carve out a distinctive voice about foreign policy issues, because, for reasons of *realpolitik*, Irish nationalists shared many of their goals. Second, by the late 1920s the Irish Free State had established the primacy of the civilian government over the army, had held a succession of free elections, had protected the rights of minorities, and had a seat at the League of Nations. The Free State had achieved the most important political goal of European socialist movements – the establishment of a constitutional democracy. While poverty, migration, and other social and economic ills continued to afflict Irish society, from the point of view of European history in the first half of the twentieth century, the Free State represented an astonishing success. The Anglo-Irish disputes of the 1930s have disguised the extent to which Britain provided a geopolitical shelter from which the Free

State could shield itself from the intervention of other great powers. The successful establishment of constitutional democracy and the shelter from the violence of the 1930s and 1940s meant that the international context of Irish political debate differed significantly from that in large parts of Europe in a way that had not been true of the first three decades of the century.

I

In the early twentieth century European socialists were the most numerous and best organised opponents of great power aggression and conflict. At meetings in Stuttgart in 1907 and Basel in 1912, European socialists affirmed their opposition to war and their willingness to call a general strike to cripple any incipient war effort. In the last weeks of peace in Europe in the summer of 1914, tens of thousands of socialist party supporters thronged the streets of French and German cities in protest against the coming war. The South Wales Miners' Federation refused to cut short its annual holiday in response to a government request, as Britain prepared to declare war on Germany during the August bank holiday weekend. A week into the war, the local newspaper, *Y Dinesydd Cymreig*, declared that 'the remains of this war will be left behind for generations, in hate, jealousy, misery and poverty.'[1]

The opposition to war was grounded in socialist theories about capitalism as well as in less abstract concerns for the welfare of workers and citizens. Although European socialists were a heterogeneous lot, they tended to view great power aggression and the risk of a general European war as embedded in capitalism. Writers such as Karl Kautsky, Jean Jaurès, and Lenin argued that advanced capitalism constantly required new markets. This explained the imperialist expansion in the late nineteenth century. As the world was divided between the great powers, acting in the interests of the capitalist elite, this resulted in international tensions and crises. According to the socialist critiques the bourgeoisie derived an additional benefit from these international tensions, as it justified the maintenance of large standing armies, which could be used to suppress domestic discontent. In place of this militarist and capitalist nexus, based on suppression at home and imperial expansion abroad, the German Socialists, for example, called for a militia army, shorter training periods, free trade, and international arbitration.[2]

This abstract denunciation of the international system was buttressed by a more immediate and visceral sense of the destructiveness of modern warfare. In the autumn of 1912 the Balkan League – Serbia, Bulgaria, Greece and Montenegro – declared war against the Ottoman Empire. The conflict lasted only a few months, but it was accompanied by atrocities, rape, famine, and epidemic diseases. Over 400,000 Muslim refugees fled to Anatolia. The Balkan Wars were reported widely in the European press, often accompanied by photographs, documenting the devastation visited upon families and communities. European socialists, fearing that the war in the Balkans would trigger a general European conflict, warned that similar atrocities and sufferings would accompany a conflagration between the great powers. 'The events in the Balkans give us an idea of what universal war would be like', Jean Jaurès, the French socialist leader, wrote. 'It is the reproduction, in a civilised age, of the great destructions of barbarous times when entire armies, entire populations disappeared.'[3] For most workers – indeed for most Europeans – in late July and August 1914 the risk of loss of life and limb, the fear of unemployment and food shortages, and the sundering of family relationships informed the sadness and despair at the outbreak of war.

European socialists, however, failed to prevent the outbreak of war or even to call general strikes. James Connolly mocked the failure of his European comrades: 'What then becomes of all our resolutions, all our protests of fraternisation, all our threat of general strikes, all our carefully built machinery of internationalism, all our hopes for the future? Were they all as sound and fury, signifying nothing?'[4] Connolly's writings during 1914 and 1915 continued the pre-war European socialist critique that the war was rooted in capitalist interests and harmed the material and physical welfare of the workers. Home Rule and the broader question of Ireland's relationship with Britain provided a particular context for the decision of Connolly and Irish socialists to oppose the war. In emerging nations in eastern Europe, in Russia, and in Italy in 1915, the majority of socialists also opposed the war. In many respects the decisions of British, German, French, and Austrian socialists to support their governments' war efforts were more similar to that of John Redmond and the Irish Volunteers. First, it was an opportunity for workers and socialist parties to demonstrate their patriotism and loyalty to the state. More importantly, it also reflected the experience of the working class in these states in the years before the war. From the late nineteenth century, governments had introduced health and unemployment insurance, primary education, and minimum standards of health and safety in the workplace. These states also guaranteed constitutional rights, such as the freedom of association and free speech. Socialist parties expected that they could more effectively champion their interests within the framework of the state than in opposition to it.

II

While German Socialist deputies were pleased to hear Kaiser Wilhelm II declare on 4 August 1914 that he no longer recognised parties, only Germans, they, like their counterparts in other countries, expected political, social, and economic benefits for their support. There were some immediate political gains, giving European socialists a voice at several cabinet tables. Members of the SFIO entered the French cabinet as part of the Union Sacrée in August 1914. The following year, Albert Thomas, on the right-wing of the SFIO and later the first president of the International Labour Organisation, entered government as the powerful Undersecretary for Artillery and later became the Minister for Armaments. In Britain, the Labour Party split, but the majority supported Britain's participation in the war. Arthur Henderson, whose son David would be killed during the Battle of the Somme, sought to give Labour a distinctive voice through the War Workers' National Emergency Committee. In 1915 he joined the government and he had particular interests in finding employment opportunities for Belgian refugees and disabled ex-servicemen.

There were more tangible achievements in industrial relations. It should be noted that trade unions, even more so than the socialist parties, were heavily involved in the economic mobilisation for war, which accelerated with the emergence of trench warfare in late 1914. Trade unions attracted an increased number of members and enjoyed a high political and economic profile. In Germany, the Hindenburg programme initiated in late 1916, which aimed to double armaments production, saw the army and trade unions cooperate, ensuring better wages and conditions for workers, as well as formal positions of authority and influence within companies. The fear that strikes would upset war production led governments to establish arbitration systems. As elsewhere in Europe, Irish workers used brief strikes as a means to improve pay and conditions. In November 1916, for example, following a railway workers' strike in Ireland, the government took the rail system under state control and awarded workers an additional seven-shilling bonus. As the German submarine blockade forced British and Irish agriculture to move from pasture to more labour-intensive tillage production, the National Agricultural Wages Board for Ireland fixed the minimum labourer's wage at twenty five shillings a week for those over twenty-one years of age and the ITGWU began to represent agricultural labourers.[5] Some socialists, such as Thomas, considered the cooperation between trade unions, employers and the state during the war as a model of industrial relations for peacetime.

European socialists were at the forefront of the debate on the post-war international system. The issue of war aims and the post-war settlement was so contentious that governments sought to avoid any public discussion. Yet the diplomatic machinations of the powers, the peace proposals from neutrals, such as the Papacy and the United States, and events such as the Russian Revolution ensured a vigorous public debate. From the perspective of European socialists, no matter what their nationality, the war had reinforced their understanding that socialism at home required peace abroad. The understanding of what constituted peace broadened during the First World War. It no longer simply meant the absence of fighting, the signing of treaties and the occasional meeting of the ambassadors of the great powers. Peace was now imagined as an interlocking system of domestic and international commitments and institutions, based on democracy and welfare at home and disarmament and arbitration at international level. The world was to be made safe for small countries as well as great powers.

Mobilisation for war had politicised the intimate, the quotidian and the private sphere. Peace, therefore, required attention to these issues: at one level, far removed from the world of diplomatic congresses, but at another level, the foundation for a new world order. Socialist groups produced a multitude of plans to improve the quality of life for ordinary workers and citizens after the war. The regeneration of towns in occupied France needed to go beyond mere repair; instead the Action Committee, composed of trade unionists and socialists, called for modern town planning, in which urban space would conform to modern needs by building 'healthier, gayer, and finer towns'.[6] Ethel Snowden, suffragette, peace campaigner and wife of the future Labour Chancellor Philip Snowden, captured this broader imagination of peace in an appeal to various socialist women's associations for a Women's Peace Crusade in September 1917: 'all can help in the general work, even children. What more pathetic appeal could be made to the hearts and consciences of men than a procession of children carrying flags with the words inscribed "I want my Daddy"?'[7]

The debate about the post-war order and peace intensified in 1917. Socialists were at the fore of these debates, from the ill-starred proposal by Dutch and Scandinavian socialists for a meeting of European socialists in Stockholm to the Peace Resolution passed in the German parliament in July.[8] Although the most dramatic interventions in the peace debate came from beyond the European socialist parties, from Lenin and Woodrow Wilson, their vision of peace was both informed by and attracted support from socialists. In contrast to the territorial ambitions, economic claims, and security issues, which filled the rhetoric of many nationalists and conservative visions of the post-war order, Lenin and Wilson cast their ideas in terms of a universal appeal. Wilson's re-election as president in 1916 owed much to the formidable American Federation of Labor and other socialist associations. In putting together his election-winning coalition, Wilson paid considerable attention to the American Left's foreign policy agenda. These aims were often vague on details, but carried a powerful emotional appeal. In March 1917 the American Federation of Labor claimed that it stood for 'Labor, Justice, Freedom, and Humanity' and that it sought 'to maintain human rights and interests the world over.'[9] Lenin's direct appeal to European workers had some resonance, particularly in cities affected by food shortages. The German soldiers occupying Russian territory after the treaty of Brest-Litovsk in March 1918 were considered particularly susceptible to Lenin's vision of a post-war order.[10]

By the end of 1917, socialists throughout Europe had crafted, with different variations and emphases, a compelling vision of the future peace, which combined geopolitics, international institutions, a constitutional and democratic state, economic and social reform, and attention to the politics of everyday life. Socialists were advocates of a 'peace culture', which reflected the experiences and lessons of the war. The ending of the war on the Eastern Front in 1917 and on the Western Front in 1918 demonstrated the importance of the ordinary soldier and citizen in the outcome of the war. Exhausted and with little hope of victory, soldiers in the Russian army and then in the German army signalled their desire for peace. 'You need war and money, but we need life', declared one appeal from a group of Russian soldiers in October 1917. A year later German soldiers retreating on the Western Front expressed similar sentiments. 'Soldiers were heard to say that they had no desire to be shot [by the enemy] now, just before the peace', recorded the war diary of the 3rd Battalion of the 33rd Landwehr Regiment. For these soldiers the meaning of peace was stripped down to its bare minimum – survival. In Germany, the stronghold of the European socialist movement, the revolution of 1918 did away with the Kaiser, and a new provisional government, composed of the SPD and the Independent Socialists (who had opposed the war), was formed.

III

The second half of the war seeped into the revolutionary post-war period, so that it is possible to view the period between 1916 and 1923 as a revolutionary era in European as well as Irish history. As in Ireland, historians of the European Left have been critical of socialist parties' performance in this period. Geoff Eley, for instance, argues that the Left's challenge to the established economic and political structure had failed by the early 1920s, though he contends that socialists were able to shape the political agenda for decades to come.[11] He attributes this failure to splits within the socialist movement, the spectre of the Bolshevik revolution, the residual strength of conservative interests, and the competing emotional appeal of the radical Right and nationalism. Assessing the achievements of the European socialist movements in the early 1920s requires a careful calibration of what constituted success and failure. While industries were not nationalised, welfare provision remained scanty in many areas and dictatorships emerged in Russia and Italy, socialists played an important role in establishing peace in Europe by the mid-1920s. The goal of many socialists was peace, improved quality of life for ordinary citizens, and the safeguarding of constitutional democracy. Charging them with failing to overturn established institutions fails to appreciate their more prosaic goals.

The policy of cooperation with parties and institutions, outside of the socialist fold, started in the First World War and continued thereafter. Leaders such as Friedrich Ebert, the first SPD Chancellor in Germany, believed that cooperation and moderation would secure domestic political order and constitutional democracy. This policy of cooperation also reflected the electoral reality. In none of the great powers did socialists gain a majority of seats or votes in an election at the end of the First World War. In France, the right proved resurgent initially and only in 1924 did the leftist bloc of parties win power under Edouard Herriot. In Britain, the elections between 1918 and 1924 marked the replacement of the Liberal Party by the Labour Party as the main opposition to the Conservatives. In 1923 Ramsay MacDonald became Britain's first Labour Prime Minister. In Germany the SPD were the dominant party of government between the revolution at the end of the war that created the republic and the elections of June 1920. Thereafter the SPD remained the largest party but only served in government during the inflationary crisis in late 1923. These parties cooperated with parties from the centre. In the Weimar Republic in 1919 the SPD rejected coalition with the Independent SPD to their left in favour of a broader coalition with the Democratic Party and the Catholic Centre Party. MacDonald's first government was a minority one, dependent on the support of Liberals. The Irish Labour Party perhaps brought this policy of cooperation to a self-defeating level by opting out of the 1918 election, but it nonetheless was acting along the same lines as counterparts elsewhere in Europe.

There was, of course, another variant of socialism in post-war Europe. In Russia the Bolshevik party under Lenin achieved power by revolution, which was followed by a bloody civil war in which an estimated 2 million people died.[12] The violence of the Russian Revolution and Civil War had an impact on the prospects for socialism throughout Europe, demonstrating the importance of the international context in which socialism thrived or withered. The Russian Revolution weakened the European socialist movements. First, Lenin opposed social democracy as representing a futile compromise with capitalism. Second, the violence of the revolution and the subsequent repression of political opponents undermined (unjustly) the cultures of peace presented by socialists. The short-lived Limerick Soviet in April 1919, for example, occurred at the same time as a Soviet Republic was declared in Munich and in Budapest. In each case the opposition of powerful institutions, such as the army and the Catholic Church, as well as middle class fears that Bolshevik-style atrocities would be visited upon them, ensured the failure of these local Soviet experiments. In Italy, Benito Mussolini's Fascists attracted considerable support from those fearful of the growing militancy of trade unions.

It has become a cliché to note that peace did not come with the armistice of November 1918 nor the Treaty of Versailles in June 1919. Only in the mid-1920s was peace in Europe seemingly secure. In October 1925 Britain, France, Italy, Belgium, and Germany agreed the Treaty of Locarno, which guaranteed the post-First World War territorial settlement in western Europe and agreed that territorial changes in eastern Europe could only come about through arbitration. The Locarno pact was significant not only because of the terms of the agreement, but also because it represented a new process in international politics after 1918, built up trust between former enemies and provided the basis for further negotiations. The key figures at Locarno were not socialist – Austen Chamberlain was a British Conservative, Gustav Stresemann a German Nationalist, and Aristide Briand a French Radical. Nonetheless the Locarno pact owed much to socialist support in each of the signatory powers and to the impact that socialist thinking on international politics had on changing perceptions of how to achieve security and peace.[13] The triumph of the French Left in the 1924 election represented a victory for a vision of international peace based on arbitration, the League of Nations and disarmament over the narrowly conceived military security policy of Raymond Poincaré. MacDonald in his brief stint as Prime Minister had pushed British policy towards a greater commitment to European stability, while in Germany, the SPD had supported Stresemann's policy of accommodation with France, which was deeply unpopular amongst nationalist and right-wing groups during the occupation of the Ruhr in 1923 and 1924. By the mid-1920s the socialist argument – that international peace and security could be best achieved through negotiation, not violence, through arbitration, not threat, and through multilateral institutions and processes, not unilateral demands – had apparently been accepted by the great powers in Europe.

Peace in mid-1920s Europe was sustained by a broader set of institutions, norms and associations, which owed much to socialist cultures of peace. The League of Nations was the most notable of these. Although derided for its weakness in the 1930s, the League had played roles in solving disputes between the Baltic states, between Yugoslavia and Bulgaria, and between Greece and Italy by the mid-1920s. It had begun to advocate minority rights and it broadened its remit to include economic, welfare and health issues. The League of Nations was charged with the preservation of peace in its broadest sense, a meaning of peace that had changed in the course of the First World War – from the rights of small states to the welfare of ordinary citizens. The International Labour Organisation (ILO) was set up in 1919. Thomas was its first president and, like the League of Nations, it too had a wide range of duties that historians are only beginning to explore.[14] The improvement of workers' conditions of employment had been at the centre of socialist ideals of a post-war peace settlement, which the ILO sought to implement. Socialists also played a key role in one of the most interesting institutions promoting peace – international veterans' associations, such as the International Federation of Ex-Servicement (FIDAC), which brought together former soldiers who had fought against each other to campaign on a range of issues from disarmament to better welfare for disabled ex-servicemen. Representatives of one national association regularly attended rallies of another. In 1929, Joseph Paul-Boncour, a left-wing French politician, and Erich Rossmann, a SPD deputy and head of the association of disabled veterans in Germany, called for international peace and adherence to the new ideas of arbitration and the League of Nations in commemoration of the 'dead of all nations, buried in the fraternity of the tomb'.[15]

IV

Rossmann and Paul-Boncour mobilised the dead to support peace. Soldiers had died in the name of their nation in the First World War, but their sacrifice had to be commemorated in the work of peace. This was a view shared by socialists throughout Europe. Nationalists, however, argued that the sacrifice of the war dead could only be redeemed through another war (in Germany's case, for example) or through the maintenance of the absolute security achieved through victory (in France's case, for example). At the same time as Rossmann and Paul-Boncour met, the bonds of peace, which socialists had done so much to knit together, began to fray. Domestic political shifts, the Great Depression and the resurgence of military force in international affairs contrived to make the socialists' culture of peace less appealing than it had been in the 1920s. Socialists had never rejected the centrality of the nation and state in politics; indeed they had embraced it during the First World War, but they embraced it on the assumption that a world of nations would also sustain a more peaceful international and domestic society, that disputes between nations could be resolved through arbitration, and that welfare could be best provided in the context of a national community.

The Great Depression had three intertwined consequences for socialist movements around Europe. Shrinking economies led to cutbacks in social welfare provision and public sector salaries as states struggled to maintain a balanced budget and avoid the reappearance of hyper-inflation, which had destroyed economies in the early 1920s. These cutbacks, often supported and implemented by socialist-led governments, radicalised domestic politics. As states cut back expenditure, governments tried to protect national economies by adopting protectionist policies, which in turn undermined international economic and political stability. The German example is perhaps the most extreme, but it illustrates how socialists failed to adapt their cultures of peace to the harsher international and domestic environment of the 1930s. In 1928 the SPD had triumphed at the polls in Germany. It was the largest party in the new coalition. Soon after its electoral triumph, the tide began to turn. Months before the Wall Street Crash, the German economy slowed down and unemployment rose. The SPD wanted to increase employers' contributions to an unemployment insurance fund, but as the crisis worsened, the coalition collapsed as employers baulked at constant increases in taxation and social insurance. The split was compounded, however, by an increase in military spending, especially on the German navy. Socialists regularly commented that money spent on armaments would be better spent on housing and welfare.[16]

This debate over welfare and armaments was a microcosm of the contest between war cultures and peace cultures in Europe. As earlier generations of radicals had argued, military expenditure diverted resources from social problems at home and exacerbated international tensions. In 1929, the Labour Party and the SPD had, independently, both produced manifestos, which had given prominence to their foreign policy ambitions of arbitration and disarmament. By 1930 the SPD had left government in Germany and would not return until the 1960s. Parliamentary government came to an end with the departure of the SPD in 1930, although it was another three years before Hitler came to power. In those years more nationalistic and militarist figures dominated German politics and dismantled the domestic and international frameworks that had sustained peace since the mid-1920s. Although the Labour Party won the British election in 1929, it was overwhelmed by the Great Depression and a National Government was formed in 1931, which removed Britain from the Gold Standard and ended free trade. These were two of the fundamental institutions of the open globalised economy that socialists had believed would bring greater prosperity to workers and peace to the international system. In Ireland the victory of Fianna Fáil in the 1932 election also led to a more autarchic policy and an economic war with Britain.

Finally, the League of Nations failed in two essential tests, marking a return to a more militarised conception of security. Japanese aggression in Manchuria in 1931 went unpunished, while the Geneva disarmament conference failed to make any progress between 1932 and 1934. Hitler took Germany out of the conference in 1933, as he continued the process of remilitarisation of German foreign and security policy, which had begun with naval rearmament in 1928. The proclamations of socialists that states could enjoy security through arbitration, disarmament and the League of Nations rang hollow by the early 1930s. The world had become a more dangerous place for small states, though compared with Poland, Czechoslovakia, and other states in central and eastern Europe, Ireland enjoyed the considerable security blanket of the Royal Navy. In 1938 while Hitler was busy dismembering Czechoslovakia, Britain was handing back the Treaty ports, which enabled de Valera, who by then had lost any faith in the League of Nations, to adopt a policy of neutrality the following year.

V

The violent legacies of the First World War have been well-documented. The more peaceful legacies remain marginal, but if we peer beyond the end of the Second World War, we find some traces which suggest that the cultures of peace, advocated by European socialist movements, amongst others, survived the Second World War. Some of these traces can be seen in minor characters, such as Leon Bagot, who led a peace strike at the Renault factory in May 1918, joined the editorial board of *L'Humanité* after the war, and was elected a municipal councillor for the French Communist Party in 1945.[17] Another was Franz Osterroth, who was born in 1900 and called up in 1918. Service at the front led him to detest war and he joined the SPD. He worked on various publications before going into exile after 1933, but he returned to play an active role in SPD politics, particularly in youth education after 1945.[18] For socialists like these, the traditional demarcations of European history – 1918, 1933, 1945 – were only part of a longer story. After 1945, the agenda set by socialist cultures of peace in the First World War – international institutions, human rights, and welfare provision amongst other issues – were renewed. This was most obvious in the case of Britain, where the Labour Party won a landslide in 1945. However, right-wing parties, such as the Christian Democrats in Italy and West Germany, also embraced the welfare state, regulated capitalism, and supported international institutions.

If we define political success and failure in terms of the ballot box, then socialism in twentieth century Europe would have a limited purchase on historians' attention. If we broaden our conception of political success, then we can see how the twentieth century was shaped by socialist ideas. The First World War marks an important turning point in this history because mobilisation led to a dramatic expansion of the state and therefore the agenda of politics. Socialists were at the fore of this expansion of politics and their ideas shaped political agendas for the coming decades. In the Irish context socialists failed to define the agenda during the First World War. Moreover, in terms of constitutional politics, most Irish nationalists (and to a lesser extent unionists) would have agreed with the political assumptions of European socialists – constitutional democracy, civilian control of the military, minority rights and security for small states through the mechanisms of international law and arbitration. Therefore, even before one looks to social structures as an explanation for the comparatively weak performance of the Irish Labour Party for much of the twentieth century, it is worth noting that it had a smaller political space in which to operate than its European counterparts.

6. 'IF IT'S SOCIALISM YOU WANT, JOIN SOME OTHER PARTY': LABOUR AND THE LEFT

NIAMH PUIRSÉIL

For most of those committed to the idea of radical change in society [the Labour Party is] the irreplaceable touchstone of political angst. For many people on the Left, it has traditionally been the party one would never dream of joining, the party one is thinking of leaving, or the party one has just left.[1]

JOHN HORGAN NEATLY sums up a problem that has afflicted Labour for much of its history. If the notion of the Labour Party being the 'irreplaceable touchstone of political angst' seems a touch melodramatic, it is true that many progressives have had great difficulties in associating themselves with Labour and those who do venture into its ranks do not always last terribly long. It is a phenomenon highlighted (no doubt accidentally) by a poster produced by Labour students in UCD in 2008. Proclaiming, 'they fought for social justice in their generation: now it's your turn. Join Labour Youth today', it featured photographs of four well-known Labour activists: Jim Larkin, James Connolly, Noël Browne and Mary Robinson, each of whom had left the Labour Party at some point (for very different reasons); James Connolly, executed before he ever had the chance, was the exception. Still, of the many individuals and some groups that have departed over the years, many did return. As one activist whose round trip had taken almost thirty years to complete explained 'you can bash the Labour Party all you like, but still on the left you come back to it'.[2] In fact, no other party has engaged in as many takeovers and mergers over the years; some were of former rivals, most notably the Democratic Left, but most were of splinter groups 'coming home'.

In his compelling but unreliable and jaundiced memoir, *Against the Tide,* Noël Browne related how his friend Johnny Byrne had been told by Young Jim Larkin: 'if it's socialism you want, join some other party.'[3] Known for his capacity for bitterness, Browne told the story against Larkin who, he claimed 'had stood for election as a Communist on his return from Moscow. He had been utterly defeated. Having "learnt his lesson", he had long since become a respected trade union leader and deeply conservative member of the Labour Party.'[4] Browne was wrong to describe Larkin as 'deeply conservative' and to imply that he was an opportunist who plumped for a respectable career after a heavy electoral defeat but the words he ascribes to him here ring true. Young Jim Larkin understood left-wing ideology better than most; he knew what Labour was and what it was not around this time (1950s) and it was *not* a socialist party, much as he would have liked it to be. The examples of how the former Communist (Larkin), the Trotskyist (Byrne) and the maverick radical (Browne) all ended up in Labour illustrate the party's capacity to attract people of different left-wing beliefs (the Labour Left often manages to be at once tiny and labyrinthine) even if none of them found Labour a particularly satisfying home. For many years, the problem for those on the Left who found Labour too conservative was that there was no alternative, as Jim Larkin knew well when he told Johnny Byrne to 'join some other party'. Occasionally there was literally no other party to the Left of Labour; more often it was the case that the Left alternatives were too small and ineffectual.

I

Writing in 1963, David Thornley began a study of the Irish labour movement by posing the question of how the 'militantly Marxist movement of Connolly and Larkin became the gradualist and scarcely socialist party of today',[5] but while he conceded later on that the 'revolutionary fervour' of Larkin and Connolly was 'never fully representative of the movement as a whole'[6], he failed to recognise that the political wing of Labour was not established as a Marxist party and that as militant as Connolly and Larkin may have been, the Irish Labour Party was set up first and foremost in order to provide parliamentary representation for workers in an Irish parliament. Its original objective was to 'organise and unite the workers of Ireland in order to improve their status and conditions generally and to take such action in the industrial and political fields with that end in view.' As such, it was labourist, not socialist, and this was reflected in the organisation's structure which was based on affiliated unions and which did not allow individual membership or membership by socialist or cooperative societies as was the case with the Labour Party in Britain which had been founded a few years earlier. Had there been socialist groups within Labour from the beginning, they might have weighted the party more to the Left but with tiny, split-prone memberships, it is questionable how much impact they could have made. Nevertheless, without such an anchor, the party was liable to float in whichever direction the political wind blew and without a grass-roots membership the party became overly reliant on trade union officials and members of the parliamentary party, which was fairly small in 1922 and, with the exception of a brief fillip at the June 1927 election, only got smaller. Individual personalities developed undue influence and the vagaries of the electorate could have a marked impact on the party's direction. Moreover, the absence of certain personalities, most obviously James Connolly, resulted in a more cautious movement overall. The parliamentary Labour Party which entered the Dáil in 1922 was led by Tom Johnson, who had been a Fabian and member of the Independent Labour Party in Britain before becoming active in the socialist movement in Ireland but, like Johnson, the party was reformist, not revolutionary.

Part of Labour's problem at the time was that its political rivals on the Left constantly painted it as being more right wing than it really was. The odium Labour instilled in those to its Left during the decade or so after 1922 was remarkable. The numerous front groups and splinter groups are too many to list here, but for simplicity, they can be reduced to a troika of communists, republican leftists (i.e. republican men and women who looked to Connolly rather than Pearse)[7] and Larkinites, with considerable overlap in sympathies. The animus towards Labour has its roots in two issues. The first related to Labour's position on the Treaty. Labour declared it was 'neutral' on the issue, a stance which opponents of the Treaty (which, as well as anti-Treaty Sinn Féin and IRA, included the newly established Communist Party of Ireland) believed was just de facto support for the settlement.[8] While Labour saw itself as an honest broker and spent a great deal of time in the Dáil speaking against the ill-treatment of republican prisoners and castigating the government for its summary executions,[9] their presence in the Free State Dáil rendered them traitors to the very people they attempted to defend[10] and resulted in death threats being issued against Labour politicians.[11]

The second matter had virtually nothing to do with ideology but sundered the trade union movement and the Left for several decades. In April 1923, Big Jim Larkin returned to Dublin after an eight-year absence in the USA, intending to pick up in his union where he had left off in 1914.[12] Not unreasonably, this was blocked by his former colleagues, people like William O'Brien and Cathal O'Shannon, who had spent almost a decade rebuilding the Transport Union from the ruins of the 1913 lockout. Strictly speaking, Larkin's quarrel was with the ITGWU leadership but since the same people were at Labour's helm, the party inevitably became a target. Moreover, since Larkin resented anything he could not control, he could not allow it to operate without him; as Emmet O'Connor observed, 'incredible as it may seem, the schism was entirely of Larkin's making. A movement that emanated from O'Brien and Labour Leader Tom Johnson had to be destroyed, simply because he could not claim credit for it.'[13]

Larkin filled his newspaper, *The Irish Worker,* with diatribes against the 'God save the King Labour Party' led by its 'English anti-Irishman' leader, ignoring the fact that both Johnson and Larkin originally hailed from Liverpool, and Larkin's accent was considerably more pronounced. The attacks were not merely on paper but occasionally degenerated into physical violence. Perhaps the nadir for Labour came at the September 1927 general election when, following a particularly unpleasant campaign by the Larkinite Irish Worker League, Tom Johnson, who had led Labour since it entered the Dáil in 1922, lost his seat in Dublin County.

It is probably no exaggeration to suggest that this triumvirate of Leftists devoted more effort to attacking Labour than to undermining Cumann na nGaedheal governments. The extent to which Labour was damaged by these campaigns is difficult to gauge but undoubtedly the Larkinites' vendetta caused real harm. Most obviously, it cost them Tom Johnson's seat in 1927 but their role in pushing working class support behind Fianna Fáil – even when instructed by the Comintern to desist[14] – is also important. It is hard to believe that a Labour Party that enjoyed Larkin's support would not have been more popular especially in Dublin, but instead, Larkin was Labour's sworn enemy. The constant emphasis on Labour's 'Englishness' and its 'Free State' outlook almost certainly damaged Labour but rather than these attacks benefiting the radical Left they merely encouraged working class voters to look to Fianna Fáil – republican, *Irish,* and styling itself as the 'real Labour Party' – as their natural home.

II

A decade of left-wing attacks on Labour came to an end in the mid-1930s but, just as the battle on one front ended, another began, which had a profound impact on the party until the 1950s at least. Jim Larkin's (temporary) retirement from party politics after the 1933 election removed one opponent.[15] The Communist/Republican Left effort in 1934 to establish a united front in the form of Republican Congress was also a factor. Several of those involved in Republican Congress, including Michael Price, Séamus O'Brien and his wife Nora Connolly O'Brien (a daughter of James Connolly) joined Labour around this time, with the goal of pushing it to the Left. The latter's brother, Roddy Connolly (founder of the Communist Party of Ireland), had already done so independently several years earlier.[16] Labour did move quite firmly to the Left around this time most obviously when the party's 1934 conference adopted a motion stating that Labour's goal was to establish a 'Workers' Republic', but the role played by the new republican members in bringing this about would seem to have been negligible. The impetus, as the ITGWU official Frank Robbins put it, was that Fianna Fáil (in government since 1932) had 'stolen' Labour's old policy and programme and they needed a new one 'in order to be in advance of any other political party'.[17] The move Left was also in reaction to the growth of Fascism in Europe and its domestic variety in the form of the Blueshirts. It should be remembered that the party had also been joined by a small number of Leftist intellectuals (mostly – if not all – from Trinity College Dublin) including Owen Sheehy-Skeffington and his cousin Conor Cruise O'Brien, but they were regarded as an irritation by some working class veterans.[18] Labour's shift Left did not last long. When a special committee of Catholic clerics declared that the Ireland envisaged in the Workers' Republic constitution was 'similar ... to Soviet Russia', its days were numbered and the republican Left could do nothing, as under William Norton's pragmatic leadership, Labour dropped its 'radical' clause almost as easily as it had been adopted.[19] As Norton once told the Labour executive, 'We should be slowest in doing anything that might make difficulties for us later on and prevent us from being in a position to manoeuvre. The political party which can't manoeuvre is dead.'[20] Having taken over a parliamentary party of seven deputies, he was not interested in doing anything which might further reduce that number. Faced with the prospect of doing anything which would probably lose votes – whether it was socialism, criticism of the Church or supporting republicans in Spain

– Norton would always walk away. In terms of influence, then, the right-wing press and the Catholic Church were infinitely stronger than the Left inside or outside of Labour and the party, which, with notable exceptions, was fairly conservative anyway, went out of its way to make sure it was seen to be so.

For the former Republican Congress man, Séamus O'Brien, dropping the Workers' Republic constitution was a compromise too far. 'You have killed the idealists in your party,' he told Norton, 'there is no future in it for them.'[21] There is, however, little to suggest there was any mass exodus in the wake of the U-turn; in fact, the opposite was the case. It was only a few months afterwards that war broke out in Europe and over the course of the Emergency, Labour became a magnet for Leftists of many hues. To begin with there were Trotskyists, some of whom had escaped from Britain when the war broke out to avoid arrest as subversives.[22] In 1941, Big Jim Larkin was allowed rejoin, despite ITGWU opposition. That same year, the USSR entered the war against Germany. National communist parties were now expected to support the allies, but rather than support Britain, the Communist Party of Ireland wound itself up.[23] It continued to exist in the six counties while the southern cadre were instructed to join the Labour Party. With an expanding, activist membership Labour appeared more vital than ever with 'Connollyites, Trotskyites, Stalinists and all kinds of social democrats' cooperating in a 'comradely way'[24] but there was one group notably absent. The decision to allow Jim Larkin back into Labour was viewed askance by the Transport Union's chiefs who threatened to disaffiliate if his membership was not cancelled. Not only was it not cancelled,[25] but after much skulduggery on all sides, he ended up standing as a Labour candidate in Dublin North East at the 1943 General Election and was elected. This was too much for the ITGWU which acted on its threat but soon found that its members did not regard Larkin's presence as good reason for leaving the party. Looking around for a better excuse, the ITGWU leadership alighted on the presence of communists in Labour who, it said, had 'infested' the party.

The union's disaffiliation was damaging enough but this disingenuous claim had a devastating effect on Labour. A party which had been on the offensive in recent years, growing in confidence and numbers, now found itself subject to lurid exposés from the breakaway National Labour Party, concerned 'friends' (like Alfred O'Rahilly) and gleeful opponents like Seán MacEntee. A problem for Labour was that, while the stories were vastly exaggerated, they were not without substance and rather than deny the accusations outright, Labour established a committee of inquiry on the matter. In the end, four members were expelled on the findings of the committee (although one was subsequently allowed back) and the Liam Mellows branch in Cork was dissolved.[26] There was certainly no purge of leftists, nor did others leave in protest, but *Torch,* the weekly newspaper of the party in Dublin, was closed down and the Left became very careful not to say anything that would give cause for alarm. This meant any mention of socialism was forbidden and anything which could be construed as being critical of the Catholic Church was avoided at all costs.[27] A fairly ludicrous situation developed whereby activists on the Dublin Left, which included a relatively large proportion of Protestants and atheists, regularly cited papal encyclicals in the party's publications and speeches because it was the only way to attack capitalism without being branded a 'Red'.[28] As galling as it was, the idea of standing against this 'intellectual terrorism' simply was not countenanced. On one occasion, Sheila Greene, the editor of Labour's weekly paper *The Irish People,* returned a piece to Seán O'Casey in which he had criticised the Roman Catholic Archbishop of Westminster as it would give ammunition to the party's enemies. 'I think if you lived here you would understand,' she told O'Casey, but clearly from his home in Devon he did not. 'Goethe's last words were "More light. More light." Mine will probably be "More courage. More courage". I am not out to force the Labour Party of Ireland. Their ways rest with their conscience'[29].

This culture of self censorship and the 'shocking belief among ordinary … members that enthusiasm is the last thing Head Office wants to see'[30] did not make Labour an attractive home for any would-be radicals, something which was highlighted all the more when the new republican party, Clann na Poblachta, appeared in the summer of 1946. As *The Irish Times* journalist and Labour activist Brian Inglis noted at the time, it was 'those who have been deterred from coming in that really matter; the number of Clann members I know, who have admitted that they would have like to have joined Labour, but who were put off by the moribund state in which they found the party is astonishing'.[31] This being the case it is difficult to understand why anyone on the Left would choose to stay but at least part of the reason was the hope or expectation that a change of leadership would revive the party and move it to the Left. The person identified as Labour's saviour was Young Jim Larkin, who had joined Labour alongside his father, Big Jim, in 1941 and who had stood successfully as a Labour candidate in successive elections since 1943 before stepping down in 1957. Unlike his father in so many ways, this cautious and diffident man refused to play the role in which others had cast him. He told his friend John de Courcy Ireland that he would leave Labour if he thought anyone was a member because of his presence in the party, telling him:

> I do want you to know that I am not of the stuff of which leaders are made, and even if I was foolish enough to let you and other short sighted persons convince me, and try to live up to it, I'd fail at a critical moment and the cost to be paid might be very heavy…I only wish I could get some other people to take the same view, not for my sake but for the peace of mind and the good of the movement.[32]

Although Larkin put his unwillingness to lead in personal terms, it was really his politics that were problematic. Larkin had not merely been an active member of the communist Irish Worker League and the Revolutionary Workers Groups but he had previously spent several years studying at the International Lenin School in Moscow, as Seán MacEntee delighted in mentioning at any given opportunity. By 1938 he had dropped out of the communist movement but as far as his enemies were concerned, he remained a dangerous Red. A 1947 Department of Justice dossier on communist activity in Ireland noted that Larkin (Junior) 'remains in the background but there is little doubt that he would resume his identity as 'comrade' Larkin if it were politic to do so.'[33] 'Little doubt' really meant 'no evidence' but there was nothing which could be done to disabuse people of the belief that he was a communist sleeper. This became most brutally clear in 1948 after Labour had entered into the broad based inter-party government with Fine Gael among others. Labour had three ministers who were selected by a vote of the parliamentary party but when Fine Gael learned that Jim Larkin Junior was one of Labour's nominees, Norton was told to find someone else, which he duly did. With Young Jim refusing to lead a revolt and no one else willing or able to take his place, the arch-pragmatist William Norton remained *in situ* until 1960 simply because the other Labour deputies were 'too engrossed in their constituencies and county councils to challenge him.'[34]

III

The unhappiness of the Labour Left was only made more acute by the party's experience in government. The most positive effect of the first inter-party government of 1948–51 was that it reunited the two Labour Parties after a seven-year breach. That administration brought some real advances, most notably in housing, but there were also disappointments and any benefits were overshadowed by the furore over the Mother and Child scheme. A cautious leadership combined with the compromises of government led some to leave while others only stayed by the skin of their teeth.[35] The second inter-party government of 1954–7 was less volatile but more troubled as unemployment and emigration rocketed after 1956. Asked about that government in later years, Brendan Corish, Labour's Minister for Social Welfare, recalled how he would 'lie awake at night, worrying about the unemployed'.[36] The government appeared unable to tackle it in the short term and the austerity policies of Fine Gael's Finance Minister, Gerry Sweetman, only made matters worse. Many on the Labour Left had concluded that it was a 'hopeless case,'[37] but there was nowhere for them to go. The Irish Workers' League had around sixty members nationwide and was being hounded by anti-communists; Clann na Poblachta was all but dead as a party and Seán MacBride (who had lost his seat in 1957) was looking to Labour to establish a Labour–Republican alliance which might provide him with a lifeline. The National Progressive Democrats, a new party centred around Noël Browne, failed to develop into more than a flag of convenience for Browne and his colleague Jack McQuillan. Labour was very damaged by its experience in government, but the lack of viable left-wing alternatives gave it some breathing space to revive. Labour's leadership issued a *mea culpa* for the previous administration and pledged not to enter into another coalition. Parallel to that, there was a strategy to rebuild the party that included an effort to unify the Left which would mean convincing smaller groups that there was room for them in Labour. This inclusiveness could be grudging as it was towards Noël Browne (a legacy of the first inter-party government) but slowly it began to reap rewards. With a new young leader, Brendan Corish, replacing William Norton in 1960, Labour began to look less reactionary and by the mid-1960s it was beginning to sound more progressive too. The word 'socialism' actually made an appearance on Labour platforms for the first time since the 1920s.

In Ireland, as elsewhere, there was an explosion of radical groups in the late 1960s. There was now a bewildering number of organisations across the left-wing spectrum,[38] while the republican movement had been shifting leftward over the course of the decade. Occupations, sit-ins, fish-ins and marches were frequent occurrences on issues as diverse as housing to the Vietnam War to architectural conservation. Despite this multiplicity of protest groups and radical sects, many enthusiastic Leftists flocked into Labour's ranks as the party promised that the 'Seventies would be Socialist.'

With the 1969 conference attended by 840 delegates, its largest ever by far, it was possible for some members to get caught up in the excitement. For a time the Left seemed to have it largely its own way and by the time the party went before the electorate at the 1969 general election it was virtually unrecognisable from that of a few years earlier, but if the party's old-guard kept quiet it was only because they knew where their power lay and that was in their own constituencies. Fianna Fáil – in its first general election with Jack Lynch as leader – ran a Red scare during the campaign. Knowing better than to smear the whole party – no one would have believed it – Fianna Fáil told voters how 'there are two Labour Parties – the traditional one… and a new group of extreme left-wing socialists preaching class warfare and who want total state control and all that goes with it'[39] or, as Brian Lenihan told a woman in Roscommon, 'your local candidates are decent fellas but what could they do with those dangerous men at the top?'[40] The 'decent fellas' did their best to avoid guilt by association, staying out of the national press, avoiding using official Labour literature sent down by head office or even posters which bore the word 'Labour.' Most of them survived; three from Labour's Munster heartlands did not. Even if this owed more to bad tactics and boundary changes than anything it still caused the Labour Right to begin its fight back.

The heady optimism of the 1960s became a distant memory as the 1970s wore on. The ascendancy of the Left came to an abrupt end and the party became best known for its squabbling. There seemed to be infinite reasons for in-fighting; within the parliamentary Labour Party, much of it was the result of dashed expectations (on the Left and centre), bitter resentment (on the Right) and the cramming of a large number of large and volatile egos into a relatively small parliamentary party,[41] but personality problems merely provided the tinder. The fuel for the fire came primarily from two issues which had begun to emerge in the late 1960s but which became acute after 1970: the troubles in the North and the question of coalition. Attitudes on the North and on the IRA campaigns, in particular, did not fall neatly into Left/Right lines, resulting in a number of somewhat bizarre alliances on the issue within the parliamentary Labour Party. On coalition, though, the ideological stance was quite clear. After the trauma of the second inter-party government, Labour's refusal to enter any coalition in which it was not the majority party had been central to the process of rebuilding the party.[42] Labour's survival depended on convincing voters that it did not merely exist to 'give the kiss of life to Fine Gael' (as Brendan Corish once put it)[43] and over the 1960s, Labour successfully rebuilt its identity based on progressive policies and political independence.

As time went on, dislike of Fianna Fáil eclipsed the perception of Fine Gael as the 'villain of the second inter-party government'[44] and there was growing frustration among some TDs that the keys to ministerial office were being put permanently beyond reach. For those on the Left, however, a coalition with Fine Gael meant inevitably abandoning the socialist policies which they had only just managed to secure, akin to 'Moses telling the Israelites that there was no Promised Land after all, but that they need not worry, since the Pharaoh had agreed to take them back.'[45] The anti-coalitionists had managed to retain the policy going into the 1969 election, but were unable to stop the move to scrap it afterwards. The issue effectively became the fault line between Left and Right for the next two decades and it was this question, more than any other, which established Labour as 'the touchstone of political angst'.

The special conference held in Cork in 1970 to decide on the matter, 'held in an atmosphere of virtual civil war,'[46] included tearful delegates and bitter words between Brendan Corish and Noël Browne, the latter inadvertently leading a walkout when he left the hall early to get the train back to Dublin.[47] For much of the 1970s, the Liaison Committee of the Labour Left (LCLL) continued to oppose coalition after the party went into government with Fine Gael in 1973,[48] although in 1977, two members of LCLL, one being Noël Browne, stood as independent candidates before setting up the Socialist Labour Party (SLP) later that year. A contemporary profile of that party observed how frustrating the previous decade had been for the Irish Left:

> Unable to harness the industrial conflict or the agitation of the sixties, the leadership of the massive upsurge in the North slipping through its fingers, the Left has had to run very fast just to stand still. Massive unemployment, reduction of living standards and a wave of political repression gave socialist groups plenty to fight. But it didn't bring in the recruits.[49]

The writer (Gene Kerrigan) observed that the Left was fragmented and that, as difficult as it was to establish 'unity of the Left', 'a rallying point which can draw in large numbers of workers who would otherwise be confused or disillusioned by the disunity of the Left can serve a useful function,' and suggested that the SLP might just be that party. Inevitably, it was not; the SLP never developed as a real party organisation and ultimately dissolved in 1982.[50] In effect, all it had done was provide a home for many of Labour's anti-coalitionists outside of the party and add another notch to Noël Browne's tally of parties. But if Kerrigan was wrong about the SLP's prospects he was correct about fragmentation, which only got worse going into the 1980s as Sinn Féin–the Workers' Party (simply the Workers' Party from 1982) won its first seat in the Dáil in 1981 and began to establish a strong base in Dublin.

In 1977, Fianna Fáil won an unexpected electoral landslide, putting the Fine Gael–Labour coalition out of office and (paradoxically) ushering in an era of great political volatility. The next few years were particularly difficult for Labour. Morale was low and a lack of strong and secure leadership did not help.[51] For those on the Left who had not defected to the SLP, coalition remained the most divisive issue and was one which was forced by successive inconclusive elections between June 1981 and November 1982. The party was largely sundered into the two camps, the PLP (and its supporters) which supported coalition and the left-wing membership, which was against. The two sides were relatively evenly matched, something which was reflected in the party's ruling Administrative Council which was split on the issue, but the coalitionists had the edge when it mattered since they got reasonably secure majorities at special conferences which were held in 1981 and November 1982 to decide the issue.[52] The November special conference approved Labour entering into coalition with Fine Gael in an arrangement which would last until January 1987 (Dick Spring had been elected leader only in October). Throughout that time, efforts were made by Labour Left, a group established in 1983 to 'Save the Labour Party,'[53] to abandon coalition and were joined in this campaign by Militant, Labour's 'small but irksome'[54] Trotskyist tendency. Adding to the Left's fear that Labour faced annihilation was the creeping popularity of the Workers' Party in working class Dublin areas at precisely the same time as Labour was becoming weaker there.[55] At Labour's 1982 conference, the party chairman and constant champion of the Left, Michael D. Higgins, had warned that 'if this party will not stand firm for socialism, it will find there are others who will';[56] less prescriptively, a report on the 1982 elections cautioned that if Labour did not start making gains in forthcoming elections it would passed out on its right and left.[57] Certainly, nothing the coalition was doing at the time – a period of mass unemployment and emigration and a huge budget deficit – was likely to win Labour any votes.

Ultimately, Labour pulled out of the coalition in 1987 but the die was already cast. The election which followed was bruising – Labour recorded its second lowest vote, at 6.6 per cent, returned with a dozen TDs (its lowest since 1957) and only narrowly managed not to lose another leader – but the one consolation was that the election had been proportionately worse for Fine Gael. Those wondering if the Workers' Party could inflict a 'death blow' to Labour were disappointed – it won only four seats – but, as Michael Gallagher noted, otherwise the results could hardly have been worse for Labour.[58] But the fact that Labour and the Workers' Party combined had less than 10 per cent of the total poll – the lowest level since 1957 – illustrates the unpopularity of the Left in the country generally, especially when the new right-wing Progressive Democrats won fourteen seats.[59] Labour's first conference after the election suggested that if the membership had its way the party might swing leftward, prompting a counter-attack by the party leadership. They expelled members of Militant (as British Labour had done some years earlier) and in so doing, fundamentally eroded the support base for the Labour Left group.[60] As a result, Labour went into the 1990s on a socially liberal, socially democratic platform.

IV

The new decade began with some notable advances; there was the success of its nominee Mary Robinson in the presidential election of 1990, the merger with the Democratic Socialist Party, bringing Jim Kemmy back to the Labour fold after almost twenty years, and then the 'Spring Tide' of 1992 surged in. Labour looked like a force to be reckoned with for the first time in years. There followed the decision to go into coalition with Fianna Fáil. As usual, a special conference had to approve the coalition and this time did so almost unanimously. Afterwards, Dick Spring remarked 'That's answered something I've always wondered about. The party isn't full of anti-coalitionists after all. They were just anti-Fine Gael all along!'[61] Perhaps Spring had a point, although it is unlikely that the event would have passed quite so smoothly had Militant not been purged a couple of years earlier. Either way, coalition was no longer the source of conflict which it had been for so many years. After the coalition with Fianna Fáil fell two years in, Labour went into a 'Rainbow Coalition' with Fine Gael and Democratic Left (DL), the party which had broken away from the Workers' Party in 1992, but had failed to develop into more than the remnants of the old party.[62] Cooperation at cabinet level laid the groundwork of a merger between Labour and DL in 1999, ushering in a brief period of the much coveted left-wing unity (although unity was not a word which described the situation at constituency level) without significant change in party policy. The new Labour Party, as it went into the twenty-first century, differed little from that of, say, New Labour in Britain; ostensibly social democratic but ultimately not challenging the economic system in the slightest, adopting the language of 'hard-working families' which had grown out of focus-group politics during the 1990s. It is worth noting that the results of general elections prior to 2011 suggest there was little demand for anything more radical than that.[63] It took an economic crisis of catastrophic proportions to secure the largest ever left-wing vote by far but without any prospect of left-wing unity.[64] Labour has identified itself as a centre party of government, ruling out any cooperation with Sinn Féin, now increasingly identifying itself as the party of James Connolly (as Fianna Fáil did in the 1920s) or with 'hard left protest parties and ragbags'.[65] The party's decision to enter government with Fine Gael and implement, or as Labour ministers might put it, temper, a regime of austerity, means that once again the battle among Left republicans and the socialist Left is over who the real Labour Party is; the one thing on which they agree is that it is not Labour.

Historically, the weakness of Labour and of the Left within the party was part of a larger issue, namely, the profound weakness of the Left in Ireland as a whole. For many years, Labour was the only party of the Left to secure any electoral representation in the Dáil and often won only 10 per cent of the poll, indeed as Tom Garvin once observed, while 'the reasons for Labour's weakness have often been debated by Irish political scientists and historians, it might be more appropriate to inquire into the reasons why it managed to survive at all'.[66] While Labour was a broad church, its membership ranging from socialist activists to the right-wing trade unionists who often dominated the parliamentary party, fear of powerful critics on the Right – whether from the Catholic Church, the press or its political opponents – frequently resulted in the party taking a cautious approach not to mention the propensity of leftwing members to self-censorship to avoid attack as happened during the 1940s and 1950s. The party as a whole may have become relatively fearless by the 1960s, promising to build the Socialist Republic, but that did not last beyond the 1969 election. The disappointing election result and a sense of frustration among members of the PLP prompted a watering-down of policy and the dropping of Labour's go-it-alone policy but the socialist genie was out of the bottle, and the new Labour left would not silence itself, as its predecessors had done, or be silenced. Ultimately, resignations and expulsions diminished the Left within the party while the arrival of former members of Democratic Left helped tip the balance still further to the right. In the meantime, the parties who placed themselves as the Left alternative – Sinn Féin and the United Left Alliance (featuring former Militants) – made uneven progress before making significant gains at the 2011 general election. That contest saw Labour at its strongest, in terms of seats, and at its most vulnerable in terms of competition from the Left. Perhaps the fragmentation of the Left is temporary, as in the past or maybe it is part of a broader realignment in Irish politics, but it does seems as though the days of Labour as a broad church as in Young Jim Larkin's time are over; the difference is unlike Larkin's time is that if it's socialism you want, you can join some other party.

7. LABOUR AND THE PURSUIT OF POWER

PAUL DALY

'LABOUR MUST WAIT', the phrase so closely associated with Labour's decision not to contest the 1918 election, still retains a hold over the collective consciousness of the party. Even as Labour prepared for what would be a historic election result in February 2011 the shadow of 1918 loomed – maybe not large, but it loomed. In January 2009, for example, party leader Eamon Gilmore, TD, at an event to mark the ninetieth anniversary of the Democratic Programme, stated: 'Ninety years ago, Labour took a patriotic and selfless decision, not to contest the 1918 General Election, so as not to split the vote of the Independence Movement. In the decades since, Labour members have often wondered about the wisdom of that decision, especially as we reflect on our seemingly permanent third place in Irish politics.'[1] In the following eighteen months Gilmore would return to the same theme at least twice in key speeches, describing the 1918 decision as one of the central 'regrets' of the party, at a SIPTU conference late in 2009.

In doing so, Gilmore was accurately reflecting a widely held belief among party members and supporters. Every party member who has stayed too long in a public house to console themselves after a becalmed day in a count centre can attest to the inevitable evocation of 1918. It was the ultimate sacrifice – the labour movement put nation before party and has been waiting ever since. The 1918 election was the first democratic election involving a near universal franchise. The electorate (which for the first time included women, albeit only those over thirty) had expanded three-fold since the previous general election in 1910. For many, the decision by Labour not to contest an election held in such historic circumstances, with hundreds of thousands of voters forming their political allegiance for the first time, was a strategic error with lasting consequences.

However, the exclusive focus on 1918 as a defining point in the development of Irish electoral politics and Labour's subsequent traditional role as the minor player in a two-and-a-half party system, fails to tell the whole story. While the 1918 election defined the immediate nature of Irish nationalism, it could be argued that it was the events of a decade later, and specifically the entry into constitutional politics of the majority of anti-Treaty Republicans under the Fianna Fáil banner, that defined the party system and by extension Labour's relationship with power. Indeed, to put forward the counter-factual question of 'what if Labour had contested in 1918?' is revealing. While the labour movement had taken a leadership role during the conscription crisis earlier that year, this should not be taken as a signal that the Labour Party was a powerful force on the brink of electoral success. In reality the development of the party had been stalled since its foundation six years earlier. Labour mobilisation and agitation was the main concern of the Irish Trade Union Congress, not the development of its political wing.

At the ITUC&LP conference in Waterford in August 1918 Labour had decided to contest the planned election and Johnson wrote the manifesto published in September. However, the sudden collapse of the German army in November 1918 fundamentally transformed the context within which the election would take place. The prospect of an international peace conference to decide the fate of nations, especially small nations, was now a reality. The nature of the electoral contest envisioned in August had been turned on its head in just four short months, as Arthur Mitchell noted: 'The principal issues in the forthcoming election has been framed by Sinn Féin: the election would be a plebiscite on the question of Irish self-determination, Sinn Féin would refuse to enter the British Parliament but would establish an Irish assembly, and they would present the united nationalist case to the post-war peace conference.'[2]

If Labour had contested in 1918, its impact might have been minimal. In September 1918 it had intended to contest fifteen seats; however, in the following weeks nominations failed to materialise. It is likely that the number of Labour candidates would have struggled to break double figures. While the party nominated candidates in four of the seven Dublin constituencies, 'in other areas of the country the appeal for Labour candidates met with a negative response. In Kilkenny, North Kildare, East Wicklow, Wexford, Waterford and Cork – centres of trade union membership – no candidates were put forward.'[3]

As Barry Desmond has commented, the Labour Party in 1918 'had no stomach, no resources and no candidates for a contest.'[4] It is hard to equate this reality with the popular view that subsequently developed about the enormity of the decision in 1918. Subsequent electoral results also point to the fact that the decision not to contest in 1918 did not have a debilitating effect on the ability of the Labour Party to attract substantial support. In January 1920, as the War of Independence raged, municipal elections were held with Labour emerging as the second largest party after Sinn Féin.[5] An even more impressive result was to come when Labour contested its first election to Dáil Éireann in June 1922. *The Voice of Labour* declared, 'The victory has been magnificent. Workers put their banner bearers at head of poll nearly everywhere,'[6] as seventeen of Labour's eighteen candidates were returned, with five topping the poll. Indeed, if organisation and finance had allowed it is likely Labour would have returned with a larger parliamentary party. The initial hope offered by Labour's breakthrough was short-lived. Within days of the June 1922 election the new Free State government began the bombardment of anti-Treaty forces in the Four Courts heralding the beginning of an eleven-month civil war – the bloody, divisive struggle that would ultimately do so much to define the Irish party system when the majority of anti-Treaty republicans regrouped as Fianna Fáil and entered Dáil Éireann.

Labour's parliamentary record in the decade 1922–1932 is dealt with extensively elsewhere in this volume. It has often been criticised for what Charles McCarthy described as the 'sensitive, mild, parliamentary socialism' that it adopted in the early years. However, the defining quality of Labour's contribution in the early years of the state was its commitment to constitutional politics and its desire to see parliamentary democracy secured. It is an honourable record and the party's role in convincing Fianna Fáil to enter Dáil Éireann during the tumultuous summer of 1927 epitomises the manner in which Tom Johnson in particular put country before party at a critical juncture.

In advance of the June 1927 election Labour had good reason to be wary of the threat that de Valera's newly founded Fianna Fáil represented to it. The new party wore its republicanism on its sleeve but its concentration on social and economic issues, as evidenced by de Valera's address at the party's founding in Dublin's La Scala Theatre in May 1926, presented a clear threat to Labour's support base. As the parties prepared to contest the June 1927 general election Johnson alleged that two thirds of Fianna Fáil's election manifesto had been lifted from the Labour programme.[7] Not only had Fianna Fáil managed to rob Labour's ideological clothes, it had also succeeded in a remarkably short time to build a powerful political machine that dwarfed the campaigning abilities of both Labour and Cumann na nGaedheal. Just six months after its foundation, Fianna Fáil speakers had addressed more than 400 public meetings.[8] By spring 1927 it had established 800 branches and launched a weekly newspaper, *The Nation*. Niamh Puirséil notes that 'While Labour had one man trying to build up a local branch network single handed, a crack team of Fianna Fáil volunteers ... were travelling the length and breadth of the country to establish a cumann in every parish.'[9] From the outset Fianna Fáil also had access to funds. De Valera had collected $20,000 in the US by 1927 and would visit that country twice before the end of the decade to establish support committees and raise more funds. Fianna Fáil also quickly leaned on its grass-roots supporters and business interests to fill the party coffers. By comparison Labour had managed to raise just £1,200 during 1927.[10]

Fianna Fáil did not decimate Labour on its first electoral outing in June 1927, although the fact that it won twice as many seats gave an insight into its intentions and potential. Labour's record in opposing the continuing authoritarianism and fiscal conservatism of the Cumann na nGaedheal government, however, ensured that it secured an impressive election result, returning twenty-two TDs, a feat that would not be bettered until 1992. The assassination of the Vice-President of the Executive Council, Kevin O'Higgins, in the weeks following the election then transformed politics. Fianna Fáil had attempted to enter Dáil Éireann without taking the oath and in the wake of O'Higgins' murder Cumann na nGaedheal forced the matter by passing legislation to prevent abstentionist candidates from contesting elections. It was a critical moment for Irish democracy with some fearing that without intervention it would result in a resumption of the Civil War.

Labour played a crucial role in July and early August in ensuring the entry of Fianna Fáil into Dáil Éireann. Not only did it facilitate the entry into constitutional politics of its greatest electoral threat, it also agreed to attempt to form an administration that would seek renegotiation of the oath and if this was not successful to put the issue to the people in a referendum.[11] On 12 August Dáil Éireann was given notice that Fianna Fáil deputies had taken their seats and four days later Johnson moved a motion of no confidence in the government with the aim of forming a coalition administration with the right-of-centre National Party, supported by Fianna Fáil. The prospects of this disparate coalition implementing a programme of reform or indeed lasting until the end of the year were remote, a fact hinted at by Johnson in his speech on the no–confidence motion, but it was a chance Johnson was prepared to take to reconcile Fianna Fáil to constitutional politics. As he stated during the debate,

> I said that there has been a new situation created by the definite, formal entry into the constitutional course of a party which has hitherto abstained from attendance at this House. That is a great new fact, and I think this House ought to welcome and recognise it. It is for themselves to say, but I believe the primary consideration determining that course was the belief which I and others have insisted upon in public that the country needed a rest from turmoil and trouble, that there was need for a period of settlement, for a period of reconstruction, for a period of devoted national service.[12]

Johnson's actions in the summer of 1927 and the Labour Party's decision to put nation above party gets little recognition within or without the party, partly because of the nature of the party system that would develop from it and partly because it is often wrongly viewed as an attempt by Labour to grab power at the head of a disparate coalition of forces. However, solely by reference to the perilous political situation that pertained that summer it was an act of patriotism, devoid of party interest. It was also an act for which Labour would pay a heavy price. The Cumann na nGaedheal government hung on to power with the casting vote of the Ceann Comhairle and subsequently called an election for September. Labour, after a historic election just months before, lost more than one third of its seats, including that of Johnson. Other smaller parties fared badly too, as Fianna Fáil and Cumann na nGaedheal increased their vote and between them secured 77 per cent of the seats in the new Dáil. The die of Irish politics was finally cast, it would be democratic, constitutional and dominated by two major parties.

In his speech on the no–confidence motion in August Johnson had pointed to a political future where coalition formations, of all hues, would compete for power.[13] It was the logic of the proportional representation electoral system. The challenge for Labour post-1927 was to rebuild the party to the extent that it remained relevant to the emerging political reality and could present itself as a third force, with a distinct appeal beyond that of the Civil War parties. To do that it needed leadership, policy focus and organisational ability, and its reserves on all fronts were low. The break from the trade unions in 1930 presented the party with an opportunity to reposition itself, but the resulting party programme failed to offer the policy definition necessary to prevent the inroads that Fianna Fáil was making into its urban working class and rural labourer vote. At a time when the party should have advanced distinct policies to secure modest electoral gains it opted for a broad policy programme that failed to distinguish it from Fianna Fáil in particular.

This strategic error was compounded by ongoing organisational weakness, financial problems and parliamentary indiscipline that led to the expulsion of two of its thirteen TDs. When the 1932 election was called, 'Labour remained on the sidelines, so irrelevant that neither of the larger parties bothered attacking it.'[14] The party vote dropped to a record low and it returned only seven TDs, again losing its leader into the bargain. Fianna Fáil triumphed at the election, winning 44.5 per cent of the vote and securing an additional fifteen seats. With Fianna Fáil just five seats short of an overall majority, the new Labour leader William Norton led the Labour Party into the Dáil to support the formation of a minority Fianna Fáil government, after agreeing a seven-point programme with de Valera. However, Labour did so from a position of weakness. Labour's policy demands of the new government were readily acceptable as Fianna Fáil had incorporated so many of them into its election programme.

The influence Labour had on Fianna Fáil's first administration was short-lived: within a year de Valera dissolved the Dáil and the subsequent election returned a slim Fianna Fáil majority government (with Labour again supporting de Valera's nomination as Taoiseach). The seminal 1932 election, which witnessed the first transfer of power since the formation of the Free State, did not herald the multi-party competition that Johnson had envisaged in August 1927. The failure to develop and grow the party from both a policy and organisational perspective in the previous five years left Labour on the periphery of politics. More importantly Fianna Fáil would, in turn, develop its aversion to any sharing of power, a position that would endure for the next fifty-five years. Irish political competition effectively developed into a contest between Fianna Fáil and the rest. Labour's attitude to power was as a result circumscribed for it rather than defined by it. Its only option for government until the last decade of the century would centre on a coalition arrangement with Fine Gael and at times other parties. The failure of Labour to limit the appeal of Fianna Fáil between 1927 and 1932 was crucial in defining political competition for the next two generations. Unlike smaller parties in other European democracies, Labour was prevented from using its electoral strength to broker the best deal for its policies and its supporters between the two large conservative parties. The question of exercising power was fundamentally restricted with one avenue effectively closed off.

Following its ascension to power in the 1930s Fianna Fáil elevated its quest for single-party government into a 'core principle'. In spite of an electoral system that encouraged plurality, and by extension implied coalition, Fianna Fáil set its teeth against the idea of sharing power. It effectively tried, and for a large part succeeded in, turning party competition into a bipolar affair, a question of Fianna Fáil versus the others. Indeed, it twice tried to change the electoral system to install a first-past-the-post system that would deliver on its conception of party competition. As Peter Mair wrote in 1987, 'The crucial period was thus that of the 1920s and 1930s, and since then little has changed. It is as if politics stopped more than half-a-century ago, as if the needle had suddenly jammed and the record had continued to repeat the same dull chorus through decades and generations.'[15] Labour's attempts to deal with the unique nature of Irish party competition were a constant source of disappointment, division, and at time, delusion throughout the following decades. As Fianna Fáil developed the critical mass to impose its bipolar view on Irish politics, Labour's attitude to power, and specifically its attitude to coalition with Fine Gael, became a fault line in the party.

For both Fianna Fáil and Fine Gael, the attitude to power was simple and straightforward – they wanted it and each general election presented the opportunity to get it. The acquisition of power was a defining *raison d'être* for both parties. For Labour, things were never so simple. Participation in government presented the party with the opportunity to access power and to implement policies and it can point to real achievements across a broad range of issues such as housing provision, liberal reform and social provision during its periods in office in the 1940s, 1970s and 1980s in particular. However, participation in government regularly created a crisis for the party. It was viewed by many as a compromise with a dominant right-of-centre party which set back the goal of re-ordering Irish politics along traditional European Left/Right lines.

According to the argument, short-term policy achievements (or indeed short-term careerism depending on how vicious the debate got) only served to copper-fasten the dominant political structure whereas Labour's challenge was to eschew power and political compromise in the interests of building an independent left-wing alternative to the politics of both Fianna Fáil and Fine Gael. The 1969 election perhaps illustrates the ambition and ultimate futility of the latter view. Labour had ploughed an independent furrow since its participation in the second inter-party government between 1954–57. Its bruising experience in this coalition, best known perhaps for the view that it is a contender, until recent times, for the worst government in the history of the state, saw the party emerge with its first preference vote in single figures and its parliamentary party reduced by one third.

Throughout the 1960s, and especially in the latter part of the decade, the party's policy platform took a genuine shift to the Left, with Brendan Corish publicly espousing the socialist nature of Labour's programme. This policy renewal was partly grounded in the swelling of the party's ranks with a new generation of activists, mainly in the Dublin area. Labour looked confident, radical and purposeful as it approached the 1969 election declaring that 'The Seventies Will Be Socialist'. After more than a decade of electoral independence 1969 was a make-or-break election for Labour's attempt to reshape the Irish political landscape along traditional Left/Right lines. Labour had not participated in government for twelve years, it was advocating a realistic, avowedly left-wing programme under a charismatic leader and its ambition for power was clear. The election campaign was a failure, however. Attacked by the two conservative parties, the Catholic Church and much of the media for having the temerity to advocate a socialist programme, the Party's expected breakthrough failed to materialise. Labour returned to the Dáil with three fewer seats, having witnessed a steady if not spectacular increase in the two previous elections in 1961 and 1965. Gains in Dublin could not make up for losses outside the capital.

The experience of 1969 is instructive. Writing twenty years later about the Labour Party and power John Horgan noted, 'One thing above all is certain, and that is that the Labour Party, when deciding its electoral strategy, should at least consciously abandon the notion that it is operating in a political vacuum.'[16] The same could be said for 1969. In attempting to force a Left/Right realignment in 1969 Labour was not just battling against the power of conservatism or the Church or the immensely popular figure of Fianna Fáil's Jack Lynch, it was also battling against the very foundations of the Irish party system. Those foundations were fundamentally based not on class but on the Civil War, and subsequently reinforced by the deadening hand of clientelism and Catholicism.

The ambition and purpose of the Labour Party in 1969 may have been admirable but the feasibility of the strategy it set itself proved beyond its capabilities. Indeed, the lack of enthusiasm within the ranks of its own conservative, mainly rural TDs, was testament to the enormous challenge in trying to instil a new ideological divide in Irish politics. For all Labour's policy innovation and socialist zeal, party competition in Ireland still revolved around the original Civil War divide; simply put, whether Fianna Fáil would hold power or not, ideas and policy came second. It may be dispiriting but not surprising that after an election when the Labour Party put forward the most policy-focused platform in its history and tried to force a debate about ideas, it was condemned by Fine Gael for its 'refusal to play a realistic role in Irish politics'.[17] For Fine Gael any strategy embarked on by the Labour Party that sought to move beyond the Civil War cleavage only served to strengthen the dominant party in that divide, resulting in Tom O'Higgins' charge that Frank Cluskey's belief in the ultimate success in the strategy pursued by Labour in 1969 rendered him 'the greatest friend Fianna Fáil have in this Dáil, and so are the horny-handed sons of toil who sit behind him'.[18]

The choice after 1969 was clear. Either the party could continue its current strategy, absenting itself from government for perhaps another generation or reconcile itself again to the idea of coalition with Fine Gael and seek support for an agenda which, although far from heralding a transformative socialist idyll, would present the opportunity to introduce social and economic reform that the Ireland of the 1970s desperately needed. In Cork in December 1970, Labour dropped its independent electoral strategy with the document submitted to the conference declaring: 'Labour's policies were not designed for permanent opposition but for implementation. To be a socialist is not to be condemned to perpetual opposition but rather is to be committed to achievement, where the opportunity arises to do so with honour.'[19] This *volte face* paved the way for Labour to enter coalition with Fine Gael following the 1973 election.

Despite the experience of the 1960s the tension within Labour about the issue of power and coalition would continue to divide the party throughout the following decade and a half. Conditioned in part by another bruising coalition experience with Fine Gael between 1982 and 1987, which saw the party emerge with just twelve TDs and eclipsed into fourth place by the newly formed Progressive Democrats, the issue of coalition again dominated internal debate, nearly to the exclusion of all else, with John Horgan remarking: 'One of the problems it creates, for example, is that for as long as it exists as the central strategic question in the party, it obscures the development of genuine Left-Right arguments. Labour activists who are opposed to the leadership for all kinds of reasons will readily grasp anti-coalitionism as their banner, no matter how conservative they may be on other issues. And the equation of 'Left' with 'anti-coalition' … stereotypes the party in such a way as to ensure that its policies and its personalities rarely get a satisfactory hearing.'[20]

The solution to emerge in the 1980s managed to avoid the dogmatism that characterised both sides of the coalition debate. The Commission on Electoral Strategy which reported in 1986 set the bar high for future coalition participation – a minimum of twenty-five seats – however, it did not end the factionalism that thrived on the coalition issue. Labour was not the only party, however, that had to struggle with the realities of power in the late 1980s. The fact that Fianna Fáil had not secured an overall majority since 1977 revealed a significant if gradual shift in the Irish party system. While still the largest party, Fianna Fáil's ability to tout itself as the keeper of the flame of single-party government was about to be snuffed out. While partly driven by the desire of Charles Haughey to remain in power at any cost the decision by Fianna Fáil to enter coalition in 1989 represented the largest transformation of the party system in the post-war period. As Peter Mair pointed out:

> In entering coalition and in declaring itself coalitionable, Fianna Fáil effectively undermined the foundation on which the post-war party system had been structured. From 1989 onwards, it was no longer the case of Fianna Fáil versus the rest. From then on … Fianna Fáil became just another party. Since both Fianna Fáil's appeal and the constraints on its opponents were based firmly on this particular foundation, its undermining opened up the entire Irish electoral market, including the support base of Fianna Fáil itself. The consequences were more than evident in 1992.[21]

Fianna Fáil's decline and its conversion to the logic of coalition between 1989 and 1992 represented a watershed for the Irish party system. Following Labour's then historic election success in November 1992 it had, for the first time in its history, alternative government choices available to it. Under Dick Spring it used this new-found power within the party system to leverage the best policy terms for entry into coalition (and settle a few old scores with Fine Gael into the bargain). The old certainties imposed by the party system had broken down and Labour was in a position of relative freedom with regard to its coalition options. It was not the realignment of Irish politics envisioned in 1969 or by some of the anti-coalitionists in the 1980s but it did offer the Labour Party a way out of the coalition straitjacket that the system had previously imposed on it. Labour's election victory gave it a mandate for real power and for once the party system allowed it to exercise that power.

The extent of the fundamentally changed nature of party competition and coalition formation was sudden and jarring, not least to many Labour members and supporters. Having fundamentally opposed Fianna Fáil at every election since the late 1930s the reality of sharing power with the party was, for many, a step too far. Fianna Fáil's attitude to power and its ability to conflate the party interest with the state's interest, especially under Charles Haughey's rule, put the party beyond the pale for many in the Labour Party. Fianna Fáil's inability to adapt mentally to partnership government, which contributed to the coalition's collapse in 1994 was, for many, proof that the experiment had failed. However, the subsequent formation of a more traditional-looking Fine Gael–Labour coalition, this time together with Democratic Left, did not reverse the fundamental change that occurred in Irish party competition. Fianna Fáil was now a party like any other, and its ability to attain power was dependent on other actors in the political system. Its subsequent hold on power for fourteen years from 1997 was predicated on that fact.

Labour oscillated in its attitude to this new-found development. It sought to exploit the situation in 2002 by refusing to rule out the prospect of a Fianna Fáil coalition, while a rejection of Fianna Fáil and all its works was a central plank of its 2007 electoral strategy. The diametrically opposed attitude towards possible coalition options espoused by two successive party leaders accurately mirrored the wider party's division on the issue. Labour's independent stance in 2002 – with Quinn refusing to categorically rule out a possible coalition with Fianna Fáil – attempted to focus debate on policy options, with Labour insisting that the core issue was not who was in the next government but what policies it implemented.

However, Quinn's approach to coalition was as much tactical as strategic. Ruling out Fianna Fáil immediately relegated Labour to being the minor party in a Fine Gael coalition and therefore sidelined the party during the election campaign. With an electorate increasingly agnostic to all political brands and forming its voting intentions later during campaigns – in the 2011 general election campaign four in ten voters decided in the last week of the campaign,[22] a trend which has been increasing steadily throughout the last decade – the 2002 electoral strategy was designed to ensure Labour remained relevant during the vital latter stages of the campaign.

After the standstill election of 2002 Pat Rabbitte's subsequent leadership reverted to a more traditional Fianna Fáil-against-the-rest typology. The 'Mullingar Accord', reached soon after the 2004 local and European elections, trailed the pre-election pact between Fine Gael and Labour in place for the 2007 general election. The logic behind the strategy, shared at leadership level by both parties, was that after a decade of Bertie Ahern-led governments, voters wanted a tangible alternative to Fianna Fáil in place before they voted – the election was effectively turned into a plebiscite between Fianna Fáil and the traditional Fine Gael–Labour alliance. Again Labour stood still.

Eamon Gilmore assumed the leadership in 2007 espousing an independent electoral strategy, which mirrored the 2002 position. Labour would advocate for its own distinct policy agenda and eschew any pre-electoral pacts. However, negotiating the party's internal conflict regarding possible participation in government with Fianna Fáil was not to prove the headache it had for Gilmore's two predecessors. As the unprecedented financial, economic and political collapse and Fianna Fáil's authorship of that tragedy unfolded between 2008 and 2010, it became increasingly clear that the next general election would produce seismic voting shifts. Fianna Fáil suffered an electoral collapse rarely equalled in modern European politics, a result so dramatic that even the future existence of the party is questionable.

For Labour, its campaign produced a historic election result and a familiar place in coalition with Fine Gael. However, the familiarity of the government that emerged out of the 2011 election should not distract from the radical transformation in party support that the election heralded. The demise of Fianna Fáil has fundamentally changed the party system but exactly how that change will evolve remains unclear. The 2011 election was the most volatile seen in Ireland since September 1927. The 1927 election witnessed a collapse in Labour's strength and the loss of its talented and principled leader. As argued earlier, the failure of the party to recover in the ensuing five years was a key factor in forming the party system that dominated Irish politics for generations. Now, however, Labour was a significant beneficiary of the volatility witnessed in February 2011.

One of the immediate challenges for Labour is to maintain its current position of strength while working in a government facing unpalatable and unprecedented policy options. It does so with an invigorated Left and Sinn Féin opposition trying to make inroads into its support base and a rump Fianna Fáil party battling for survival. Labour can rightly claim significant policy success through its involvement in government, perhaps most notably between 1992 and 1997. However, it has never secured two successive terms in power and its experience of coalition has often been accompanied by electoral setback. Experience of government has tended to confirm rather than transform Labour's position as the half party in the two-and-a-half-party system. The 'earthquake' election of 2011 and its continuing fallout may well give the party the opportunity to break out of this historic cycle.

It is perhaps after the next election that Labour, if it retains its current status as the second largest party in Ireland, can look to shape, rather than be shaped by the party system. The old Civil War division has long been viewed as an anachronism. Yet that original cleavage was sustained over the decades by many factors, including a real division on attitudes towards Northern Ireland, social class, the dominance of Catholicism and latterly the reduction of political debate to a contest of managerial competence between two centrist groups. Developments in the past decade or so, both positive and negative, have removed or transformed the issues that sustained the Irish party system.

Yet the shape of things to come remains unclear – can Fianna Fáil continue and if so can it come to terms with being a minor party, as seems certain for the foreseeable future? Does Fine Gael have the driving ambition to govern alone and will it try to attract right-of-centre independents (and even Fianna Fáil members!) into its ranks to achieve that goal? Where does Labour see itself in Irish politics – as the leading Left party opposing conservative policies and willing to sacrifice power to realign politics or alternatively as a natural party of government, the fulcrum for coalition formation around which every other party must turn? Is it possible that from the embers of economic and social ruin a new political party will emerge, as was threatened but not delivered in advance of the last election? These are just some of the questions that politics may have to grapple with after the landslide witnessed in February 2011. Little is clear as of yet but for the first time in its history Labour can claim that its future rests in its own hands.

8. 'No good Catholic can be a true Socialist': The Labour Party and the Catholic Church, 1922–52

Diarmaid Ferriter

In March 2011, the new Minister for Education, the Labour Party's Ruairi Quinn, announced the establishment of a forum on school patronage. While this development was broadly welcomed and regarded by many as long overdue, due to the extent of the historic and continued control of schools by the Catholic Church, some found it disquieting that Quinn felt it necessary to deny the Labour Party had a 'secular agenda'. One critic argued that a secular state school system was a legitimate and necessary aspiration, making room 'in the spectrum of belief for those who have no religion. It is nothing short of intolerance that this has not been the case in our state-funded primary schools up to the present time'.[1]

Quinn is the first self-declared atheist Minister for Education in the history of the 26-county Irish state. Born into a devout Catholic family, he was a student at Blackrock College in the early 1960s and was active in the Legion of Mary, but a few years later he abandoned the Catholic faith while a student at University College Dublin (UCD). Socialism for him became more important than Catholicism, and he found the body of orthodox Catholic doctrine 'impenetrable to reasoned critique or analysis', even when he was a teenager: 'I was by now an atheist'.[2]

When he was Minister for Finance in 1996, Quinn declared that Ireland was a 'post-Catholic pluralist Republic',[3] which was somewhat premature given the control the Catholic Church retained over education and other sectors. His school patronage initiative in 2011 was perhaps an indication that the Republic was edging closer to a situation that would justify the description of post-Catholic, but that this development was also coupled with an emphasis on the lack of a secular agenda is indicative, not only of power politics, but an inbuilt caution in the Labour Party about appearing overzealous in taking on Church power. Arguably, it is a reluctance born of its historical experience in the twentieth century and the frequency with which it faced accusations of godlessness and found itself affirming its Catholic credentials. This was particularly apparent in the first three decades of independence for the 26-county state, from the early 1920s to the early 1950s, which is the main focus of this chapter.

There is little doubt that from its earliest days the Labour Party was targeted specifically on the question of the religious faith of its leaders and members locally and nationally. The Dublin Labour Party put forward candidates at the annual municipal elections in January each year from 1912 to 1915. Five councillors were elected in 1912 but there was little progress made thereafter, with only six Labour councillors in 1915 on a council of eighty members. Arthur Mitchell's *Labour in Irish Politics 1890–1930,* published in 1974, maintained that 'the lack of support for the party made it clear that a majority of Dubliners accepted the image of Larkin, Connolly and the other leaders as anti-clerical, socialist revolutionaries', a picture painted by nationalist politicians, the press and the Church.[4]

James Connolly was well used to this, given the alliance of 'priests and publicans' that had prevented his election in Dublin's Wood Quay ward as an Irish Socialist Republican Party candidate in 1902.[5] It was clear, it seemed, that hostile propaganda ensured Irish socialists were often on the defensive, and declared their Catholic faith loudly, raising the question of the degree to which Ireland was an exception to the rule enunciated by historian Eric Hobsbawm in 1978 in *Marxist Studies.* Hobsbawm maintained that the modern working class socialist movement 'has developed with an overwhelmingly secular, indeed often a militantly anti-religious ideology … the rise in atheism … so far as many of the militants were concerned, [was] an essential content of the rise of the Labour movement'. It was claimed that in public Connolly 'went out of his way to appear to be a Catholic', and while he was often involved in bitter disputes with the clergy, he was moved to declare in 1913 that 'the most consistent socialist or syndicalist may be as Catholic as the Pope if he is so minded'.[6]

During the first decade of its existence, however, the fortunes of the Irish Labour Party developed in stark contrast to that of the Catholic Church. Michael Laffan has characterised the party during the War of Independence as a 'delicate and neglected creature, vulnerable and totally lacking in self-confidence'. Its robustness was surely undermined by hostile media comment from, amongst others, the *Irish Independent*, which maintained in October 1919 that 'the socialist party of Ireland' distributed the doctrines of Marx and Engels and James Connolly 'among the illiterate in Dublin from their headquarters in Liberty Hall'. Laffan points out that the same year, an issue of the *Watchword of Labour* devoted half of its front page to elaborating on the headline 'A Catholic may be a socialist' and while some in Sinn Féin, like Michael Staines, were keen to insist that in 1916 'Connolly died as a brave Irish Catholic', the godless image of socialism suited the Sinn Féin party in that it made it easier for it to do 'what many of its supporters were inclined to do in any case' which was keep a distance from the Labour movement.[7]

Notwithstanding its broad appeal, divisions within Sinn Féin did provide the Labour Party with the opportunity of a breakthrough in the June 1922 general election when it decided not to repeat its stance of 1918 and 1921 when it had opted out of contesting the Dáil elections. Its success in this election at the outset of the Civil War was significant; it won seventeen seats, suggesting that many of the electorate were prioritising social and economic issues rather than debates about oaths, symbols and constitutional conundrums. In securing 21 per cent of the votes cast, Labour performed better than anti-Treaty Sinn Féin in terms of votes (though not seats), 'a performance which surpassed all expectations'.[8]

But the extent to which it represented a breakthrough it could confidently build on is debatable. It may have been that it profited from the discontent with the Sinn Féin divisions over the Anglo-Irish Treaty, but it was also a party now operating in a partitioned island. In the mid-1920s, 35 per cent of the working population in Northern Ireland was engaged in industry while the figure was only 14 per cent in the Free State; the respective figures for agriculture were 26 per cent and 51 per cent and in the Free State, of 'the sections within the working class on whom the Labour Party might rely, the agricultural labourers were declining in numbers and the skilled and semi-skilled working class constituted a relatively small segment of the political nation'.[9]

That, however, was only one complicating factor; another significant drawback was the extent to which nationalism and Catholicism continued to perform 'an integrating function' which was manifest in the 1920s. In contrast, unity in the Labour Party and the Labour movement generally proved elusive with the return of Jim Larkin to Dublin in 1923 and the attendant power struggles his reappearance created. The question of religion was of central relevance; during the 1923 general election Cardinal Logue, the Catholic Archbishop of Armagh, intervened to urge support for Cumann na nGaedheal and warned against votes for alternative candidates; he did not mention the Labour Party, but his command cannot have done the Labour Party's electoral fortunes any good.[10]

The split in the Labour movement also exacerbated tensions about its international links; in 1927 an Irish Dominican proposed that the party congress affiliate with the Christian International of Trade Unions, an organisation of Catholic unions established in 1922, as the socialist and communist internationals were 'distinctly … anti-Catholic in tendency', while 'Labour in Ireland is essentially Catholic; should it not openly show itself proudly in its true colours?' Such an initiative, he suggested, might allow the Labour movement to recover from the 'disrepute' it had fallen into 'due to anti-Catholic leaders', an obvious reference to Larkin and a convenient overlooking of the dilemma the Labour movement faced in seeking to maintain an all-Ireland structure with large numbers of Protestant workers in the North.[11]

The Labour Party leader Tom Johnson was careful in how he used language with religious overtones, maintaining in July 1925 that his party was hungering 'for an opportunity to go out and preach the gospel of reconstruction and national development', but he lost his seat in the September 1927 General election. The *Irish Labour Party and Trade Union Congress Report* for 1928 maintained that during that election campaign, time had been insufficient to enable them 'to meet the unscrupulous campaign of lying and innuendo touching the motives and personal character of Johnson' and lavish full-page advertisements with misleading and inaccurate stories.[12]

The election of September 1927 was disastrous, Labour dropping from twenty-two to thirteen Dáil seats; it did not help that in the same year the Synod of Maynooth instructed priests that 'care should be paid to the working class, lest lured by the promises and deceived by the fraud of socialists, it loses its ancestral faith'.[13] For the Labour Party it also marked the beginning of a long period of decline – by 1932 its representation in the Dáil had been slashed by two thirds in just five years – which was compounded by the extent to which 'Red scares' developed momentum in the 1930s and led to a relentless onslaught from the *Irish Rosary*, *The Standard* and *Irish Catholic* publications.

Such was the extent of the invective and accusations that Labour Party members were tacit supporters of communism that William Norton, who took over the leadership of the party in 1932, succeeding Thomas O'Connell, wrote a letter to the Papal Secretary of State, Cardinal Pacelli, to complain. He pointed out that at the Labour Party's 1934 conference a motion had been adopted which 'strongly opposed any attempt to introduce anti-Christian doctrines into the movement'. His action in writing to Pacelli angered Tom Johnson who objected to this move on the grounds that expressing a belief in an economic creed was not a question concerning faith and morals.[14]

In *The Irish Times* in May 1931, at a time when it was estimated that in the heart of Dublin city 4,830 tenement houses sheltered 25,230 families, it was suggested that 'it is indeed something of a miracle for which we must thank the boundless resignation of the Irish poor – that the slums of Dublin have bred no violent revolt against the social order'. It was no miracle, however; it was partly as a result of the Catholic Church's determination to narrow the ground available for socialist agitation by insisting that 'no good Catholic can be a true socialist'.[15] This was also part of an effective Church campaign to divide and conquer. At the October 1934 Labour Party Conference, Roddy Connolly proposed a resolution calling for 'a truce among all who stand for an Irish worker's republic and a united front against the common enemy' and an invitation to them to exchange views with the Labour Party, but his resolution was voted down and an alternative resolution was passed – that 'the aim of the Irish labour movement must continue to be the establishment of a just social order based on Christian teaching'.[16]

There was worse to come between 1936 and 1940 as a result of Labour's new constitution in 1936, committing the party to the establishment of a workers' republic. The words of William Norton at the Labour Party's annual conference in 1936 made clear the extent to which the party was on the defensive over what constituted a workers' republic: 'It has become fashionable … to address admonitions to Irish workers warning them of the dangers of Godless communism and suggesting in these admonitions that there is a danger that Irish workers would embrace communism as an economic and religious creed. I say, as one Irish Catholic worker, such admonitions addressed to us are quite unjustified by the facts of Irish history and that they betray a deplorable want of faith in the deep-seated religious convictions of the Irish working class'.[17]

This was a crucial point, as what Norton maintained about the faith of the working classes was also something the Church was moulding and monitoring and it took advantage of occasions like the celebrations of the centenary of Catholic Emancipation in 1929 and the Eucharistic Congress in 1932 to underline this. As was pointed out in *The Standard* newspaper in June 1929, 'the poorest of the slums proved that in the most priceless of treasures they are rich indeed. The papal colours are appropriate emblems of the faith that dwells there'.[18] In 1932, Éamon de Valera, who had led Fianna Fáil to power in that year's general election, made pointed reference to 'our people ever firm in their allegiance to our ancestral faith', highlighting the extent to which the Eucharistic Congress provided public opportunities for the new government to repair its damaged relations with the Catholic Church as a result of the Civil War and the excommunication of some republicans. At a time of great political tension and economic stagnation, the emphasis on shared values and faith helped temporarily to mask the bitterness that riddled the Irish body politic but it also served as an opportunity to stress that there were no class tensions in Ireland, therefore no need for class politics and it was a time when statements denouncing political radicalism were given maximum coverage.

As pointed out by Fearghal McGarry, it was unfortunate for the Labour Party that its shift to the left coincided with the resurgence of a popular anti-Communism which was deepened by the outbreak of the Spanish Civil War and the emergence of the Irish Christian Front, which could even rely on a Labour Party TD, Michael Keyes, to speak on its platform. Well-known academics and Catholic social activists like Alfred O'Rahilly, James Hogan and Fr Denis Fahey also assumed key frontal positions in the battle against supposed subversion on the Left. Cardinal Joseph MacRory, Archbishop of Armagh from 1928 to 1945, added to the expressions of worry about Labour's perceived radicalism.[19] At a mass meeting in Limerick city in 1936 Michael Keyes hailed the work of the Irish Christian Front in its efforts to 'bring into existence in this country a social and economic system based on the Christian ideals of life as expressed in the Papal encyclicals and thereby to overcome the evils of socialism which are altogether contrary to Christian principles'.[20]

John H. Whyte has characterised the Irish Labour Party's position in relation to sympathy for Spanish republicans in the late 1930s as 'muted and uncertain'. While de Valera refused to withdraw recognition from the Spanish government, senior Labour Party figures 'seem to have avoided referring to events in Spain and when, at the party's annual conference in 1936, a young delegate from the TCD branch, Conor Cruise O'Brien, made an attack on Franco, he provoked protests from a section of the delegates'.[21]

Another difficulty in sustaining the aspiration for a workers' republic was the decision by the Irish National Teachers' Organisation to seek clarity from the Catholic hierarchy on the appropriateness or acceptability of the Labour Party's constitution, which was considered by the bishops in October 1937.

Predictably, they did not approve and this was an important turning point; early in 1939 the Labour Party leadership conceded the hierarchy's demands for the removal of the objectionable part of the constitution. The motion to delete 'workers' Republic' was passed by eighty-nine to twenty-five votes at its April 1939 conference and in the words of Fearghal McGarry, 'with it also passed Labour's last tentative commitment to socialism until the 1960s',[22] or in Niamh Puirséil's description, it demonstrated 'Labour's apparent craven kowtowing to the Hierarchy's demands'. There was, of course, a broader international context to all this; McGarry makes the point that while the bishops seemed unwilling to make any distinction between communism and moderate socialism, 'in fairness to the Church, however, it should also be noted that its opposition to increasing state intervention was not entirely unreasonable in a decade which saw democratic government increasingly undermined by authoritarianism throughout Europe'.[23]

Had the Labour movement really desired to move Left in any case? It was, after all, a trade union that had approached the hierarchy seeking guidance on what was acceptable, and from a party political viewpoint, solving the constitutional dilemma was, for William Norton, about the need to prevent the party 'foundering on a rock which might mean its political end'. Niamh Puirséil suggests it was a party that from here on would go out of its way to be seen to be conservative, an assessment given credence by the assertion of Labour TD Gerard McGowan at the annual conference of the Labour Party in 1938: 'with respect to everybody's religious beliefs, he said they were Catholics first and politicians afterwards'.[24]

John H. Whyte points out that its amended constitution of April 1940 prompted Belfast Protestant Sam Kyle to protest that the Labour Party was 'granting an outside body the right to say that the movement must act in accord with their ideas and not its own', but that diluting the socialism of its constitution was electorally beneficial. It experienced extensive gains in the local elections of 1942, winning 100 out of 630 county council seats compared to 37 out of 757 in 1934, and in the general election of 1943 it won 17 seats compared to just 9 in 1938.[25] While there were different reasons for this change in fortune, putting the controversy over the constitution to bed was one of them.

When proponents of Catholic social teaching succeeded in persuading de Valera to establish a Commission on Vocational Organisation in 1939, many in the Labour movement remained sceptical, some more so than others. Like many examining the issue, the Labour movement struggled to find an adequate definition of what vocational organisation or Corporatism actually was and there was concern that it had Fascist overtones. Jim Larkin was appointed a member of the Commission, chaired by the Bishop of Galway Dr Michael Browne, but he was suspicious that Corporatist proposals would not be compatible with democracy; likewise, Luke Duffy, the secretary of the Labour Party, was a member of the Commission and did not think Ireland was ready for any elaborate scheme of vocational organisation which could, in his words, lead to a 'bureaucratic fascism'. Their views, however, exerted little influence on the Commission whose report noted that there was 'very little danger of socialism or communism obtaining a footing' in Ireland. Both men declined to sign the report; Duffy 'ridiculed the recommendations' it contained while Larkin regarded the Commission 'with more or less silent contempt'.[26] The subtext of their opposition was a preference to let parliament reign supreme; the report of the Commission had recommended reorganisation of the distribution of power based on vocational councils which would regulate sectional interests and be answerable to a national vocational assembly.

Labour continued to be on the defensive in the 1940s over how it was being depicted. Now firmly ensconced in power, Fianna Fáil became adept at using the Red scare against any smaller party claiming to offer a more radical alternative. In this pursuit, Fianna Fáil minister Seán MacEntee became the chief communist denunciator, declaring in a 1943 election leaflet that 'even in these most dangerous days when the Nation should be firmly united, the Labour Party seeks to set class against class'.[27] The entry of Jim Larkin into the parliamentary party in 1943 – from 1933 to 1941 he had styled himself as 'independent labour' and he was elected again for Dublin North East in 1943 before losing his seat in 1944 – ultimately split the party, leading to the formation of the National Labour Party. In the first six weeks of 1944, the ultra-Catholic *The Standard* had run a series of supposed exposés of an alleged communist takeover of the Labour Party in Dublin. According to Barry Desmond, there was a high degree of collusion between different elements, to the extent that 'there were a large group of ITGWU anti-Larkinites, Catholic actionists and Archbishop informants who peddled every nuance of radical opinion into communist subversion'.[28]

The National Labour Party emphasised its commitment to Catholic social teaching and *The Standard* described the programme it set out as a 'forthright social and national document full of sound Catholic principles with practical application to our country'. James Everett, the Wicklow TD who championed the new party, also gave his view on the split, suggesting there was, before the party divided, 'intrigue and infiltration among members of the Labour Party and those who had spent time in Moscow and fighting for Marshal Tito were the real rulers behind the scenes'. He also called on the Labour Party to have allegations of communist infiltration investigated 'by the Bishops or any impartial body'. Everett continued to play the Red-scare card for all it was worth, creating serious tensions between himself and Roddy Connolly. Frequently articulating allegiance to the Vatican, Everett claimed he was proud that the fundamental purpose of the National Labour Party was 'irrevocably committed to the papal encyclicals and also to implement the Christian philosophy of social justice enshrined therein'.[29]

In 1948, both Fianna Fáil and the National Labour Party espoused the anti-Communist theme and Everett said his party aimed to assist in 'setting up a vocational order of society under which the common good will always be considered'. But Labour Party public representatives also had opportunities to continue to emphasise their anti-communist credentials; on May Day in 1949, John Breen, the Labour Party Lord Mayor of Dublin, presided over a rally of over 100,000 people in solidarity with those who opposed the Hungarian people's government and the persecution of Cardinal Mindszenty.[30]

Both Labour parties formed part of the first coalition government that took office in 1948 (the Labour split was healed in 1950 with the reunification of the parties) and were quick to cooperate in displays of extreme subservience to the Church. It was significant, for example, that it was Maurice Moynihan, secretary to the Department of the Taoiseach, and not the Labour Party or Clann na Poblachta that objected to the new government offering, in correspondence with Archbishop of Dublin John Charles McQuaid, to 'repose at the feet of your holiness' and stating 'our firm resolve to be guided in all our work by the teachings of Christ' as inappropriate.[31] But there were considerable strains as a result of preferred Labour Party policies in government, despite its insistence that its policies were compatible with Church teaching. The dilemma for those in power was undoubtedly exacerbated by McQuaid's calculated use of language and his penchant for using the phrase 'Atheistic communism' which had, he maintained 'openly pronounced its brutal sentence on all the principles of our Catholic faith and culture. Its agents have been content to disguise their aims under the mask of socialism'.[32]

William Norton, Minister for Social Welfare in that government, was also a member of the Knights of Columbanus and he quoted Pope Pius XI's encyclical *Divini Redemptoris* in support of his proposals for a social welfare bill. He argued that 'as a Christian nation we must give practical expression to our Christianity – surely it would not be suggested that it is a Christian attitude to allow unemployed men or women or widows or orphans to beg from door to door; nor would it be the Christian attitude to pay such low rates of benefit as bear no relation to the requirement of the time'.[33]

Angela Bolster in her history of the Knights of Columbanus argues that, given that not a single voice was raised in favour of Norton's proposals from the ranks of the Knights, the rejection of his Bill amounted to a rejection of Norton by the order 'of which he was a member of considerably high standing'.[34] Another difficulty for Norton was the opposition from the Catholic hierarchy to any comprehensive social welfare scheme, as articulated by Dr Joseph Rogers, coadjutor Bishop of Killaloe: 'state grants and social services, no matter how generous, are cold and impersonal and do not take into account the spiritual requirements of the recipient'.[35] This was an indication that Norton's insistence that a Christian welfare state – 'a place where Christian people under a Christian government taking direction from Almighty God' could provide benefits to the vulnerable was possible in Ireland and was 'the most practical approach to applied Christianity' – was not going to soften Church opposition. Fine Gael TD Liam Cosgrave suggested his party would be prepared to support a watered-down version of the Bill because it would provide 'a bulwark against communism'.

In his ministerial portfolio of social welfare, Norton increased pensions to widows, orphans, and the elderly and introduced reforms in workmen's compensation; he was also responsible for a social welfare act in 1950 that absorbed into his department the functions of the National Health Insurance Society that insured one fifth of the population against loss of earnings through illness. But his desire for a complete overhaul of social services, published in a white paper on social security in October 1949 and involving the replacement of all existing social welfare and insurance schemes by a single comprehensive scheme funded by contributions from workers, employers and the state was doomed after it was denounced by conservative Catholics, and resisted by several Fine Gael ministers. His Social Welfare (Insurance) Bill of December 1950, which incorporated modifications of his original proposals, expired in committee stage when the coalition government fell.[36]

How the Labour parties reacted to one of the most celebrated controversies of that era, the Mother and Child debacle of 1951, is also revealing of what was by then a well-established deference to the Catholic Church. But again, such obedience was not without its tensions. The proposal to provide a free health scheme for pregnant mothers and postnatal care of mothers and children, vigorously promoted by Minister for Health Noël Browne, would have enjoyed the support of many ordinary Labour Party members and supporters. Prior to the Irish Medical Association and bishops' objections it had been supported by William Norton; he was keen to reach a compromise and was active in trying to keep the scheme in some form.[37] According to Archbishop McQuaid's biographer, John Cooney, Taoiseach John A. Costello revealed to McQuaid that some Labour Party members had been 'worked up to a defence of Browne's scheme' and that Costello had to deal 'very firmly with several of their members' misconceptions'. According to Cooney, 'within the Labour Party there had been a propaganda attempt to secure a confidence vote on the scheme following the TUC's call on its 200,000 members to support it', but the Labour Party chairman and deputy leader William Davin countered this move. Davin was also a member of the Knights of Columbanus.[38] While it was undoubtedly the case that with Labour in coalition Norton was determined to avoid more 'Red scares' it should not be overlooked that the Mother and Child Scheme enjoyed significant support within Labour, and it has been observed that there were tensions between the 'Dublin Left' of the Labour Party and the leadership for many years to come.[39]

Niamh Puirséil suggested the whole business 'left Labour looking very shabby indeed'; Michael Keyes, who was Minister for Local Government, agreed that with the opposition of the bishops it was the end of the scheme but also added 'they shouldn't be allowed to do this'.[40] Norton's contribution to the Dáil discussion on the resignation of Noël Browne in April 1951 included the following: 'if this question is raised as one in which the Bishops are to be on one side and the government are on the other, I say, on behalf of the government, that issue is not going to arise in this country. This government will not travel that road.' He accused Browne of seeking a 'head-on collision' with the Catholic bishops, and asserted that the issue of whether the country was governed by elected public representatives or the Catholic clergy was 'not going to arise in this country' because the government would not countenance any 'flouting of the authority of the Bishops in the matter of Catholic Social Teaching or Catholic moral teaching'.[41] James Everett, Minister for Posts and Telegraphs in the coalition government, remained almost childlike in his expressions of shock that controversy could have been generated or that it had been allowed to reach boiling point, concluding mournfully, 'It is a terrible thing in a country like this that you have fighting and flouting of the Bishops until the Bishops would have no negotiating with the government.'[42]

Despite the Mother and Child Scheme row, McQuaid was much happier with a coalition government in power than with Fianna Fáil; significantly, when he corresponded with the Apostolic Nuncio, Rev. Gerald O'Hara in November 1952, when Fianna Fáil was back in power, he referred to his strong preference for the coalition government over the new one. He criticised de Valera for failing to consult with the hierarchy over health legislation: 'to deal with Mr Costello's cabinet was, with the exception of Dr Browne, Minister for Health and Mr McBride, Minister for External Affairs, a very pleasant experience, for one met with a Premier who was not only an excellent Catholic, but an educated Catholic, in immediate sympathy with the Church and the teaching of the Church ... to deal with Mr de Valera and his ministers is indeed a different matter. From Mr de Valera's re-assumption of political leadership, the chief element of note as far as the church is concerned, is a policy of distance'.[43] Quite clearly, on the evidence of this letter, the Labour Party ministers were regarded as compliant, obedient Catholics, unlike Fianna Fáil and some members of Clann na Poblachta.

There is little doubt that many Labour Party TDs and members felt strongly about social issues and made housing a priority but when it came to the fundamental issue of state intervention, the party was no match for the machinations of McQuaid and some of his episcopal colleagues, including Bishop Michael Browne of Galway and Bishop Cornelius Lucey of Cork who were also vocal in resisting state intervention. The Labour Party's caution was not born only of the genuine Catholic conviction of its representatives, but also lack of experience of power. It is significant, for example, that when the hierarchy again attempted to scupper a health bill when Fianna Fáil was back in power, the bill was passed with only cosmetic changes because this time the hierarchy faced much more experienced and cannier political operators like Taoiseach Éamon de Valera and Minister for Health James Ryan. In contrast, the Labour Party had decided, in the face of episcopal wrath, to fold its tent, a century after the Synod of Thurles had condemned 'the apostles of socialism and infidelity'.[44] Labour Party members preferred to engage in semantic caution in order to present themselves as socially progressive, but ultimately unthreatening to the Catholic Church, rather like Cardinal Tomás Ó Fiaich decades later who, after speaking about social justice and poverty, was asked if he was a Christian Socialist. He replied, 'I would prefer to describe myself as a social Christian'.[45]

9. 'A PARTICULAR VIEW OF WHAT WAS POSSIBLE': LABOUR IN GOVERNMENT

DAVID MCCULLAGH

'ABOVE ALL, THE task of the first coalition must be to elect the second.'[1] Wise words from key Labour strategist Brendan Halligan, as the party prepared to enter coalition with Fine Gael in 1973. The party, however, has found this advice extraordinarily difficult to follow: with the exception of February 1982, Labour has lost seats after every spell in government.[2] Labour has never won successive terms in power and has spent just over one fifth of its first century in government. An impartial observer might wonder if there was something about how it handled power that made Labour unelectable after a term of office.

Although Labour did not actually enter government until 1948, it came close to forming a coalition with the National League, supported by Fianna Fáil, in 1927. However, the plan was dashed by the infamous absence from the vital vote of Alderman Jinks of the National League (as well as Labour's deputy leader T. J. O'Connell who was at a conference in Canada).[3] Labour twice supported Fianna Fáil minority governments, in 1932 and 1937. In theory, this offered the party the attractive combination of power without responsibility. The reality was rather different. In 1932, the new government did introduce progressive legislation on issues such as pensions, price control and housing, but Fianna Fáil took the credit as it favoured these policies anyway. When party leader William Norton warned that Labour would vote against proposed public spending cuts, de Valera called a snap general election,[4] winning his first overall majority. Although no longer needed, Labour voted for de Valera when the new Dáil met in 1933 and remained largely supportive of the government. A former Labour TD described his erstwhile colleagues as the 'tin-whistle players in the Fianna Fáil band'.[5] When de Valera again found himself in a minority after the 1937 election, Labour supported him once more. But in May 1938, after a Fine Gael motion calling for civil service arbitration was passed with Labour support, de Valera called another snap election, and won another majority. The electoral impact of minority government support was decidedly mixed. In 1933, the party's vote fell, but thanks to Fianna Fáil transfers it gained one seat to reach eight. But in 1938, although the Labour vote held relatively steady, it lost four seats. While opponents of coalition consistently urged Labour to support minority governments rather than joining right-wing parties in Cabinet, the experiment was not repeated.

I

An innovation came in 1948 – Ireland's first coalition, known as the Inter-Party Government because Fianna Fáil had succeeded in making 'coalition' a by-word for instability. The idea, proposed by Fine Gael leader Richard Mulcahy, was enthusiastically taken up by Norton, who raised the question of who should lead the proposed government, indicating that Labour would not want to serve under the leader of another party. The objection was tactfully phrased; the real reason was Mulcahy's Civil War record. Norton also appears to have been the first to suggest John A. Costello (a Fine Gael front bencher and former Attorney General) as an alternative.[6] When Costello tried to argue against his own elevation, he was flatly told by Norton that 'they were wasting their time unless I agreed, as his group would have nobody but me'.[7] There were a number of reasons for Norton's support for Costello – he had no Civil War record; he was (relatively) progressive; and the two men had worked together when Costello was Attorney General.

The ten-point programme agreed by the parties, the modest precursor to modern programmes for government, showed plenty of Labour influence, with commitments to reduce the cost of living, tax 'unreasonable' profits, provide a comprehensive social security scheme, modify means tests, and remove unpopular taxes imposed by Fianna Fáil on tobacco, beer and cinema tickets.[8] However, coalition with Fine Gael was not popular with the membership. The US Embassy noted that while Norton had 'capably defended the Government's actions' at the 1948 Party Conference, a warning shot had been fired by Young Jim Larkin, who said 'he would not wait indefinitely for the … Government to act' on issues like prices and excess profits tax.[9]

In January 1949, the Fine Gael advisory committee, made up of senators and other party heavyweights, complained that 'Labour doctrine and false philosophy, social and economic, is being imposed on the Government.'[10] Costello was concerned enough about suggestions that the Labour tail was wagging the Fine Gael dog that he addressed them head on at his party's Ard Fheis in February 1950. He said nationalisation was only used where necessary, and the social security plan was not 'the first step on the road to totalitarian socialism'.[11] On occasion, Labour asserted its independence in government, as when it voted against compensation for directors of CIÉ after nationalisation in 1950.[12] But Norton was more likely to take a conservative line – as in his decision to accept the advice of the Department of Finance to follow the devaluation of sterling, rather than taking the more radical option pushed by Seán MacBride.[13]

The party had considerable achievements in government, particularly in the work of Tim Murphy, and after his death, of Michael Keyes, in the Department of Local Government, which oversaw and funded a massive increase in house construction. There were significant increases in welfare rates, as well as reformed means tests, CIÉ nationalisation and the introduction of arbitration for civil servants and teachers. On the debit side, James Everett walked the government into a major row, the Battle of Baltinglass, over the appointment of a crony to run a post office in that Wicklow village, while Norton failed in his main aim, the introduction of a comprehensive social security scheme. His proposals were stalled for years by Fine Gael, and the government fell before legislation could be passed.

It is arguable that Norton was far more successful as Tánaiste, keeping the government afloat, than he was as Minister for Social Welfare. Costello later said, 'Any time I ever had any trouble … I always sent for my friend Bill Norton for his sage and wise advice and counsel.'[14] One sympathetic profile described him as the coalition's 'tactician-in-chief'.[15] *The Irish Press*, less sympathetic, claimed that he spent 'most of his time with party matters and leaves his Department to run itself'. An ill-advised libel action saw Norton win the princely sum of £1 in damages, leading Fianna Fáil's Seán MacEntee to label him 'Billy the Quid'.[16]

Norton's role as coalition trouble-shooter was most evident during the protracted wrangling over the Mother and Child Scheme. The Tánaiste was the key figure in attempting to broker a deal between Health Minister Noël Browne and the medical profession. An experienced negotiator, he came up with a compromise scheme imposing an upper income limit of £1,000 a year for free treatment, but his efforts foundered on Browne's insistence on a universal scheme. Norton's efforts at conciliation gained the approval of the Archbishop of Dublin, John Charles McQuaid, who was worried about 'leftist Labour elements, which are approaching the point of publicly ordering the Church to stand out of social life'.[17] There was no danger of Norton supporting such calls, and other leading Labour figures at the time like Brendan Corish shared the widely held deference to the Church authorities. Noël Browne also publicly accepted the ruling of the bishops, but his effective presentation of his case made Labour, and particularly Norton, look bad in comparison. And Browne and some of his independent supporters put paid to Labour's continuation in government, voting for de Valera when the new Dáil met.[18]

Labour had learned some lessons in government, and decided that things would be different when the opportunity arose again. Before agreeing to support the second Inter-Party Government in 1954, the party insisted on a detailed agreed policy, while Norton successfully sought the Industry and Commerce portfolio, giving Labour a direct input into economic policy for the first time. The new government got off to a cordial start, with James Larkin overheard telling Taoiseach John A. Costello, 'Don't you know that we would do anything for you?'[19] One of its first actions was to reduce the price of butter – a key Labour demand (though Costello claimed it was his idea).[20] Health Minister Tom O'Higgins skilfully defused a potential row when he had to delay introducing new services which Labour had backed in opposition. O'Higgins met Labour TDs to convince them the Health Service was not yet ready – the Fine Gael man was so persuasive that a vote of confidence in him, proposed by Larkin, was passed.[21]

But the overriding impression created by the second Inter-Party Government was of lethargy. There was certainly no radicalism supplied by Labour. According to the current affairs journal *The Leader*, 'a stranger visiting this country … would find in office a government recognisable to any student of politics as conservative; he might discover that certain Ministers bore the label 'Labour' … but he would be unlikely to pick them out from their colleagues on the strength of their public utterances'.[22] Frustration with this situation, and with the deteriorating economy, was voiced in September 1956 by Larkin, who warned against the government's austerity measures. 'Labour has a positive policy, and before it is too late Labour must declare for progress and against retrogression and decline.'[23] His comments came just days before the Taoiseach unveiled a new economic strategy but while Costello's proposal included many progressive elements, it had been proposed by O'Higgins, and drafted by the Taoiseach himself with help from advisors and Fine Gael ministers. Labour appears to have had very little to do with it, although the party's TDs enthusiastically supported it.

While Labour ministers, especially Norton, fought many battles behind the scenes against Finance Minister Gerard Sweetman, these were mainly defensive. Norton robustly challenged Sweetman on various issues relating to his own department, refusing to accept a cut in the ESB budget for rural electrification in August 1956,[24] and telling him in September 1956 that he was 'appalled' at Finance's 'unpardonable breach of propriety' in trying to influence an inquiry into the future of the railways.[25] There appears to have been no coherent challenge to the underlying issue, Sweetman's economic policy, and Labour in Government failed to provide the fresh thinking that Ireland desperately needed. In fact, Norton used his position in Industry and Commerce to delay moves to end protection.[26]

The other major point of difference between Labour and Fine Gael was on Northern Ireland. In 1954, the party, including Norton as Tánaiste, voted for a Clann na Poblachta motion calling for Northern representation in the Dáil. As the British Ambassador dryly noted, Labour 'displayed a marked independence of their major allies in one of the first important divisions under the new Government.'[27] The Irish Ambassador in London, Freddie Boland, told British officials the following month that Labour Ministers 'had been rather half-hearted in the discussions of anti-IRA policy'.[28] He went further in December, claming that Labour still had 'a sympathetic attitude to IRA activities against Partition'.[29] This was put to the test when the IRA Border Campaign began in November 1956. The US Embassy reported 'violent cleavage within Cabinet, with Labour leader Norton opposing Government action' against the IRA.[30] But action was taken – resulting in Clann na Poblachta withdrawing its support, precipitating a general election in March 1957. The results were dismal for the government, for Labour, and for the prospects of any future coalition. Costello rather pompously wrote of his pride in being 'instrumental in permitting representatives of the Labour movement to take part in the Government ... enabling them to see the difficulties of Government ... and shoulder responsibility.'[31] Labour, though, was in no mood to repeat the experience, especially with Gerard Sweetman – Brendan Corish swore he would never again serve in government with him.[32]

II

That view had changed by 1973, partly through the experience of sixteen years in opposition, where principles are unsullied but achievements are rare. The Arms Crisis had heightened concerns about Fianna Fáil's continuance in office, while an influx of prominent intellectuals had increased Labour's belief in its prospects of holding its own in government. And Gerard Sweetman's death in a car crash in 1970, along with Fine Gael's adoption of the Just Society programme in the mid-1960s, made that party a more attractive coalition partner. The two parties agreed an outline programme, and effective transfers increased their joint total of seats despite a drop in Labour support.

In Labour's two previous spells in government, ministers were chosen by vote of the parliamentary party. This time, Corish, who had taken over as leader in 1960, insisted on choosing his Cabinet team – if the party did not like it, they could find another leader.[33] Despite his mild manner, Corish could be tough. A British assessment said he 'has considerable presence and comes over well on television. He is vigorous in debate, but modest and easy in manner.'[34]

He also got on well with Liam Cosgrave, who said he was 'a man of integrity and honour … once you made an agreement with him, that was it.'[35] Cosgrave actually agreed to Labour getting one Cabinet seat more than the relative strengths of the parties indicated. And the Labour team was a talented one. Apart from Corish in Health and Social Welfare, it included Michael O'Leary, the Minister for Labour; Justin Keating in Industry and Commerce; Conor Cruise O'Brien in Posts and Telegraphs; and Jimmy Tully in Local Government. Frank Cluskey, Parliamentary Secretary to Corish, effectively took over the Social Welfare part of his brief.

An influential Cabinet subcommittee on the economy had three Fine Gael members (Finance Minister Richie Ryan, Agriculture Minister Mark Clinton, and Garret FitzGerald, the Minister for Foreign Affairs) and three Labour (Tully, O'Leary and Keating).[36] Given FitzGerald's propensity to side with Labour, the conservative Fine Gael position was in a minority on the committee, and had a bare majority in Cabinet as a whole. The most symbolic Labour victory was the introduction of the Wealth Tax. Although Richie Ryan had severe misgivings, it fell to him to introduce it. As it happens, so many loopholes were introduced that it was largely ineffective. During the Dáil debate, Ryan accurately complained: 'Never were there so many words said about a measure that will affect so few people.'[37] But the Wealth Tax caused a huge backlash, which was blamed by many in Fine Gael for the party's defeat in 1977.

Much of the tension between the two parties involved Ryan. In

September 1976, as the Cabinet Economic Subcommittee worked on a Green Paper on the economy, Corish complained that 'the Departments concerned with social affairs were being ignored'. Ryan insisted that resources had to be targeted first at areas which would generate growth; Corish replied that the public would not accept cuts in health spending.[38] Not for the last time, Labour and Fine Gael priorities were opposed.

One of the issues facing Keating in Industry and Commerce was the development of natural resources. At the 1974 Party Conference, Noël Browne called for the nationalisation of the Bula zinc mine in Navan, County Meath. The issue was not simply one of socialist economics – it was also about coalition. According to Ruairi Quinn, the aim was to have the conference direct the leadership 'to take a course of action which it could not deliver in government'. But Keating delivered an impassioned reply to Browne, securing the support of members with the promise to obtain the 'best possible deal'.[39]

As John Horgan points out, Keating was working to an unstated objective, 'the creation, in Bula, of a company which would, with state involvement, be the nucleus of an Irish multinational, strong enough to engage the other multinationals on their own terms ... [It was a] strategy, based on a particular view of what was possible for a Labour minister playing a minority part in a coalition government'.[40] Keating also pursued an imaginative approach (much to the annoyance of Finance) to mineral exploration, for instance securing investment in Avoca Mines in part payment for an offshore oil exploration licence.[41]

A further indication that Labour was capable of original thinking came in mid-1975, when Corish pushed for radical changes in economic policy, writing to the Taoiseach that there were 'unmistakable signs of growing uneasiness among the supporters of the Government at the Government's apparent unwillingness to give a clear lead in the economic crisis. If this uneasiness develops further it could be fatal to our Government, and perhaps quite soon.'[42] The Labour proposals, which matched similar ones by FitzGerald, led to a mini-Budget on 26 June 1975, which temporarily introduced food subsidies and reduced VAT on a number of items in order to reduce inflation.

In return, unions were expected to moderate wage demands. Richie Ryan worried that the unions would not live up to their side of the bargain, but was pleasantly surprised by the tough negotiating stance of Michael O'Leary. 'I think it was a shock to his friends in the trade union movement that he made it perfectly clear that the Government was in earnest about

... this reduction ... and that if it wasn't done the Government would withdraw the subsidies.'[43] The result was a reduction in inflation, followed by some moderation in wage demands.

By the time the election came around, the economic situation was on the turn, not that the Coalition got any credit from the electorate. The Cabinet was evenly divided on the timing of an election: half wanted to hold off until the autumn of 1977, half wanted it at the start of the summer. The decision was left to Taoiseach Liam Cosgrave, who went for the earlier option, apparently under the influence of Corish,[44] who was under pressure from his parliamentary party. In common with Labour's previous coalition experiences, the subsequent election saw Labour lose seats and returned to the opposition benches.

III

Just four years later, in 1981, the two parties were back in power, in Garret FitzGerald's short-lived first government. Having succeeded Frank Cluskey, who lost his Dáil seat, Michael O'Leary became Tánaiste and Minister for Industry and Energy. Though charismatic, his commitment left something to be desired at times. One party activist remembers O'Leary going missing for a couple of weeks. It turned out he was staying in a hotel suite while his house was being renovated, and completing his legal studies so he would have the option of practising as a barrister[45] – hardly a vote of confidence in Labour's political future! The other Labour ministers were Jim Tully in Defence, Eileen Desmond in Health and Social Welfare, and Liam Kavanagh in Labour and the Public Service.

Some in Fine Gael felt that Labour was now a tougher proposition than in the National Coalition of 1973–77. Trade Minister John Kelly felt they 'were looking over their shoulders at the Workers' Party and ... pursued a much more independent, left-wing stance in government'.[46] But there was one similarity – once again, a coalition faced terrible economic problems, in this case exacerbated by the outgoing Fianna Fáil government's deliberate underestimation of the likely Budget deficit. An emergency Budget followed the coalition's formation in June 1981, which pulled the current budget deficit back from a projected £950 million to £450 million, through increases in VAT, excise duties, and postal charges, a 1 per cent Youth Employment Levy and the reintroduction of road tax.

Further problems arose when the following year's Budget had to be agreed early in 1982. The Cabinet initially agreed to abolish food subsidies, an agreement which O'Leary reneged on in a 3 a.m. phone call to FitzGerald. Faced with a potential split, ministers eventually reached a compromise, which saw the retention of some subsidies, paid for by an increase in VAT to 18 per cent, and its extension to clothing and footwear. O'Leary said the compromise 'was greeted with relief … we were at the end of a desperately intensive period of panic and pressure. We were an exhausted government'.[47] That exhaustion showed in political misjudgement by the Taoiseach and the Tánaiste, neither of whom realised the impact of the VAT changes on the independent TDs. Jim Kemmy's refusal to vote for the Budget plunged the country into an election.

After the exciting interlude of a controversial Fianna Fáil minority government, an election in November 1982 opened the way for another coalition. Labour had a new leader, the 32-year-old Dick Spring, catapulted into the position on the eve of the election after O'Leary resigned following a conference defeat on coalition. Negotiating a programme for government was a daunting challenge – as Vincent Browne said, 'Prior to these talks the biggest thing Spring had ever negotiated was his mortgage'.[48] However, Spring quickly put FitzGerald on notice that he was no pushover. The Fine Gael leader had planned to leave the coalition talks to attend a European conference. Spring made it clear 'that if the putative Taoiseach was not prepared to cancel his plans for a weekend in Paris, he could regard the negotiations as being over'.[49] Spring put together a good back-room team. He also brought Frank Cluskey along for one of the sessions, in order 'to frighten the shit out of Fine Gael', as one of his advisors elegantly put it.[50]

Labour sought taxes on wealth and property, and indexation of welfare payments; Fine Gael opposed these measures, but wanted a commitment to balance the books in four years. Foreshadowing the positions of the two parties in 2011, Labour feared the deflationary effect of closing the budget deficit so quickly and, again foreshadowing 2011, the compromise was to push the target date out to five years. A National Development Corporation (NDC) was included in the programme, though it was significantly different from the Labour proposal – John Bruton had his own ideas about how an NDC would operate, which later caused further tensions.

More immediate problems developed with Minister for Finance Alan Dukes, a tough and abrasive personality. As Barry Desmond put it, 'I always thought that I was a particularly intransigent person on political issues until I experienced Alan Dukes at first hand.'[51] Four weeks after the formation of the government, Dukes announced he would be aiming to reduce the current budget deficit to £750 million. This figure was swiftly repudiated by Spring, whose position was subsequently backed by FitzGerald and the Cabinet. The Labour view was that if Spring had not objected, 'he would never have had the authority in his own ranks to keep that government alive'.[52] For those who favoured fiscal rectitude, though, it showed 'fundamental divisions ... in a government not yet a month in office. It was an ominous development.'[53]

The stark realities of government sank in fast. When trying to persuade Fergus Finlay to join the Labour team, Spring explained that 'when we opened the books we discovered there isn't a spare penny ... I'm offering a very bumpy ride. I have no idea whether this government will last a fortnight. What do you say?'[54] Finlay said yes, embarking on a very bumpy ride indeed. He found that the key relationship was between the party leaders who 'were determined that they were not going to be brought down by internal wrangling ... Even when they disagreed, they stood by each other.'[55] Gemma Hussey wrote of 'the affection and respect in which the Taoiseach and Tánaiste held each other, the almost fatherly concern of Garret for Dick ... [they] sorted out a great many potentially explosive items before they ever came to Cabinet, quite often in Garret's basement sitting room ...' Hussey, not a fan of Labour, also wrote of Spring's 'bad-tempered, often sulky demeanour which irritated many of us in Fine Gael.'[56] FitzGerald frequently showed his liberal instincts, for instance casting the decisive vote in favour of a Labour proposal to ban South African produce, against a majority of his Fine Gael colleagues.[57] However, his instinctive search for consensus led to overlong Cabinet meetings which 'wore his government out'.[58]

FitzGerald himself provoked a row with Spring in September 1983, when he said on radio that the next year's Budget would have to include half a billion pounds in spending cuts. In response, the Labour ministers boycotted a Cabinet meeting for a time, until FitzGerald met Spring and agreed that there would be no further 'off the cuff' statements giving such figures.[59] It was further agreed that Spring would spell out his approach in a public speech, in Millstreet, County Cork. The Labour leader said the government was committed to correcting the public finances, but only in a way that did not impede recovery or damage the country's social fabric. 'It was a blunt put-down for Fine Gael ... FitzGerald had a choice: to pursue fiscal rectitude or to keep power. He and his colleagues chose the latter option.'[60]

The Taoiseach also emerged with a bloody nose from a botched Cabinet reshuffle in February 1986. Under pressure on the Right from the new Progressive Democrats party (PDs), he decided on a number of changes. He felt Dukes, Desmond and Hussey had suffered the brunt of public criticism and deserved a move to less contentious portfolios. Part of his plan involved a division in the Department of Foreign Affairs to give Hussey a post covering European affairs, a move successfully resisted by Peter Barry, determined to hang onto his empire in Iveagh House.

Even more of a problem was the other deputy party leader in the coalition, Barry Desmond (who, like Peter Barry, was a Corkman, which might or might not have been a coincidence). Although Spring had agreed to the move, Desmond flatly refused to surrender his dual Health and Social Welfare portfolios, at one point barricading himself into his office. As Fergus Finlay dolefully recounted, 'It was like a Gilbert and Sullivan version of *Mutiny on the Bounty*'.[61] Eventually, Desmond agreed to give up Social Welfare (which went as a not very satisfactory consolation prize to Hussey) but retained Health. It was, until January 2011, the most bungled reshuffle in Irish political history. In his memoirs, a still defiant Desmond admitted that his actions 'had seriously diminished the government's credibility. A major reshuffle had turned into a complete shambles. The Taoiseach could not exercise his most fundamental constitutional entitlement – the right to hire and fire his own government ministers.'[62] It was an episode Brian Cowen could have studied to good effect.

It also left lasting ill-feeling in the coalition. In her diary, Hussey described herself as being 'in black depression' and referred to 'the sordid details of Barry's refusal to move'.[63] Ruairi Quinn – who did well out of the reshuffle, managing to add Public Service to his Labour portfolio after suggesting it would not be a good idea to put it with Finance – said 'the damage to the cause of the coalition was almost terminal'.[64] One by-product was the return to Finance of John Bruton – who had already been central to some tough clashes with Labour. Fergus Finlay later claimed that 'most of the rows in that government involved John Bruton ... He could never allow an argument to end until he had won it. He caused more trouble in that government – with his own as well as with Labour ministers – than any other member.'[65] This tension would have important political consequences some years later, as Bruton came to represent for Labour the unacceptable face of Fine Gael, as Sweetman had to an earlier generation.

The most severe tension initially was between Bruton and Frank Cluskey, the Minister for Trade, Commerce and Tourism. The two were described by a Cabinet colleague as 'sparking off each other – both are like very large little boys'.[66] The immediate cause of combustion was Dublin Gas. This private company was being bailed out by the State, but Bruton refused to nationalise it, which prompted Cluskey to resign. Many believed Dublin Gas was a pretext for Cluskey, who had not been particularly happy in government.[67] In the wake of Cluskey's resignation, Spring insisted on Labour getting the Energy portfolio – much to the annoyance of Bruton, who considered resignation as a result.[68] Spring also tried to persuade Mervyn Taylor to take Cluskey's place at Cabinet, but in the end the left-winger baulked at the idea.[69] Spring saw the advantages of drawing anti-coalitionists into Cabinet, an idea he would act on the next time. After Taylor's refusal, Ruairi Quinn was promoted instead.

By mid-1986, Spring and Desmond had agreed that the party would not accept any more health cuts[70] (which were certain to be proposed by Bruton for the following year's budget). As early as July, FitzGerald was telling one of his ministers that 'he couldn't see a Budget being put together' and floated the idea of 'Fine Gael parting company from Labour at some stage during its preparation'.[71] FitzGerald apparently considered parting 'amicably' from Labour in October 1986, introducing a tough Budget and then fighting the election on that platform.[72] However, the government limped on until January, when the Labour ministers withdrew in protest at the Book of Estimates being proposed by Bruton.

A predictably horrendous election campaign ensued; Spring almost lost his seat, famously saving it by a margin of four votes. Other seats teetered on the brink through the long count, but in the end the party retained twelve TDs, although this left Labour in fourth place, behind the Progressive Democrats who had fourteen. Ominously, the Workers' Party now had four TDs as well, and posed a potent threat to Labour in a number of other constituencies. The scars of government would remain – but lessons had been learned. The next time, Spring determined, he and Labour would be treated with more respect. And he would be very reluctant to work with John Bruton.

IV

Just five years after the disaster of 1987 came the triumph of the Spring Tide election of 1992, with thirty-three TDs returned. The surge to Labour had been evident from opinion polls during the campaign. Outgoing Fianna Fáil Taoiseach Albert Reynolds drew the correct conclusions, saying to his Press Secretary after one such poll: 'Labour will strike a hard bargain.'[73] But a deal between Fianna Fáil and Labour seemed unthinkable to many in both parties – and to Fine Gael leader John Bruton. His refusal to include Democratic Left in a possible deal with Labour, and insistence on including the PDs instead, was described by Barry Desmond as 'our coalition of nightmares ... He pushed Spring into the loving Longford embrace of the astounded Albert Reynolds'.[74]

Reynolds took full advantage of Bruton's failure to reel in the Labour leader. His advisor Martin Mansergh had already drawn up a positive response to the Labour manifesto, accepting some proposals word for word. A key line suggested that a 'partnership Government between two substantial parties would inevitably be different in character to a traditional coalition involving one large and one small party'.[75] Ruairi Quinn was 'taken aback', telling a journalist it was like getting not just a free ticket to the dance, but 'the guarantee of a good time as well!'[76]

But could this guaranteed good time endure? Spring spelled out the importance of how he and his party were treated in a speech to the conference which approved coalition with Fianna Fáil: 'This government will stand or fall on the issue of trust ... If it does not conform to the highest standards of accountability and openness, it will cease to exist – it is as simple as that.'[77] But Labour sometimes seemed to forget that Fianna Fáil had sensitivities too; as Noel Dempsey put it, 'It's important that Labour realises that we're still the majority party, and that we're not going to be pushed around.'[78]

Spring was well aware of the potential for disagreements between ministers to clog up Cabinet meetings. When he was Tánaiste to Garret FitzGerald, disagreements were referred to 'facilitating meetings' where Chief Whip Seán Barrett and senior civil servant Seán O hUiginn would attempt to broker a compromise.[79] In the inter-party governments, such issues were referred to Cabinet committees for resolution. The new solution was a system of Programme Managers – one for each Minister – to identify potential areas of conflict. 'The frayed nerves and the hurried compromises, which had characterised the 1982–87 Fine Gael-Labour government, were to become a thing of the past ... The new structure ... would enable ministers to take strategic political decisions with a minimum of damage to the cabinet's operational morale and cohesion.'[80]

The Labour Programme Managers and advisors met on Monday afternoons to discuss the agenda for the following morning's Cabinet meeting. Labour Ministers met early on the Tuesday morning to prepare the line for Cabinet. Then Spring would meet Reynolds to see if any remaining logjams could be cleared.[81] It was a tight and effective way to ensure a united Labour front. Seán Duignan was somewhat jealous of Labour's superiority to Fianna Fáil in 'their tightly integrated approach to every aspect of government, with Labour members of the cabinet, junior ministers, programme managers and special advisers uniting in highly effective common cause and action'.[82] However, the Programme Managers – as well as Labour's insistence on having a separate Office of the Tánaiste which would receive all documentation at the same time as the Department of the Taoiseach – led to media criticism that the party had lost the run of itself.

Spring had the option of Labour holding Finance or Foreign Affairs. Given his own lack of confidence in economics and his desire to have a role in Northern Ireland (for reasons that were to become obvious), he chose the latter.[83] Reynolds had briefed him on the possibility of a major breakthrough on the North, and the Labour leader understandably wanted part of the action. This was, arguably, a massive strategic blunder. Spring got little enough credit for his role in the peace process, while the amount of travel involved was a huge and distracting burden for a party leader (as Seán MacBride found). Instead, Labour's economic input was secured by Ruairi Quinn in the new Department of Enterprise and Employment, which took in the old Department of Labour, as well as Industry and Commerce. The party also secured Education (Niamh Bhreathnach), Health (Brendan Howlin) and two new departments – Equality, held by Mervyn Taylor, and Arts, Culture and the Gaeltacht, under Michael D. Higgins.

Spring's advice to his new ministers was succinct: 'Keep in touch with the backbenchers, do not abuse the car and be careful about foreign travel.'[84] Sound advice, but Labour quickly came under intense fire in the media for alleged jobbery and over-indulgence in the luxuries of office – and much of the fire was directed at the Tánaiste. Some of the criticism concerned the employment of relatives at the taxpayers' expense – Niamh Bhreathnach offered to resign because of the attacks on her employment of her daughter as constituency secretary.[85] Spring refused to discuss resignation.

After being at the receiving end of Labour criticism for years, Fianna Fáil could hardly believe their luck. Transport Minister Brian Cowen teased his Labour colleagues: 'Jaze, lads, ye're giving us an awful bad name.' The Taoiseach confided to his press secretary: 'There are no better lads than Labour for ethics in politics, and there are no better lads than Labour for grabbing every job they possibly can when they get half a chance.'[86] Fianna Fáil's schadenfreude boded ill for a harmonious working relationship.

Spring himself became a target of attack for staying in the Waldorf Astoria rather than the Irish-owned Fitzpatrick's in New York. While the criticism may have been ill-informed and unfair, it stuck. 'The image of Dick as a jet-setter was firmly established, and would be replenished every now and again by stories about the use of the government jet.'[87] In other circumstances, Labour might have been given a free pass by the media over such issues. But having set the bar so high for itself and others, the backlash was to be expected.

One of Spring's strengths was his team of advisors: Programme Manager Greg Sparks, press secretary John Foley, organisation overseer Pat Magner, and Fergus Finlay. Finlay was seen by Fianna Fáil as a manipulative influence. Many in Labour agreed. At one point Labour ministers complained to Spring about 'the heavy hand of Fergus Finlay'.[88] I experienced this feeling myself at a Labour Party conference in Limerick. One senior Minister sardonically told journalists that if the entire Cabinet team went on stage and announced their resignations, the media would immediately attribute it to another masterstroke by Finlay!

As always, the relationship between Taoiseach and Tánaiste was the key to the government's success, and the dynamic between Reynolds and Spring quickly became a problem. As Seán Duignan noted, 'Reynolds was manipulative and impatient of opposition to his wishes. Spring was moody and quick to take offence … he's touchy, and when he's not being touchy, Fergus is touchy for him.'[89] Finance Minister Bertie Ahern also noted that Spring was 'a prickly character. As time went on, he and Albert seemed increasingly uncomfortable in each other's company … Usually it was something and nothing – Albert saying something, Dick taking offence …'[90]

An early test for Labour came in March 1993. Reynolds and Ahern disagreed over a proposed tax amnesty. Reynolds insisted to his press secretary: 'I can carry the Cabinet if I want!'[91] Spring realised that whoever he sided with would win, with implications for the standing of the Taoiseach or his most powerful Fianna Fáil minister. He also believed a majority at Cabinet would vote against the measure, and therefore 'it would be infinitely better if the amnesty were quietly buried without any difference emerging, this early in the life of the government, between the partners.'[92] Not surprisingly, Ahern felt differently, describing the Labour ministers in cabinet: 'They just sat on their hands looking sheepish.'[93]

Labour paid a price for their sheepishness, as the media went to town on their surrender of principle. Reynolds had won, but Labour had learned a lesson about him. Labour press officer John Foley told his Fianna Fáil counterpart, Seán Duignan: 'We've seen enough of Albert to recognise that he is the most pleasant and reasonable of men – provided he gets his own way.'[94] When a similar issue arose the following year, Spring determined that Reynolds would not get his own way.

The Taoiseach was anxious to introduce changes to the tax regime for expatriates. Spring refused to allow the measures come to Cabinet. Reynolds, on holiday in Cyprus, was incensed: 'Yet again Labour threatened that if I didn't agree with their decision it could lead to a general election – in other words, back off or else!'[95] He told Duignan that he would not be dictated to: 'I will not be a half Taoiseach ... this could be the breakpoint.'[96] Spring, meanwhile, told his closest advisors that 'he had come to the conclusion that the government would be over on Monday'.[97] In the end, Reynolds backed off, but was, in Spring's words, 'pretty pissed off'.[98] As Ahern noted, it was 'not the sign of a relationship which was going to last'.[99]

A succession of further incidents sapped confidence between the parties – the Masri passport affair, TEAM Aer Lingus and, most dramatically, the Beef Tribunal Report, parts of which Reynolds insisted on publicising, to Labour's fury. Finlay later wrote that Spring should and would have resigned over the latter incident had he not known how delicately balanced the peace process was at that point.[100]

Despite the triumph of the IRA ceasefire, the relationship between Reynolds and Spring was now toxic, and it was only a matter of time before something finished it off. That something was Reynolds' insistence on appointing Attorney General Harry Whelehan to the Presidency of the High Court against Labour objections. The details are extremely convoluted, and need not detain us. Suffice it to say that Reynolds rejected the very idea of giving in to Labour demands. 'No Taoiseach can survive having to publicly knuckle under to that kind of blackmail.'[101] Labour not unnaturally held him personally responsible for the debacle: 'a good government was ended by one man's stubborn refusal to accept that he couldn't win every argument.'[102] A *Sunday Tribune* poll at the time found blame evenly divided between Reynolds and Spring.[103] The public was undoubtedly right: there was a pair of them in it.

But while Reynolds paid the ultimate political price, Spring had another spin on the merry-go-round, as by-election results and a Fine Gael change of heart about coalition with Democratic Left made an alternative government possible. Two days before John Bruton was elected Taoiseach as head of that alternative, Spring told Ruairi Quinn that Labour could not achieve a 'rotating Taoiseach', but they might be able to get the Department of Finance.[104] Quinn assured his party leader that he would be up to the job, and so Labour held both Finance and Foreign Affairs in the new government. With two of the three top jobs, and essentially the same programme for government as was agreed with Fianna Fáil, Labour was in an immensely powerful position.

The key imponderable was Bruton, Labour's *bête noire* just two years before. In the event, the Fine Gael leader was a revelation. Finlay later admitted he viewed Bruton 'with some trepidation ... I was wrong – or else he had changed quite a bit ... [He was] open, honest and always willing to listen.'[105] Quinn too enjoyed 'a good and constructive working relationship' with the Taoiseach.[106] Ironically, the Finance Minister found his relationship with his own party leader under some strain, feeling that Spring had undermined him by agreeing a higher pay increase as part of a national agreement with the unions than he had wanted. Quinn felt 'gazumped and bushwhacked', telling Spring in the course of 'the only intense, awful row we ever had' that he was on the point of resigning.[107]

There was no resignation, but there were other clouds on the horizon. Finlay, back working at party headquarters, had research conducted which showed the public had not forgiven Labour for campaigning against Fianna Fáil in 1992, and then entering government with them. In addition, the Labour Ministers were perceived as competent, but also 'technocratic, distant, arrogant'.[108] There was a strong argument for the government going its full term – to November 1997 – as the economy was improving, but as always it would take some time before the improvements were noticed by voters. However, Quinn, for one, preferred a June election, feeling the government would be prey to special-interest pleading if it tried to go to the autumn.[109]

Despite filling the Department of Finance at a time of strong economic growth, despite Spring's high-profile and successful tenure in Iveagh House, and despite delivering on an extraordinary proportion of its 1992 manifesto, Labour lost all the gains it made in that election, dropping sixteen seats. It was a particularly disheartening result after a strong performance in government. By contrast, Fine Gael gained nine seats. It was the same old story: a spell in government hollowed out Labour's support, while the bigger party got the electoral benefit.

V

It is perhaps significant that one-time Labour TD John Horgan titled his 1986 study of the party's participation in government *Labour: The Price of Power*.

Anti-coalitionists through the years have argued that entering government with a larger party inevitably means that Labour policy is diluted, which leads to electoral defeat. Noël Browne put this argument in a nutshell in February 1973:'A compromise when you are in a minority is likely to be the compromise which suits the majority in that coalition government.'[110] This is not entirely accurate. There have been plenty of occasions when Labour has won policy arguments with its larger partner. But it has not reaped any electoral benefit from so doing, and its biggest loss of seats came in 1997, after its most productive and successful period in government. The question is what lessons, if any, Labour has learned from this dispiriting record.

In 2011, that question arose again. Labour had had its most successful election ever, winning thirty-seven seats and becoming the second biggest party. But unlike 1992 when it negotiated with a demoralised Fianna Fáil, its prospective partner, Fine Gael, had also had its best ever result, and was less prepared to give in to Labour demands. Even some party activists who had always been on the pro-coalition wing of the party conceded there might be an argument for Labour staying in opposition, aiming to gain more support and lead the next government.

During the 2011 election campaign, Labour's 'Gilmore for Taoiseach' posters attracted a considerable amount of derision. As polls showed the party's support dropping, Labour's aim lowered, and the final week of the campaign became a desperate struggle to convince the voters that Gilmore should be Tánaiste. But those posters at least showed a party with ambitions, a party that realised that to implement its objectives, it needed to be the biggest party in that government, and to control the key posts. As it enters its second century, one wonders whether Labour has forever foreclosed that option by yet again entering government as a junior partner.

10. LABOUR AND THE MEDIA: THE PROMISE OF SOCIALISM, NEGATIVE CAMPAIGNING AND *THE IRISH TIMES*

KEVIN RAFTER

On 28 May 1969 – six days into that year's general election campaign – Sir Frederick Sayers from Camlagh, Greystones in County Wicklow, wrote to *The Irish Times*. The correspondence, printed on the 'Letters to the Editor' page, was headed 'Irish Labour's Intellectuals'.[1] Sir Frederick was concerned about the newspaper's recent editorial direction and what he saw as a trend in favour of 'any form of Government which is not F.F.' The Wicklow voter wanted in particular to warn 'the plain people of Ireland' about the Labour Party's 'extreme socialism' and 'utopian doctrines'. Sir Frederick's letter continued: 'I regard those extreme socialists as people who want a job themselves in parliament in order that they may spend other people's money, extracted from all grades in society, on people who, for the most part, do not want such help, but now find that they are better off sitting idle and, probably spending national assistance in the locals.'[2]

The 1969 contest was predicted as Labour's breakthrough election. The party was not only running more candidates than it had done previously but it had also succeeded in recruiting several high-profile individuals including Conor Cruise O'Brien, David Thornley and Justin Keating. Many were well-known television figures, although the main political parties were still adapting to the new medium: the 1969 contest was only the second Dáil election since the arrival of a national television service. Newspapers remained the most influential news medium – possibly, however, the last time they held this position. In the latter regard, Sir Frederick's 'Letter to the Editor' raised an interesting issue – was *The Irish Times* soft on the opposition parties, and Labour in particular, with a partisan editorial agenda that discriminated against Fianna Fáil? This chapter focuses on Labour's embrace of socialism in the late 1960s and examines to what extent did *The Irish Times* rally to the party's cause in the 1969 general election. The discussion illustrates how Fianna Fáil measured its message to respond to the Labour threat – and how a ruthless, negative campaign successfully dominated news coverage and overpowered the Labour agenda.

In very many ways the 1969 contest was a transition election. Across Irish society there was evidence of a nascent modernisation agenda while in the realm of political campaigning a new professionalisation was evident. Campaign techniques – recently seen in the United States and United Kingdom – were being adopted, in varying degrees of sophistication, by the three main Irish parties. Jack Lynch's 'meet-the-people tour' was a central part of a highly personalised Fianna Fáil campaign. Lynch's party was well resourced – budgets even paid for the hire of a helicopter for the leader's tour. Fine Gael still lagged behind its larger rival but there were signs of a new attitude from a party whose senior members were described only a few years previously as part-time politicians more devoted to other professional activities than to politics.[3]

Labour also displayed a more professional approach in its quest to break the stranglehold of its two main rivals. The party had an election budget of £25,000 while the Irish Congress of Trade Unions (ICTU) provided another £17,000 for promotional spending.[4] Labour also proudly revealed that it had commissioned 'a professional psephological survey of Ireland' – which showed that its support was strong in working class areas and that the bulk of its support base was aged between twenty-one and forty.[5] Some elements of 'modern' political campaigns elsewhere were, however, still resisted particularly by Fianna Fáil, which opted not to publish an election manifesto. Those interested in its policy agenda were directed to the outgoing governmental programme, the most recent budget speech and Lynch's script delivered at the start of the election campaign. 'Manifestos have a Marxist ring about them,' Charles Haughey, the Minister for Finance, declared as he dismissed Fianna Fáil's opponents: 'Fine Gael is dead and many people are afraid of the extreme socialist policies of the Labour Party.'[6]

Irish politics had for the previous half century been defined in non-ideological terms with the partitionist hangover from the independence era still influencing the shape of the party system. Labour remained the third party, and had struggled to match the electoral dominance of Fianna Fáil. When government did beckon – in 1948 and in 1954 – it was as a minority partner in a Fine Gael-led administration. The latter years of the 1960s, however, saw the commencement of a brave, but ultimately unsuccessful, departure to promote a distinctive socialist programme.

I

It remains one of the best-known sound bites in Irish political history: 'The seventies will be socialist.' These were the first five words spoken by Brendan Corish in his leadership address at his party's national conference in October 1967. The speech, which had been three months in the making, was billed as heralding 'The New Republic' as Labour sought to tap into a nascent national mood for change and modernisation.[7] The continued contemporary usage of the phrase – more often than not as a political put-down – has a great deal to do with Labour's failure to convince the electorate ultimately of the value of its socialist programme at the 1969 general election.

Yet when Corish stood at the conference podium in late 1967 there was a real sense in Labour circles that the party was on the verge of a historic breakthrough. Corish was intent on broadening his party's appeal, and wanted to provide a genuine alternative to Fianna Fáil and Fine Gael. The speech was – according to one of its authors – 'a statement of socialist intent'.[8] There had been a long-standing timidity in embracing socialism (never mind communism or Marxism), reflecting not just the non-ideological nature of Irish politics but also a genuine fear of alienating a largely conservative population by incurring the wrath of the Roman Catholic hierarchy. One Labour TD went so far as to sue a local newspaper in 1964 for printing an opponent's claim that he was a communist.[9]

'Socialist' was a word 'rarely uttered by the party' and even when Corish assumed the leadership he preferred to talk about 'Christian socialists, not rip-roaring Marxists'.[10] On one occasion when rejecting a Fianna Fáil attack Corish declared, 'Our policy is based on good, sound, Christian principles and always will be.'[11] Garret FitzGerald recalled attending a media briefing in 1962 concerning Ireland's application to join the then European Economic Community (EEC) at which a Dutch reporter asked the Labour leader if he was a socialist. Addressing FitzGerald and the journalists Corish replied, 'Garret, imagine what would happen if I got up on the platform in Duncannon and announced that I was a socialist. Sure, I wouldn't get a vote in the place!'[12]

The 1960s, as mentioned earlier, saw the commencement of a process of modernisation and secularisation – a process which was 'complex, confused and very far from a linear narrative'.[13] In the political arena post-de Valera

Fianna Fáil embraced a more outward-looking industrial policy and deepened links with the world of business. Pressure for fresh thinking within Fine Gael divided the party along liberal and conservative lines. In this environment Corish and his supporters believed there was an opportunity for Labour. Although a Dáil deputy since 1945 Corish had shown few signs of being a political radical. The first time he actually described Labour as a socialist party was in June 1964. Interestingly, however, the word did not feature in the party's 1965 general election manifesto. An explicit endorsement eventually came at the party's national conference in October 1966 when Corish referred to a 'coherent socialist philosophy'.[14]

The Labour leader was heavily influenced by a group of modernisers including Michael O'Leary, a trade union research officer who had won a Dáil seat in 1965, Brendan Halligan, an economist who was appointed as a full-time party organiser in 1967, and Barry Desmond who became party chairman. O'Leary later said that with the new strategy Corish's 'every action as leader between 1965 and 1969 threw the legendary caution of the political culture from whence he hailed, to the winds.'[15] But Corish was not a puppet on a string manipulated by a cabal of ideologues – as Fianna Fáil would allege during the 1969 election campaign. Halligan explained: 'These were his ideas not anyone else's. Others, myself particularly, wrote down the words which he then read. But the sweep of ideas, the inner feelings and the most telling phrases were his alone.'[16]

Having spent most of its history out of power – and all of the previous decade in opposition – Labour had reason to be optimistic that its fortunes were about to change. Notwithstanding electoral defeats in 1961 and 1965, there had been tangible progress – the twenty-two seats won in 1965 had been equalled only once previously (in June 1927). There were increased numbers of party branches, more members and record attendances at national conferences. Many new younger members favoured a more radical bent to the party's policy outlook. The intention was to rebrand the Labour Party, and to recast Irish politics. Halligan later recalled the energy driving this new socialist departure: '... the party took off in the giddy excitement of believing that anything was possible.'[17] There was for some time, however, a vagueness in the party's new-found public attachment to socialism and also how its policy ambitions would be realised, and funded. In the words of one writer, the party was 'faced with the task of coming up with the policies to go along with its slogans'.[18]

Throughout 1968 a raft of policy papers were published. This new socialist agenda was eventually aggregated into a 150-page booklet and later distilled into the party's election manifesto 'The New Republic' in May 1969. The process was described as involving 'a complete critique of Irish society' where all possibilities were open for discussion including consideration of replacing Ireland's parliamentary system of government with a presidential system.[19] Corish claimed that Labour's 'socialist principles' would aim at greater mobilisation of national resources to secure full employment; he said that, 'Private enterprise has failed to establish the industries needed and that public enterprises under some form of State organisation will have to play a larger part in the economy and the search for jobs.'[20]

A newly established State Development Corporation was to be tasked with securing full employment; a Rural Development Agency would focus on similar issues in non-urban areas while the promotion of enterprise would be facilitated by providing businesses with cheaper credit. The provision of a free national health service and decent modern housing were central components of the policy plan. A new department of housing was proposed to deliver promises including bringing building land in urban areas under state control and providing 100 per cent loans at low rates of interest. Some issues were, however, fudged – the party's exact stance on bank ownership was vague and, despite references to more state control, stopped short of proposing full nationalisation.

The programme has met with almost universal dismissal from leading historians with assessments ranging from 'intellectual window-dressing'[21] to 'careless socialist rhetoric'[22] to 'naive logic and clueless political analysis'.[23] More generously, Gallagher has argued that the final programme 'represented a rare infusion of idealism into the political system' although he still accepted that at the heart of the manifesto was 'a rather starry-eyed naivety' particularly when it came to the costs involved.[24] The long list of policy promises undoubtedly offered many hostages to fortune, and despite having a great slogan many Labour policies were not fully developed.

There were also communication problems – internal and external. The internal process had been largely leadership driven and this top-down strategy received a distinctly lukewarm response from rural members, not to mention many rural TDs. Despite the new spirit of openness and changing attitude to authority a significant section of the population still held to a conservative outlook. Labour's embrace of socialism did not find universal favour. As John Horgan noted the new policy direction 'would have been anathema, not only to a previous generation of Labour parliamentarians, but also to some of those who had survived'.[25]

These internal issues were evident from the start of the change process.

For example, there was, according to one reporter at the 1967 conference, 'a frenzy of enthusiasm' when Corish declared his opposition to entering a coalition government. But, interestingly, the same writer observed of the leader's embrace of socialism: 'The delegates loved it too, but curiously, during the course of the debate it seemed to have made little impact.' Most speakers from the conference podium, journalist Donal Foley noted, 'failed to apply socialist planning theories to the question under discussion'.[26]

This resistance – and failure to comprehend fully the implications of party policy – obviously persisted. One political correspondent – writing many years later – was particularly critical of the approach of some parliamentary party members: 'unfortunately, many deputies only glanced at the proposals before being sent on radio and television to explain them to the public. It became obvious they had no great notion about what they were talking about and they were not helpful to the promotion of the ideas.'[27] Any weakness within Labour at communicating its own platform only further assisted the party's opponents who were intent on pursuing a deliberate policy of negative political campaigning against Corish and his colleagues.

The eighteenth Dáil was dissolved on 22 May 1969 with polling day set for 18 June 1969. Fianna Fáil was fighting its fourth election in a decade under a third leader – de Valera in 1959; Lemass in 1961 and 1965; and now Lynch in 1969. Fine Gael's Liam Cosgrave was also a new party leader, having come to the position after the 1965 election. Corish was the veteran – he had led Labour in the two previous contests.

Lynch succeeded Lemass in 1966 but the leadership transition had not been easy for Fianna Fáil. Several of Lynch's cabinet colleagues retained aspirations to lead the party and, at best, an uneasy internal truce existed. Lynch actually consolidated his position with by-election successes – seven in all – between December 1966 and May 1968. But, 'after such a good electoral run, Lynch made a bad decision' when calling a referendum in October 1968 seeking to change the electoral system.[28] The proposal to switch to a straight vote system was rejected; the voters had also said no in 1959. Lynch's government responded by redrawing Dáil constituency boundaries in its favour. The legislation passed into law in early spring – following the introduction of a positive budget – and a general election was called immediately to take full advantage.

In total, 373 candidates contested the election – the highest number since 1948. Fine Gael had 125 candidates; Fianna Fáil 121 while Labour had 99 (compared with 43 in 1965). The election was framed as a contest of equals. One newspaper report observed that, 'The picture now emerges – for the first time in Irish politics – of three parties fully equipped with policies, candidates and calibre fully competent to form a Government'.[29] Corish said his party had been 'almost overwhelmed' by the number of people seeking to be Dáil candidates. There was for the first time in a Dáil election at least one Labour candidate in every constituency although some outgoing TDs had resisted party policy of having a running mate. Labour's election message was consistent with that articulated over the previous eighteen months – implementation of a socialist policy platform and adherence to an anti-coalition agenda. Corish said Labour was offering a real alternative based on the 'fundamental principles and policies' agreed at its recent conference.[30]

The decision to rule out a pre-election pact was a source of annoyance in Fine Gael, which believed the real beneficiary would ultimately be Fianna Fáil. It was said that 'relations between the two opposition parties were at their lowest ebb since 1948'.[31] The strains were evident even before the election was called. Dublin South candidate John Kelly warned that the Labour leadership needed to 'temper its ideals with realism'.[32] Former Taoiseach John A. Costello even rowed into the debate: 'I believe the Labour leadership, caught in a mesh of socialist theorising, will be forced to abandon an untenable position, particularly when they reflect on the election results.'[33] It was a prophetic assessment but as the country headed to the polls on 18 June 1969 the overwhelming view in Labour circles was that a socialist era was about to commence.

II

The Irish media sector in the late 1960s was small in size and 'very homogeneous' in its content.[34] There were four main newspaper groups and a state-owned broadcast service – all devoted considerable editorial space to political news and also to coverage of electoral contests. But according to one writer, in this period 'certainly in the area of political communication, the morning papers play[ed] the primary role'.[35] Newspaper analysis and comment pieces were far less prominent in 1969 than they would become in subsequent elections.[36] There was only a small number of journalists covering politics while specialist correspondents were still only emerging. There was a distinct passivity in reporting politics – in the words of one correspondent, a 'quieter pace' – and this situation only strengthened the ability of the main parties to influence the news agenda.[37]

During the 1969 contest the newspapers provided significant space to candidate scripts issued by the main parties. As part of the professionalism of campaigning in the 1960s the parties set up 'speech factories' where supporters with expertise in particular policy areas wrote speeches for candidates in the hope of securing 'some press coverage'. This was – according to Farrell – 'an attempt to manufacture news' as it was unclear if many of the scripts were ever delivered. By the 1969 general election *The Irish Times* – while still providing extensive space for these scripts – introduced many news stories with the phrase 'according to a supplied script'. A more robust and personalised approach to the coverage of politics emerged in later years. Indeed, by the 1977 general election, newspaper coverage of supplied scripts (measured in column inches) had declined significantly – for example, down 32 per cent in *The Irish Times* and down 41 per cent in *The Irish Press*.

The available evidence suggests there was a fairly even balance in the amount of space devoted to reporting on the campaigns of the three main political parties. Coverage of Labour scripts was almost approximate to the party's share of the total number of nominated candidates. Indeed, Labour received more space in two of the main morning newspapers than Fine Gael as evident in Table 1. These figures led one authority to conclude that Labour's campaign was 'fairly covered by the mass media'.[38] But while Labour could have had few complaints about the extent of newspaper coverage this raw data reveals little about the nature of the coverage and even less about how successful Labour was in getting across its socialist message.

Table 1: Coverage of Party Speeches in the 1969 General Election

	The Irish Times	*Irish Independent*	*The Irish Press*	*Cork Examiner*
Fianna Fáil	1,568	857	1,602	971
Fine Gael	966	628	556	395
Labour	1,114	536	569	395
Others	90	208	138	26

(Measured in column inches). Source: Carty, 1969

The morning newspapers displayed considerable similarities in their selection of news stories but they did adopt differing editorial stances in relation to the main political parties. It is difficult to dispute one assessment of newspaper coverage in the 1969 campaign which concluded, 'As usual *The Irish Press* supported Fianna Fáil, the *Irish Independent* opposed it, while *The Irish Times* found it increasingly difficult to discover differences between the two main parties.'[39] While *The Irish Times* stopped short of formally endorsing Corish's party in the general election campaign, one authority has said 'the paper veered towards supporting the re-invigorated Labour Party'.[40]

Somewhat like the Labour Party, *The Irish Times* had embarked upon a process of renewal and reorientation to take advantage of the changes in Irish society. Douglas Gageby, who had been appointed editor in 1963, was intent – in the words of one of his successors – in moving *The Irish Times* 'from the margins to the mainstream of Irish life'.[41] Nevertheless, at the time of the 1969 election the newspaper still had the smallest circulation in the morning market although it was 'regarded as the established quality paper'.[42]

Gageby instilled a liberal ethos in his newspaper's editorial stance as he pursued a strategy to reflect the aspirations of 'the most influential, intelligent and enterprising elements of the population'.[43] Several of his contemporaries have, however, acknowledged that he had a strong regard for Charles Haughey and he was, according to one, 'under the spell of John Healy'[44] who, in his political columns, was sympathetic to Fianna Fáil. Yet, not even the editor's sympathetic leanings towards Haughey could lead *The Irish Times* to embrace Fianna Fáil. The newspaper's staff contained many journalists who were strongly supportive of Labour's new political positioning. Its Foreign Editor James Downey did back-room work for Labour, and was nominated as a Dáil candidate in 1969.[45] More significantly, and without any apparent acknowledgement of journalistic impartiality, Michael McInerney, the newspaper's political correspondent, was effectively an unofficial Labour advisor. McInerney was close to Halligan, involved with drafting the 1967 conference speech, and was instrumental in candidate recruitment. Indeed, the first meetings between Halligan and O'Brien and Keating, respectively, were instigated by McInerney and took place over lunches in the home of *The Irish Times* journalist.

The next section will examine how successful Labour was in setting the news agenda with its socialist programme during the election campaign but beyond the news pages there were only a handful of opinion pieces in *The Irish Times* which actually addressed the party's programme. Overall, by the standards of election coverage in subsequent decades – and in the early years of the twenty-first century – few analytical articles appeared. One rare example was an assessment of the foreign policies of the three parties. Written by the newspaper's 'diplomatic correspondent', the piece assessed the contribution of Cruise O'Brien to Labour's policy positioning. 'Many people, including a few inside the party, regard his famous advocacy of an embassy in Havana as a major political gaffe', the writer concluded, but noted that opening an embassy in any socialist capital would be a symbolic reassertion of non-alignment and neutrality.[46]

The absence of writing that critiqued the different party programmes was to the disadvantage of Labour, which could have hoped for at least balanced, and possibly favourable, treatment. If anything in its analysis/comment articles *The Irish Times* did Labour few favours. Several comment articles were openly dismissive of Labour's campaign strategy – many were written by the paper's political commentator, John Healy. Moreover, the unsigned 'Inside Politics' column was used at the midpoint in the campaign to criticise Corish strongly:

> the evolution of Brendan Corish must be the greatest piece of forced growth this country has ever witnessed. There he was three years ago leading a nice gaggle of second rate men who called themselves The Labour Party ... Then they became – what was it – the Socialist Labour Party. And before you could say "Up the Republic" there was another wing-ding in Liberty Hall and this time it was the Socialist Workers' Republic, and everything in sight was to be nationalised ... and the day of the working man was on hand and Dr Noël Browne was feeling comfortable for the first time.[47]

Alongside these comment/analysis articles the newspaper's editorials were at best lukewarm in their support for Labour. One editorial, headlined 'How?', picked up the Fianna Fáil questioning of Corish's exact intent towards the banking system and what was to be understood by 'control' if nationalisation was not being pursued. The editorial went to the core of the difficulty with the Labour Party manifesto – the uncosted promises – but must have raised a few smiles in Fianna Fáil election headquarters. When Cruise O'Brien sought to raise public interest issues over Haughey's sale of his house and adjoining land for £204,000 to a property developer, the newspaper actually spun the spotlight back on Labour, and wondered in an editorial if the reaction was based on 'the politics of envy'.[48] O'Brien said the transaction deserved 'critical comment' as it emerged that Haughey had failed to disclose his interest when he introduced legislative changes which appeared to benefit him financially. The intervention, however, did Labour little good and, in fact, drew censure on the letters pages – one correspondent asked would O'Brien 'confiscate or 'nationalise' the land?'[49]

Despite this opprobrium, O'Brien was the subject of an uncritical three-part profile just before polling day in one of the few tangible signs that Labour had friends in the newspaper's editorial offices.

III

One means of measuring Labour's success, or otherwise, in promoting its policy agenda in the newspaper most benign towards the party – and testing the claims of bias by the letter writer mentioned at the start of this chapter – is to examine the use of the word 'socialist' during the election campaign. The word 'socialist' appeared in 129 individual articles in *The Irish Times* from the dissolution of Dáil Éireann on 22 May 1969 to polling day in the general election on 18 June 1969. Half of these 129 references appear in articles relating to the general election campaign – the others feature in foreign coverage (40 per cent) and in other articles with Irish-related content (10 per cent) not relevant to the electoral contest. A significant number of the election news articles covered Fianna Fáil attacks on Labour, and provide convincing evidence that if *The Irish Times* displayed biased coverage towards Labour the newspaper certainly did not reflect its views in its news coverage during the campaign.

From the outset of the election campaign Labour was a specific target for Fianna Fáil with evidence of a well-planned strategy to undermine any potential Labour momentum by putting doubts in the minds of voters who were thinking of backing Corish's party. There is mixed international evidence about the success of negative campaigning but in the context of the 1969 election in Ireland the Fianna Fáil approach was particularly successfully in terms of framing the media's coverage of the campaign.

The scripts supplied by Fianna Fáil to the media primarily focused on the dangers of Labour's socialist programme, the hidden plans of Corish's party and the gap between the socialist stance of the Labour hierarchy and the party's 'ordinary' membership. Like the other national newspapers, *The Irish Times* gave daily coverage to these Fianna Fáil claims – and not just those uttered by senior party figures but also backbench TDs and first-time candidates. The Fianna Fáil attacks were consistent throughout the campaign and received generous coverage as illustrated by the following headlines from *The Irish Times*:

- Browne denies alien influence in Labour – 26 May 1969
- MacEntee asks what would Connolly think – 29 May 1969

135

- Labour accused of policy cover-up: Challenge from Haughey
  – 4 June 1969
- Socialist ideas discarded, says Lenihan – 9 June 1969
- Socialist take-over of land feared – 11 June 1969
- Blaney warns against collectivisation – 12 June 1969
- Warning of danger to savings and property: MacEntee fears Marxist influence – 14 June 1969
- Choice is reality or Cuban myth – Lynch – 17 June 1969
- Marxist infiltration warning by Blaney – 17 June 1969

Fianna Fáil pursued a negative and highly personalised campaign as it sought to secure a fourth consecutive electoral victory. According to one of Lynch's biographers, the tone of the campaign was set by Haughey and Blaney but most likely with 'the tacit approval of Lynch'.[50] At the outset of the campaign Lynch spoke about 'the capture of the Labour Party by the extremist Left'.[51] Fianna Fáil sought to drive a wedge between Labour and its support base. 'There are Labour followers, of course, who had never read the Labour policy outline and their hair would stand on end if they did,' Erskine Childers claimed.[52] The theme that Labour was hiding its true policy intention was also one to which senior Fianna Fáil figures returned repeatedly throughout the campaign. Haughey claimed Labour was hiding its 'extreme form of socialism' with 'a very watered-down version because they know that their real policies were unacceptable to the vast majority of the people'. He said socialism created 'a joyless, soul-destroying, materialistic concept of life'.[53]

Some of the most abusive language – and the most extreme allegations – came from Agriculture Minister Neil Blaney who warned farmers that Labour's 'sinister' policies where based 'along Soviet lines in collectivisation'.[54] Fianna Fáil clearly felt it had Labour under pressure or, to use Blaney's phrase, 'Mr. Corish was beginning to squeal'.[55] Blaney had had a difficult relationship with farmers' leader Rickard Deasy, who was a Labour candidate in Tipperary North: 'The advent of Mr. Rickard Deasy as a socialist in flaming pink is the spectacle of the year. He boasts he sat in the gutter outside the Department of Agriculture. If he did, it was all mod con, with his meals sent round from the Shelbourne Hotel'.[56]

But even Blaney's language was mild in comparison to the invective from retiring Fianna Fáil minister Seán MacEntee, who had no difficulty in revisiting his 'Red baiting' from an earlier era. MacEntee claimed 'a red rash had broken out all over Dublin and presumably elsewhere' and warned that 'above all Red stands for danger to everyone's savings, to everyone's land, to everyone's property, large and small…'[57] The Fianna Fáil attacks were also highly personalised. There were repeated references to intellectuals and graduates of Trinity College Dublin. Noël Browne said such attacks set 'one particularly ugly pattern of debate … [with] a particularly sinister bigoted and sectarian overtone'.[58]

At the end of the first week of the campaign John Healy observed that the two main opposition parties were ahead in the publicity stakes with Fianna Fáil being slow to get into the election mode. But on the pages of his own newspaper, the well-planned Fianna Fáil attack strategy – based on consistency of message – was dominating news reports. It was classic attack-based negative campaigning – criticism directed at political rivals regardless of the kind of criticism or accuracy.[59] The absence of opinion polling meant it was impossible to really know how the various campaigns were actually connecting with the electorate. The Fianna Fáil attacks continued until the eve of polling day. At the party's final rally Lynch predicted that voters would show that they 'prefer the reality of progress and prosperity to the Cuban myth'.[60] While Lynch was attacking in Dublin Blaney had a last tirade in County Donegal. 'The red sunset is about to go down,' he forecast.[61]

Prior to the election being called, Corish had warned that Labour would be painted as 'a party of bogeymen bent on destroying national sovereignty and individual freedom'.[62] Indeed, the nature of the Fianna Fáil attacks should not have surprised Corish and his colleagues. Fianna Fáil had actually introduced an element of 'Red bashing' into the 1965 campaign when Blaney had also spoken of 'extreme socialism'.[63] Moreover, a canvassers' booklet for the 1969 contest provided Labour members with specific answers to potential claims about the dangers of socialism (although distribution of the booklet to local constituencies was not ideal). The evidence suggests that with respect to promoting its socialist agenda Labour singularly failed in terms of news coverage in *The Irish Times* – the newspaper that was apparently on its side. Indeed, even when Labour representatives were explaining what they meant by 'socialism' they were forced to do so in a defensive manner in response to Fianna Fáil attacks.[64]

IV

Labour had genuine hopes of real electoral success right up to polling day in the 1969 general election. From this distance there is an obvious naivety about the talk of winning a majority of Dáil seats. The context of the election must, however, be considered with a more passive media and an absence of public opinion data accounting for a lack of real information beyond the unreliability of what was being fed back from canvassers in the constituencies. At the core of Labour's difficulties, however, was the party's failure to counter Fianna Fáil's negative campaign strategy which, cynically, cast doubt on Corish's true intent and, highly effectively, exploited gaps in Labour's policy programme. The newspapers, which were the main means of communication, followed the Fianna Fáil agenda, and Labour's strategy was unable to circumvent the direction of news coverage. Even in *The Irish Times,* which was perceived by readers like Sir Frederick Sayers as closely aligned to Labour, the Fianna Fáil negative campaign undermined Corish and his socialist programme. When the ballot papers were all counted the results showed that, rather than heralding a new socialist dawn, in fact, the election had actually only 'consolidated the status quo'.[65]

An editorial in *The Irish Times* predicted the best ever Dáil and noted somewhat optimistically that Labour had emerged from the campaign 'as an unmistakably socialist party'.[66] The reality was somewhat different. Indeed, in terms of Labour's policy ambition the impact of the 1969 election outcome was dramatic and lasting. As Horgan more accurately concluded, 'The loss of confidence in the party was so great, it seems, that never again would it stick its collective neck out in quite such a dramatic fashion.'[67] In the end the seventies were not socialist, *The Irish Times* was not Labour's house newspaper and in subsequent contests a new professionalism swept over election campaigning as greater attention was paid to communication strategies – amid more assertive and aggressive media coverage – and a more dominant role for television coverage of politics.

11. Labour and the Making of Irish Foreign Policy, 1973–77

Eunan O'Halpin

This chapter discusses the Labour Party in terms of foreign policy, the European Economic Community (EEC) and Northern Ireland following the eruption of the Troubles in 1968–69. It concentrates on the years up to the end of the Fine Gael–Labour coalition in 1977, making only passing reference to subsequent developments. The chapter argues that Labour's contribution both to national discourse from 1969 and, during its time in government between 1973 and 1977, its input to national policy relating to Northern Ireland must be appraised in tandem with another crucial development – membership of the EEC. It argues further that Irish membership of the EEC changed the terms of the state's relationship not only with Britain and with her new European partners, but with the United States. This was a matter essentially of international trade and commercial policy, not of Cold War geopolitics, although the United States had long advocated Irish membership as the only means of effecting economic and social modernisation and thereby continued political stability. No one in Washington in 1973 appears to have raised an eyebrow at the advent to power in Ireland of a left-wing party that included many prominent critics of United States policy in Southeast Asia, a handful of committed Marxists such as the formidable Justin Keating, and not a few starry-eyed admirers of Fidel Castro and his revolutionary Cuba. The performance of the coalition in managing the three subtly interconnected issues of Northern Ireland, Europe, and bilateral relations with the United States, and the role that Labour played in these, invites re-examination.

What follows focuses on the parliamentary party, its policies and personalities. This allows us to explore the question of whether there was a unitary, consistent and distinct Labour Party approach to the Northern Ireland issue before and during the period of office of the Cosgrave coalition. Analysis of this question is complicated by the fact that, alone of the three major parties, on Northern Ireland as on Europe and wider international issues, Labour experienced never-ending internal debate after 1969 (by contrast in Fianna Fáil, for all the infighting and intrigue about the leadership and direction of the party in relation to Northern Ireland, there was never a remotely reasoned discussion of the core issue).[1] I argue that, while there were clearly different shades of opinion within Labour, and considerable pressure from various ginger groups and from a few spirited and articulate individuals, at national level the party's public position was broadly consistent. This was despite the fact that one key personality, Conor Cruise O'Brien, developed and loudly advocated views about Northern Ireland which challenged the mawkish attitudes to be found on the left, right and centre of Irish politics towards Northern Ireland and partition, thereby offending not only Fianna Fáilers but many of his own colleagues.

O'Brien was not the only Labour TD with strong views on Northern Ireland. In the aftermath of the disappointing general election of 1969, party leader Brendan Corish found among his colleagues other powerful, independent-minded individuals who were not prepared dumbly to follow their leader. The British ambassador reported that 'the Labour Party prepared itself for the election by a strong intake of intellectuals … The said intellectuals, standing for sophisticated Dublin constituencies, duly secured election; but the Left-wing and anti-clerical views with which they were associated themselves proved disastrous for their party when paraded in religious-minded country districts. The intellectuals undoubtedly raised the standard of debate in the Dáil, particularly when speculative questions like foreign affairs are under discussion'.[2] A year later, the ambassador reported that 'Labour is split on just about everything'.[3] It was ever thus.

Amongst the new talents were David Thornley and Justin Keating, who took positions on Northern Ireland which, while not identical, put them broadly into a republican Left camp.[4] On the other hand the mercurial Noël Browne, once an impassioned exponent of anti-partitionism, actually came out in defence of Taoiseach Jack Lynch following the Arms Crisis of May 1970. This 'Maverick of long standing', as a British diplomat described Browne, expressed his hope that Lynch would remain Taoiseach and leader of the 'peace party'. For this he was repudiated by the Labour leadership, which reiterated its call for a general election. (Within months Browne had, characteristically, completely reversed his position, saying there was no difference between Lynch and the Provisional Sinn Féin leader Ruairí Ó Brádaigh.)[5]

From 1969 onwards, Corish came under intermittent attack from within his party on a portfolio of issues centred on the question of participating in a future coalition government. In the course of those struggles there were efforts on the fringes to forge a cross-border socialist alliance, looking to groups associated with the civil rights movement that argued for a wider social and economic revolution on the island of Ireland. In 1970 there was talk of a Dublin-based Trotskyite element within Labour forming a link with the People's Democracy in Northern Ireland: after the Labour Party conference that year, the Socialist Labour Action Group was addressed by Eamonn McCann and Bernadette Devlin. A resolution was passed 'that socialist organisations, in a labour socialist alliance throughout the 32-counties, should begin to carry out the task which the Labour Party had failed to do'. Quite how such an alliance would attract rather than terrify and antagonise Northern Ireland's Protestant working class and trade union movement was not explored.[6]

The course of affairs in Northern Ireland after 1969, as what one experienced British official characterised as essentially 'a civil rights problem' mutated into an armed inter-communal and anti-state conflict, challenged the reflective anti-partitionism of many Labour politicians and of Irish public opinion generally.[7] What had appeared an opportunity for radical non-violent change in Northern society took on the appearance of a proto-civil war along ethnic and sectarian lines. Some on the Labour Left, noticeably the erratic David Thornley, remained sympathetic to an analysis of the deepening crisis similar to that of militant republicanism and of at least some Fianna Fáil politicians: if Britain would indicate her determination to depart, the contending parties in the North would come to an accommodation and Irish unity would inevitably follow. Others, not only Conor Cruise O'Brien, disagreed profoundly. The growth in violence from 1970 – 29 fatalities in that year, 180 in 1971, and 497 in 1972 – driven primarily by catastrophic British security policy decisions, and by republican and loyalist terrorism, had a generally sobering effect upon southern attitudes across the political spectrum. Within the Labour Party, most people adopted a cautiously reformist perspective on Northern Ireland.[8]

The reality is that, at the constituency level, Labour's members and supporters were preoccupied with domestic economic and societal challenges.

Fianna Fáil and Fine Gael were in the same position. Notwithstanding the emotional pull of Northern Ireland on politicians of all parties, particularly in terms of the treatment of the minority community, it is clear that at no point in Irish political life between 1969 and 1998 did Northern Ireland become a major electoral consideration. There were few votes to be had in beating the anti-partitionist drum.

I

Labour, republicanism and Europe, 1969–77

In parallel with the growth of the Troubles from 1969, Labour leader Brendan Corish had to cope with two other new major sources of potential division. These were the vexed question of whether or not Labour should offer itself at the next election as a party willing to consider entering a coalition, and Irish membership of the EEC. Corish was leader of a parliamentary party whose membership spanned an ideological spectrum from committed Marxists to near-Tridentine Catholic conservatives, and of a wider organisation engaged incessantly in ideological civil war fomented by a congeries of lightly disguised Trotskyites, semi-detached republicans, displaced Stalinists and untameable individualists. The Labour Left were against coalition, and in general also hostile to EEC membership; so too were their Northern contacts, some of whom came south to campaign for a 'No' vote in the 1972 referendum. Every Labour leader has had to cope with such pressures both from Left and Right, but Corish had a particularly difficult task.[9]

There were clear divisions within Labour on EEC membership. The majority of members and elected representatives were against it. This was despite the fact, as had become clear during campaigns for reform of Irish society in the 1960s, that in matters such as gender equality and workers' rights, the EEC offered a clear way forward for social progress which continued economic isolation did not – by 1970 the Fianna Fáil government had accepted the principle of equal pay explicitly as a requirement of EEC membership, while in matters such as the secularisation of Irish society close to many Labour hearts it was self-evident that Europe offered the best hopes for progress.[10] The roots of Labour's opposition to the EEC in the 1972 referendum, having been cautiously in favour for most of the preceding decade, lay variously in fear of the impact on manufacturing employment, in legitimate concerns about sovereignty, and in a desire to stay in step with the trade unions (some of them very influenced by British trade unionists' antagonism towards membership, and by the prevailing European left-wing hostility towards economic integration).

Through this opposition, described by Gary Murphy as 'tokenism of a high order', Labour found themselves in curious company in the accession debate.[11] The No groups ranged from Provisional Sinn Féin, whose exiguous discourse on social and economic issues owed more to Catholic than to socialist thought, to assorted Trotskyites from north and south, to the ageing Stalinists of the Irish communist movement, still loyally following Moscow's line, and to followers of the Communist Party of Great Britain's (CPGB) Irish specialist Desmond Greaves, who for decades sought, through a variety of front organisations, to harness Irish republicanism and anti-partitionism for communist ends. As early as 1947, he was 'upset by the slowness of the Irish [comrades] to realise the value of the Party' – this was a few years after a bitter struggle over communist entryism within the Labour Party culminated in the abolition of the communist-dominated Central branch.[12] Through the Connolly Association, a notionally independent body under CPGB control, Greaves sought to mobilise the Irish diaspora in Britain on the intertwined issues of ending partition and bringing about an Irish revolution. In the 1950s he was still casting around for a means of galvanising the communist movement in Ireland that would bypass stalwarts such as Michael O'Riordan and Sam Nolan, whom he believed unclear about their aims. He took some soundings with trade unionists and Labour Party figures including Donal Nevin, which he hoped might yield some results.[13] In the succeeding years, while direct Soviet interest in Ireland waxed and waned, Greaves kept chipping away, seeking people who would energise the Irish Left and build links into the republican and the trade union movements. There were countervailing factors: leading Irish communists resented CPGB attempts to act as a superintending authority over them, and some republicans mistrusted any ideas emanating from Britain.[14] There is evidence of Irish communist unilateralism in response to the Northern Ireland crisis – for instance, in 1969 Michael O'Riordan made a direct appeal to the Soviet Union for arms and money, which he believed would enable him to bring a faction of republican activists led by the energetic Seamus Costello under his control to further wider revolutionary aims.[15] On the other hand, it is also clear that from the early 1960s a handful of Greaves' acolytes acquired considerable intellectual influence within the republican movement, arguing cogently for a focus on economic and social issues and involvement with progressive forces in civil society north and south. Greaves has been beatified in Irish radical memory, represented as begetter of the Northern Ireland civil rights movement, and intellectual architect of the reorientation of the republican movement from violence towards social and economic agitation as a means of achieving all-island revolution. Secular sainthood cannot be that far away. But in the 1950s and 1960s this Stalinist intellectual was a malign influence in Irish radical politics, faithfully pushing Moscow's objectives from London and scattering the Soviet-incubated germs of a paranoid Euroscepticism. Many Labour left-wingers caught the infection.[16]

Labour opposition to EEC membership cannot, however, be explained in simple Left/Right terms. Party leader Brendan Corish, whose active Catholicism was sometimes held against him by left-wing critics, was as convinced an opponent of Irish membership on the terms agreed as Keating, Labour's EEC spokesman, who had been involved with various communist groups. This may partly be because, as Niamh Puirséil observes, 'anti-EEC resolutions' were the one thing on which the party could unite in the early 1970s. Some years ago I asked Keating about Labour's opposition to EEC membership: he rather brushed the question aside, not out of embarrassment, but rather because of what he regarded as its sheer irrelevance in modern conditions. The European Union, he argued, had evolved into a key driver for greater fairness and equity.[17]

Keating's energetic performance in the 1972 referendum campaign was not forgiven by colleagues such as Barry Desmond, who believed he had cynically used the EEC issue 'as an opportunity to become the leader of the old republican left, the hard-core trade union left and the new *avant garde* of the 1969 Labour Party'.[18]

Corish had a stroke of fortune, having to tend such a contrary bag of cats and constantly to guard the party against Leftist infestation, that by the time the Fine Gael–Labour coalition was formed, the EEC die was already cast. This meant that the new government could concentrate on getting to grips with Europe, for which they, like the civil service, industry and Irish society generally (with the exception of organised farming interests), were distinctly underprepared. Labour ministers including Keating pragmatically embraced the new European dispensation. He gained the reputation both publicly and, more tellingly, with his officials of being a clear-sighted and decisive minister. A CIA report paid him a compliment in noting that he 'drove a hard bargain with US mineral exploiters' seeking mining licences.[19] Rather to the irritation of the Department of Foreign Affairs, Keating ensured that his department got its elbows on the table when foreign trade issues were discussed in Brussels, and he generally led rather than followed the reorientation of the policy system towards Europe. In 1976, Foreign Minister Garret FitzGerald angled for this erstwhile anti-EEC campaigner to be the next Irish European Commissioner, considering him intellectually superior to Fine Gael's Dick Burke. This scheme failed and Burke was nominated. FitzGerald was surprised to find that some of Keating's colleagues regarded his quick coming to terms with EEC membership as a cynical ploy to strengthen his leadership credentials.[20]

The speed with which the coalition government got to grips with European affairs produced a significant dividend in Irish–American relations. In September 1973 the United States National Security Advisor Henry Kissinger was briefed on how to handle Garret FitzGerald. The Irish, 'as newcomers to the E[E]C', were being very 'cautious' generally: 'it might be very helpful generally if you were to give FitzGerald the benefit of your views on the need for meaningful US-E[E]C progress'. Despite a surprisingly constructive meeting – FitzGerald recalled that Kissinger was at first taken aback by, and then responded positively to, his combative approach – the Americans continued to fret, as US/EEC relations deteriorated. During the French EEC presidency in 1974 a CIA document observed that, while 'the [EEC/US consultation] process has been free of open acrimony, Paris has sought to impose a total embargo on communicating to Washington the proceedings of some meetings of the E[E]C-Nine'. President Gerald Ford was advised that Ireland, with its Francophile leanings, 'will be under pressure from Paris primarily to withhold information' when it took over the E[E]C presidency in January 1975.[21] In fact the Irish presidency became a significant milestone in EEC/American relations. This in turn rendered American policy makers more inclined to take the Irish seriously in bilateral business (where Ireland had in any case become more significant through the simple fact of EEC membership). In September 1975 Kissinger advised Ford:

> US-Irish relations are excellent and devoid of any major bilateral problems. Both countries agree that we should endeavour to develop our friendship beyond our traditionally strong ties of friendship and kinship. An excellent beginning in intensifying the US-Irish dialogue was made during Ireland's first six-month EC presidency ... We intend to continue close consultations with the Irish on matters of mutual concern.[22]

Labour ministers such as Keating and Michael O'Leary at the Department

145

of Labour were at the forefront of engagement with Europe. More generally, EEC membership brought the party into far closer contact with its western European analogues, further diluting Europhobia and sterile isolationism within the party and the trade union movement, strengthening Labour's social democratic ethos, and enabling it to draw on policy ideas and experience from across Europe. Irish accession also led to the adoption of a coherent policy on development aid, and a consequent expression of Irish diplomatic engagement with emerging states, especially in post-colonial Africa, a strategic shift which all in Labour could welcome. The paranoid hyperbole of the 'No' campaign was finally discarded within the party, to the great benefit of Irish public life.[23]

By contrast, after the IRA split, both Provisional Sinn Féin and the still Marxist Official Republican Movement remained resolutely anti-EEC. Official Sinn Féin was, however, soon to embark on a tortuous journey away from political violence, revolutionary politics and naive internationalism alike, a process accelerated though not initiated by the end of the Cold War: by the mid-1990s, there were no more begging letters to Moscow for arms and money, and no more fraternal visits to such weird outposts of Stalinism as North Korea, with whom an incongruously warm relationship had developed in the early 1980s.[24] If it is true that the contemporary Labour Party is dominated by people who, a couple of decades ago, were firmly associated with the Official Republican Movement, this is surely a demonstration not of the efficacy of the entryist tactics so beloved of the conspiratorial Left, but rather of mainstream Labour's capacity for quiet incorporation into the social democratic fold of those previously wedded to anti-democratic authoritarianism.

II

Labour, the Cosgrave coalition, and geopolitics

That EEC membership was a done deal when the Fine Gael–Labour coalition took office was a great stroke of luck for Labour (and for Ireland). Another happy chance was geopolitical. In Paris in January 1973, North Vietnamese and American representatives signed a peace accord. This dramatic development, which earned its principal negotiators Henry Kissinger and Lee Duc Tho the Nobel Peace Prize, reduced pressure on Labour figures to declaim against the United States as a neo-imperialist power, lines of argument that TDs such as Keating and O'Brien had advanced forcefully in opposition.

The coalition also moved quickly to address what successive American presidents since Lyndon Johnson had been told was the one significant bilateral issue between Ireland and the United States. This was the American request for limited landing rights for civil airlines in Dublin (American airlines were restricted to landing at Shannon). The Lemass and Lynch governments had shied away from addressing this long-held American grievance for years. The Johnson and Nixon administrations tried and failed to extract any movement from the Irish, retaliatory action against Aer Lingus being stayed on a number of occasions only on the two presidents' direct decision.[25] The logic of the American request for limited rights to use Dublin was unimpeachable; the problem was essentially that the Shannon region feared losing business. In November 1971 the Fianna Fáil Minister for Posts and Telegraphs Gerry Collins, a Limerick man, abruptly confronted an American diplomat at a dinner, telling him in highly coloured terms that the Irish people would not submit to bullying from Washington. Shortly after taking office, the coalition secured a decade of Irish–American harmony on the issue through a relatively minor concession, which allowed one American carrier limited Dublin landing rights and secured Aer Lingus' vital New York slot, which the Americans had given notice of withdrawing. These measures did not lead to the predicted impoverishment of the Shannon region; furthermore they removed an important irritant for Washington, where officials hailed a new-found realism in Irish bilateral diplomacy – hitherto, as is clear from State Department, National Security Council and CIA records, Washington made a sharp distinction between Irish multilateral diplomacy at the United Nations, generally regarded as organised and purposeful, and the inconsequential performance of the Irish in bilateral matters – Irish–American relations were characterised as 'limp as a wet noodle' by one American official in 1972.[26]

The compromise with Washington on landing rights also served as a balancing item for developments in Irish diplomacy towards the Soviet Union more likely to appeal to left-wingers. The Irish decision to establish diplomatic relations and to exchange ambassadors with the Soviet Union had caused considerable unease in Britain – Prime Minister Edward Heath sent a personal message to Taoiseach Jack Lynch on the matter in 1972, pointing out the subversive and espionage threats involved. Implementation of the decision was delayed for some time, firstly by Fianna Fáil and then by the coalition. The concerns were twofold: how best to address American and British concerns, and how to meet the domestic challenge of preventing

Soviet intrigue with either the Official IRA or the Provisionals, or both: in October 1972 the Irish ambassador in Washington told American officials that the delay in opening embassies was 'on security grounds. The police did not feel they had sufficient manpower to keep tabs on a large group of Russians.'[27] Garda reservations were partly borne out in subsequent years, although intermittent Soviet support for the Provisionals was provided only indirectly through proxies such as Libya.[28] On the other hand, the opening of a Soviet embassy in Dublin and an Irish embassy in Moscow in 1974 can have done the Labour leadership no harm with some of its more unruly left-wingers, who could interpret the development as evidence of Ireland's independence from the western bloc. They could scarcely have been more wrong.

There is no evidence in American or British records of anxiety about Labour's left-wing credentials generally, nor worry about Keating's Marxist pedigree, nor O'Brien's generic hostility towards American power. In 1974, a CIA report fairly observed that the coalition's foreign policy reflected 'basic Irish opposition to communism and colonialism' alike. The United States embassy commented that 'the new ministers are a very talented group, and they appear to have pooled their talents effectively on the northern problem. It has certainly been their first priority, and basic work has been done'. In general, the government 'offers an improvement on its predecessor, if only because it has more ministers who are competent to face problems. Major issue is US/E[E]C relations, where we face [an] uphill fight. A Fianna Fáil government would probably be even more difficult to deal with on this problem.'[29]

III

Labour and Northern Ireland, 1973–77

At the first Anglo-Irish heads of government meeting following the 1973 election, 'Mr Corish in particular stressed that the minority should be protected by a bill of rights'.[30] In practical terms, however, the loudest Labour voice within the coalition on policy relating to Anglo-Irish relations between 1973 and 1977 was not that of the party leader and Tánaiste Corish but of Conor Cruise O'Brien. It might have been thought that making O'Brien Minister for Posts and Telegraphs would keep him well away from Northern policy; in practice it did not. This was not simply a matter of his own strong interest and distinctive views on the general issues, but of his departmental remit in the area of public broadcasting. O'Brien made the case against allowing advocates of political violence access to the state broadcasting networks publicly, coherently and consistently, rather than through the hints, oblique threats and occasional ministerial tantrums which had characterised the Fianna Fáil government's management of the problem. In January 1977 O'Brien introduced an unambiguous and complete legal ban on broadcasts by persons associated with named organisations including the Provisional IRA and Provisional Sinn Féin. This action was, naturally, deeply unpopular amongst journalists and liberals generally, the very milieu to which he belonged. But it dealt with the issue unequivocally, and during the peace process negotiations of the 1990s the possible removal of the broadcasting ban became a significant bargaining chip.

The collapse of the Northern Ireland Executive in May 1974 was a low point, sweeping away the cross-community power-sharing so painstakingly negotiated in the Sunningdale Agreement. Defending the British government's craven failure to keep the roads and other key infrastructure functioning during the Ulster Workers' Council strike, the Northern Ireland Secretary Merlyn Rees wrote plaintively that 'it's one thing to fight the ... IRA, it's another to fight the Community as a whole which is what was happening with the Protestants'.[31] A CIA document commented that, 'Unless a formula like the power-sharing concept can be introduced in Ulster, the resentment that has produced violence for the past five years will continue. If the British withdraw their security forces, thereby allowing large-scale clashes between Protestants and Catholic extremists, the Republic could be drawn into the conflict and a very bloody north-south civil war could result.'[32] The latter part of this assessment, entirely at odds with Fianna Fáil's fatuous policy declarations at the time, would have been music to O'Brien's ears. We now know that British Prime Minister Harold Wilson had begun to think seriously in just such terms, and that Merlyn Rees was all in favour: 'It's coming near the time now when I must speak out in favour of leaving Northern Ireland. Not straightaway, but gradually.'[33]

There appears to have been little contact and less sympathy between the Irish and the British Labour Parties in this era. There were few meaningful fraternal links that could be used informally to augment or to circumvent official intergovernmental exchanges between the Cosgrave coalition and the Labour governments of Harold Wilson (1974–76) and James Callaghan (1976–79). How narrow was the common ground and sympathy, whether on Northern Ireland or on other issues, between the British and Irish governments is illustrated in a characteristically peevish entry in Merlyn

Rees's journal. Dismissing the Cosgrave coalition as comprising two essentially conservative parties, he wrote that 'this explains I suppose, why they are extremely suspicious of a Labour Party. They prefer a Tory Party which is Unionist.' He continued: 'The very fact that they are keen on the Common Market is I suppose one thing that will rub them up anyway because it's a sign that they like the Market and that a Labour Government doesn't in general … the fact they in the South are keen and we are not illustrates the gap of thinking between us.'[34]

In 1974, the United States embassy reported two exceptional contributions at the Labour Party conference: one was a powerful speech in defence of coalition from Justin Keating, which they judged had increased his chances of eventually succeeding Corish; the other was Conor Cruise O'Brien, whose speech on Northern Ireland castigating the Provisionals was 'warmly applauded'.[35] The following spring, O'Brien informed the Americans of his intention to use a forthcoming ministerial visit to the United States to make further attacks on Irish republican fund-raising and the Provisionals' American apologists, amongst whom he included the leading Irish-American lawyer and civil liberties activist Paul O'Dwyer.[36] His contributions to debate, while powerful, were not always regarded as helpful. In May 1975, he caused consternation when in a radio interview he dismissed hopes for a new power-sharing arrangement in Northern Ireland. This threw the Social Democratic Labour Party (SDLP) into a frenzy and it had to be rubbished quickly by the coalition.[37] A Department of Foreign Affairs official, John McColgan, briefed the United States embassy: O'Brien had been completely isolated in Cabinet, and there was 'deep chagrin' at his latest statement. The Americans believed that the government

> has overcome an internal crisis of sorts in restraining … O'Brien without a serious public split. He must be well aware that he has been chastised, although the world at large may not have gotten the message so clearly. We have long felt that O'Brien's brilliant intellect and undisciplined ego would present a challenge to G [overnment] O[f] I[reland] which would have to be faced at some point. If this has now been done successfully, GOI should be able to speak much more clearly in the future on N[orthern] I[reland] policy.[38]

At the 1976 Labour annual conference, nevertheless, O'Brien gave 'easily the best speech' in which he 'castigated the Fianna Fáil quote support of the Provo demand for British withdrawal quote as the height of irresponsibility.

He also strongly condemned the continued sectarianism in the Republic. These positions are not new with O'Brien, but he expressed them with a particularly caustic brilliance.' This may have contributed to a 'crushing victory' for Corish over 'left wing mavericks' led by David Thornley, John O'Connell and Noël Browne on the coalition issue, where their 'left alternative' talks with the two 'tiny' left-wing parties, Official Sinn Féin and the Communists, were effectively banned. The small parties themselves were dismissed as electoral irrelevancies because of their atheism.[39]

In early 1977 the coalition's handling of Northern Ireland came under attack from Jack Lynch, who emerged from a long period of uncertain quietude in opposition to make a series of speeches on Northern Ireland which called for a phased British withdrawal as the precursor to a settlement acceptable to all communities on the island of Ireland. The coalition, in the persons of Corish and O'Brien, deplored these fatuities, arguing that the only sane policy in Northern Ireland was to remain 'in support of reconciliation and the suppression of terrorism', although unease was growing in government circles at London's evident determination, embodied in the appointment as Northern Ireland Secretary of the blunt former Defence Secretary Roy Mason, to concentrate on security rather than continuing the search for new political solutions. When Labour and Fine Gael left office and Lynch returned, instead of pursuing the Northern Ireland policy he had advocated in opposition he took up where Cosgrave and Corish had left off.[40]

O'Brien clearly did not speak for his party: his views on the futility of resurrecting power-sharing, and on attempts to develop an 'Irish dimension' in the future governance of Northern Ireland, were at odds with coalition policy. Time was to show that while his analysis of the ideological underpinnings and vicious nature of militant republicanism was acute, his utter dismissal of nationalist aspirations north and south blinded him to the possibility that an 'Irish dimension' would help to create movement towards peace in Northern Ireland. But his sheer ability in argument upped the stakes for anyone wishing to make the traditional nationalist case: the only opposition politician whom the United States embassy thought might fit the bill was the 'roly-poly stage Irish' Brian Lenihan, whose 'talkative extrovert manner conceal[s] a very tough politician and quite a reflective individual. We have been quite impressed with some of his speeches on the future of the E[E]C … He is one of the few in Fianna Fáil fully capable of debating with such formidable government personalities as Garret FitzGerald and Conor Cruise O'Brien.'[41]

O'Brien lost his seat in 1977. On Northern Ireland he grew more strident and less perceptive by the year, the power of his earlier critique of militant republicanism and sentimental nationalism diluted by his own increasingly uncritical and sentimental portrayal of Ulster unionism. In 1979 Sir Nicholas Henderson, newly appointed as British ambassador in Washington with a brief to tackle Irish-American support for the Provisionals, hosted a lunch in O'Brien's honour. He was, oddly, surprised that 'none of the Four Horsemen [the leading Irish-American political figures Tip O'Neill, Daniel Moynihan, Ted Kennedy and Hugh Carey] nor any of the Congressmen involved in Irish affairs was prepared to come'. The consolation was that 'Conor was brilliant as usual. He said that the best thing was for the Americans to keep quiet on the subject of Northern Ireland'.[42] The irony is that the gradual development of an autonomous American government interest in the Northern Ireland issue which began to develop in the mid-1970s owed a good deal, particularly within the American foreign policy machine, to increased interaction with and respect for Ireland as a proactive and perceptive interlocutor in US–EEC affairs. That seachange in Ireland's bilateral standing with the United States was the work of a government of which O'Brien had himself been a prominent member.

When President Ronald Reagan came to Ireland in 1984, visiting his ancestral home place of Ballyporeen, County Tipperary, and accepting an honorary degree from University College Galway, the Irish Left, including many in Labour, recoiled in horror as a Fine Gael–Labour government extended the normal courtesies to this implacable Cold War warrior. Yet a few months later, Reagan made what in retrospect appears a decisive intervention on Northern Ireland with Britain. This came following Margaret Thatcher's clumsy 'out, out, out' press conference remarks dismissing the New Ireland Forum report and humiliating Taoiseach Garret FitzGerald. The following month Thatcher travelled to Camp David for a summit with Reagan, her Cold War brother-in-arms. Reagan told her: 'Know this can be a difficult problem, but hope Anglo-Irish dialogue can be intensified. Need at least the appearance of progress at next spring's Anglo-Irish summit'. Less than a year later, in what seemed a spectacular reversal of attitude, Thatcher signed the Anglo-Irish Agreement at Hillsborough, copper-fastening an 'Irish dimension' in the affairs of Northern Ireland. Reagan and Speaker of the House of Representatives Tip O'Neill held a joint press conference to underline American support for the initiative. Dermot Nally and Robert Armstrong, who were at the heart of Anglo-Irish negotiations throughout the 1980s, agreed that Reagan's intervention was decisive in persuading

Thatcher to come to terms with the FitzGerald coalition and to seek a new way forward in Northern Ireland. O'Brien turned out to be utterly wrong in dismissing the likely value of Irish and of American government involvement in the evolution of a peaceful settlement in Northern Ireland.[43] Yet his lack of foresight in these areas should not lead anyone to undervalue the immense contribution he made during the 1970s, particularly while in government, in challenging the naivety and ignorance of much Irish political discourse on Northern Ireland.

IV

Conclusion

In the first decade of the Northern Ireland crisis, and particularly between 1973 and 1977, the Labour Party played a consistently constructive role. This was both because of and, to an extent, despite the activities of some of its brightest stars. Some on the Left could not resist the temptation to make common cause with militant republicanism on issues such as the EEC while averting their eyes from what republicans were doing in Northern Ireland. On the other hand O'Brien so relished the battle with exponents of unthinking, outmoded anti-partitionism that at times his Cabinet colleagues had to disown him, not for the vehemence of his attacks on Fianna Fáil and on the Provisionals, but for his eclectic and increasingly one-eyed advocacy of a policy which would have consisted essentially of staying out of the Northern Ireland issue and treating the fears, aspirations and security of the minority community entirely as an internal British problem.

Neither O'Brien nor his Leftist critics within Labour approved of the coalition's policy of attempting to persuade the United States to take an independent interest in Northern Ireland. But it is clear that the coalition's management of foreign affairs, and in particular their handling of the 1975 EEC presidency and relations with the United States, transformed American assessments of Ireland's general competence, and made American officials more amenable to Irish analysis of the Northern Ireland issue. The seeds of autonomous American engagement, so pivotal in the negotiation of the Good Friday Agreement of 1998, were planted during the term of the Cosgrave coalition in which Labour collectively and individually – ministers such as O'Brien, O'Leary and Keating in particular – served with determination and distinction.[44]

12. Labour and Europe: From No to Yes

Stephen Collins

The Labour Party's attitude to the European Union, and Ireland's role within it, has been broadly positive since the Irish people voted overwhelmingly in favour of joining the then European Economic Community (EEC) in 1972. Before accession, however, the party was strongly against full membership and, for much of the time since, a negative undercurrent has lingered. The Labour Party had opposed entry to the EEC in the referendum of 1972, even though some its leading members were strongly in favour of joining. Since then the party has taken a pro-European line and campaigned for a 'Yes' vote in a succession of referendums but a steadily shrinking minority have retained the initially hostile attitude.

While some people in Labour always saw the party in terms of a broad international movement, during the 1950s it remained part of an inward-looking political consensus that continued to regard Irish sovereignty as the overriding imperative. William Norton, who led the party from 1932 until 1960, was a little more outward looking than some of his colleagues and was open to the long-term advantages of free trade as a way of improving the lot of Irish people. The general mood in the party, though, was strongly protectionist and suspicious of foreign investment.[1]

The Labour Party's initial attitude to the decision of Seán Lemass to make a formal application to join the EEC in 1961 was favourable. At the party's annual conference in 1962 the prevailing view was that Ireland should do whatever Britain did as such a high proportion of the country's exports went to the United Kingdom. However, when the small left-wing National Democratic Party advocated that Ireland should seek only associate, rather than full, membership, to allow for a much longer adjustment period,

154

Labour seemed to get cold feet. Party leader Brendan Corish, who had succeeded Norton in 1960, suggested that more thought should be given to the association option. In the event the British application for membership was turned down in January 1963 at the behest of President de Gaulle of France, the Irish application went into abeyance and the issue faded from the political agenda.[2]

In 1966 the party conference backed a resolution from Dublin Central TD Michael O'Leary that Labour should join the Socialist International. By coming in close contact with other European social democratic parties some leading Labour figures developed the view that Ireland needed to become involved in the European project.[3] However, party leader Brendan Corish went to few of the Socialist International meetings and was unmoved by the European idea. That proved important when the EEC came back onto the political agenda in 1969. Labour under Corish's direction opposed entry, arguing instead for associate membership. That position had popular support in the party despite the pro-EEC views of some of its leading members. Labour had moved decisively to the Left during the 1960s with the slogan: 'The Seventies will be Socialist.' An anti-EEC line tallied with Labour's opposition to coalition with Fine Gael, which was strongly in favour of EEC entry, as was the Fianna Fáil government.

Brendan Halligan, the general secretary of the party at the time, recalls three main grounds for opposition to joining the EEC. The first was simple old-fashioned nationalism that would have influenced Corish and powerful figures like Meath TD, Jimmy Tully. The second was a left-wing view that regarded the EEC as a capitalist plot. That appealed to many of the younger party members who believed Ireland was on the road to a socialist future. The third ground for opposition was a pragmatic view that entry would cost jobs in protected industries. This view influenced many trade union leaders who were able to point to the loss of 100,000 jobs in the decade after entry as proof that they were right. By contrast, some Labour TDs like Barry Desmond, a leading light in the European Movement, Michael O'Leary and Conor Cruise O'Brien favoured joining. They were conscious of Labour's credentials as a social democratic party and could imagine the modernising influence membership would have on Irish society. However, they shied away from an open breach with the party.

'The key issue was the personal position of Brendan Corish. The party was riven on the North and the issue of coalition. His attitude was that he was not going to introduce a third issue that could divide us,' says Halligan.[4] In the summer of 1970 Corish told the Dáil of his opposition to full EEC membership: 'I favour association because I believe this country is not equipped for full membership apart from the fact that full membership means a loss of our sovereign independence. Our influence within the European Economic Community will be marginal if not minimal. The institutions are undemocratic and all the signs are we will have to abandon our traditional neutrality. The Labour Party, therefore, proposes that we seek a treaty of association.'[5]

The Labour Party conference of 1971 came out strongly against full membership of the EEC in line with the position adopted by most trade unions and smaller left-wing groups. Sinn Féin was also strongly against the EEC and campaigned hard against it. Finding themselves on the same side as Sinn Féin was embarrassing for many Labour TDs, particularly leading critics of republicanism like O'Brien and Desmond.[6] Suggestions from Dublin delegates at the 1971 conference that the party should mount street demonstrations and coordinate a campaign with republicans were received without enthusiasm from most of those present.[7]

During the run up to the referendum on entry the lead role for Labour was taken by the party's spokesman on the EEC, Justin Keating, a former member of the Communist Party, who denounced the European project in trenchant terms. 'The origin of the EEC lies in Hitler's new order,' he declaimed. 'There is no difference in the basic outlook, the morality, the social system, between the Germany of 1914, the Germany of 1939 and the EEC of 1970,' he added.[8] He was more nuanced in the Dáil, giving long, detailed speeches during the debates on the Referendum Bill in November 1971 and the debate on the White Paper spelling out the terms of entry in March 1972. 'Our state of economic development renders full membership exceedingly dangerous. My belief is that it would be nationally fatal for us,' said Keating who insisted that Ireland was, in fact, economically a colony of the United Kingdom. 'If this referendum is passed we will not alone be abolishing the chance of ever growing to nationhood, which we have not yet done, but, in regard to community, population and tradition, we will be abolishing a good deal of Ireland. As somebody said recently, it will be the last action we will ever take as something almost a nation if we vote ourselves in.'[9]

During that debate Conor Cruise O'Brien could not contain his amusement at the comments of the colourful Fine Gael frontbencher Paddy Donegan who poured scorn on the notion that Irish sovereignty was the supreme value which had to be guarded regardless of the consequences. Donegan said bluntly that 'it is all a cod' for people to say sovereignty would not be affected, but he argued that Ireland would be a better place for all that. 'It is like the girl who got married. You might say she lost her virginity, but if she did she gained something very much more important and more enlivening for herself in this world.'[10] In fact, Donegan's views were shared by O'Brien, as well as by Desmond and O'Leary, two Corkmen elected to represent Dublin constituencies.

Desmond was actually vice-chairman of the Irish European Movement and had to grit his teeth, out of loyalty to the party, to avoid speaking out in favour of a 'Yes' vote. At a meeting of the parliamentary party to discuss the campaign strategy he put forward the view that an advantageous relationship between Ireland and the EEC, including Britain, was vital for future employment and an improved standard of living. 'I said that emotional opposition or opposition in principle often linked with a convenient disregard for economic reality was a political luxury. I stressed that Labour did not have a real political choice,' he wrote later.[11]

In the Dáil Desmond focused on the alleged weakness of the constitutional amendment permitting entry rather than commenting on the intrinsic merits or demerits of joining the EEC. O'Leary said as little as possible but, like Desmond, avoided getting involved in the 'No' campaign. After the referendum O'Brien revealed just how uncomfortable his position had been. 'I felt, and probably looked, like a dog being washed. I am not temperamentally "anti-European", and dislike anti-foreign enterprises of all descriptions, however rationally they may be grounded. And I disliked some of our allies even more than I disliked either set of our adversaries.'

O'Brien could not disguise his revulsion at being on the same side as Sinn Féin. He explained that he spent most of his time during the campaign trying to explain that Labour's case was entirely distinct and separate from that of 'the rather strange-looking people who seemed to be uttering the same monosyllable.' He took the view that Sinn Féin involvement in the 'No' campaign actually increased the 'Yes' vote. 'There were quite a few people who, in their hearts, were frightened at the idea of being locked up alone in the cold, clammy, dark with Cathleen Ní Houlihan and her memories of the dead.'[12] Fianna Fáil and Fine Gael campaigned strongly for a 'Yes' vote, leaving the anti-EEC position to Labour, Official and Provisional Sinn Féin and the Irish Congress of Trade Unions. The Workers' Union of Ireland, led by James Larkin Jr, took a different view from most other left-wing organisations and supported a 'Yes' vote. During the referendum campaign Labour maintained that joining the EEC would raise food prices, would jeopardise 35,000 jobs because Irish industries could no longer be protected from competition from other EEC countries and would open

Irish territorial waters to all other EEC fishermen. It suggested that associate membership could be considered instead and called the government's pro-EEC case 'unsustained and dishonest'.

The party distributed 1.5 million pieces of literature during the campaign. Halligan recalls that the party leadership was aware well before the referendum that the result would be 'Yes'. 'Although some Labour TDs, particularly Justin Keating, campaigned vigorously, others did not feel strongly on the issue or had reservations about the campaign and were absent from the fray,' according to Gallagher. He added that Labour also feared that the government might call a general election once the campaign was over in the belief that the opposition parties would be unable to form a credible coalition, so it was reluctant to expend all its resources on the referendum campaign.'[13] Halligan recalls that at the start of the campaign he told pro-EEC TDs like Desmond, O'Leary and O'Brien either to support the party position or make themselves scarce. 'Barry and Micko disappeared. Conor Cruise came out and campaigned but was very uncomfortable, particularly as we had some very uncomfortable bedfellows.' When the referendum was held on 13 May 1972, it was passed by a massive majority with 83 per cent voting in favour of entry. One estimate at the time was that 60 per cent of Labour supporters voted 'Yes'.[14]

Less than a year later, in early 1973, Labour found itself in office in a coalition with Fine Gael, almost immediately after the country joined the EEC. The rhetoric of the 'No' campaign was forgotten as the party adjusted to power and to Europe. Keating and O'Brien were sent as Labour representatives to the European Parliament where they joined the Socialist Group. They were there for only two and a half months as they were appointed ministers in the coalition government. They were replaced by David Thornley and Liam Kavanagh, and Labour became a loyal member of the Socialist Group.

In government Labour quickly adapted to EEC membership and Keating, who had been such an arch-opponent of joining, insisted on accompanying the Minister for Foreign Affairs, Garret FitzGerald, to European Council of Foreign Ministers meetings when trade was up for discussion. Keating developed a good relationship with FitzGerald, in contrast with his poor relations with his Labour Cabinet colleagues who suspected him of manoeuvring for the party leadership. Keating lobbied hard to be appointed Ireland's European Commissioner when Patrick Hillery, the Fianna Fáil nominee, returned home as the agreed candidate for President in 1976 to replace Cearbhall Ó Dálaigh. FitzGerald backed Keating's claim on the basis of his intellectual capacity but Taoiseach Liam Cosgrave was having none of it. Instead he appointed his loyal ally, Minister for Education Dick Burke of Fine Gael, to the post.[15]

Labour became actively involved in the Socialist Group at European level. The international affairs committee of the party with Halligan as chair and Niall Greene and Tony Browne as secretaries joined wholeheartedly in the European project. According to Barry Desmond they opened up the 'isolated political culture and organisation of Labour to the policies of the social democratic parties of Europe. They were three of the foremost advocates within Labour of a positive contribution from Ireland in the development of European integration and enlargement.' Halligan and Browne were also largely responsible for the establishment of the Institute of European Affairs (now the Institute for International and European Affairs) which, according to Desmond, had a considerable impact on Irish society. The Institute has promoted a positive engagement with and understanding of the European Union at every step along the way.[16]

In the first direct elections to the European Parliament in 1979 Labour did spectacularly well, winning four of the country's fifteen seats and taking two out of four in Dublin. Michael O'Leary and Dr John O'Connell were elected for Dublin with Liam Kavanagh winning Leinster and Eileen Desmond winning Munster. After the party entered coalition with Fine Gael in June 1981 the European seats became a game of musical chairs with three of the MEPs being appointed to Cabinet and the fourth, John O'Connell, becoming Ceann Comhairle. Labour never did as well again in a European election. In fact, the party failed to win a single seat in the 1984 European elections. This was partly to do with its role in taking unpopular decisions in government, but was also a response to the way leading party figures had juggled with the European seats in the 1981–82 period.

By this stage, most of the party had embraced Europe, even if a minority remained suspicious of the EEC and all it stood for. The leading light in this group in the 1980s was party chairman Michael D. Higgins. Europe and neutrality were touchstone issues for the Left wing of the party, which engaged in open warfare with the leadership throughout the decade. By the time the party entered its second coalition with Fine Gael, Dick Spring was leader and Barry Desmond was deputy leader. Both, with the backing of the parliamentary party, were strongly committed to the EEC. Nonetheless, a group led by Michael D. Higgins, a senator at this stage, and left-wing activists like Emmet Stagg and a range of anti-coalition party members continued to take an anti-EEC line.

The Fine Gael–Labour coalition engaged positively in the negotiations that led to the Single European Act (SEA) of 1986 designed to streamline the decision making process in the EEC. It involved amending the Treaty of Rome, which had established the Community in 1960. The SEA was approved by the national parliaments of the member states and it was assumed that the same would happen in Ireland. The process was delayed, however, because of internal strife in the Labour Party. Because of fears that the European issue could give his internal Labour enemies ammunition to undermine his position, Spring approached FitzGerald in the early summer of 1986 and asked him to postpone ratification of the Treaty by the Dáil until after the Labour Party conference in the autumn of that year.[17]

FitzGerald agreed, although he was worried about allowing ratification run so close to the deadline of 1 January 1987. 'I agreed with this request in order to minimise problems the Labour Party might face in mobilising support by its deputies for ratification in the Dáil,' wrote FitzGerald later. Labour's position was thrashed out at the Administrative Council (now the Executive Board) of the party and the full parliamentary party. The protagonists divided along the usual lines with the pro-coalition faction led by Spring coming out on top, but only after a bitter battle with the anti-coalition group led by Michael D. Higgins.

Fianna Fáil and its leader Charles Haughey behaved with typical opportunism in the debate that took place in December 1986 and argued that there should be a referendum on the SEA. Fianna Fáil voted against ratification on this basis in order to embarrass Labour. In the event, the Act was passed by the Oireachtas, but the Supreme Court decided in early 1987 that there would have to be a referendum after all. By this time Haughey was in office and he was incensed by the Court's decision.

The decision also created a fresh quandary for the Labour Party. Now that it was in opposition, the anti-European group in the party mobilised again for the referendum. A Labour 'No' group, led by Higgins and newly elected Kildare TD Emmet Stagg, took to the hustings. Higgins argued that there was 'a moral distance between Ireland and the larger individual nations in the EEC in the areas of disarmament, world peace, aid in the Third World and arms procurement policies which necessitates a rejection of the Single European Act'.[18] Stagg claimed that the SEA would 'effectively co-opt Ireland into NATO's political and diplomatic sphere'. The Workers' Party led by Tomás MacGiolla, which won four seats in the 1987 election, also campaigned for a 'No' vote. For their part, Spring and the party leadership endorsed a 'Yes' vote and campaigned for the SEA but sought to avoid creating further antagonism over the issue in an already divided and demoralised party. In the end, the SEA was carried comfortably with 69.9 per cent voting 'Yes'. However, the 'No' vote at 30.1 per cent had almost doubled since 1973 and this marked the beginning of a trend as further referendums on closer European integration became a feature of the following two decades.

Labour made a return to the European Parliament in 1989 with Barry Desmond winning a seat in Dublin. Also elected in the capital was Proinsias De Rossa of the Workers' Party, who was soon afterwards to become leader of the breakaway Democratic Left. Only five years after the SEA another European referendum was held, this time on the Maastricht Treaty, which paved the way for the single currency. A Fianna Fáil–Progressive Democrat government was in office and by this stage Michael D. Higgins was the Labour Party spokesman on Foreign Affairs. He again called for a 'No' vote, but this was in contradiction to the stance taken by the party's national executive. Party leader Dick Spring said he was in favour of 'a qualified Yes' and the bulk of the party ultimately supported a 'Yes' vote. A complicating factor was the protocol on abortion designed to protect the ban in the Irish constitution. It was that factor that accounted for Spring's qualification.[19]

The Democratic Left, which had split from the Workers' Party, also campaigned for a 'No' vote. The director of elections for the party's 'No' campaign was Dun Laoghaire TD Eamon Gilmore. 'We have a particular burden of responsibility as we are the only party in the Dáil urging a "No" vote. The people have heard all about the advantages; they must also hear about the problems and disadvantages of the agreement,' said Gilmore.[20] On 6 June 1992, after the referendum was rejected by the Danish electorate, Gilmore accused the Minister for Foreign Affairs, David Andrews, of being part of a conspiracy involving the European Commission and the other member states to frustrate the democratic decision of the Danish people. He said their strategy was 'to ignore the legal reality that the Maastricht Treaty was now null and void, go into a phoney ratification and put a political and economic gun to the heads of the Danish people'.[21] When the Irish people went to the polls on 18 June 1992 the result was almost identical to that on the SEA five years earlier with 69.1 per cent voting 'Yes'.

Six months later Labour was in coalition with Fianna Fáil. Agreement on an EU package of structural and cohesion funds for Ireland worth £8 billion, attained by Taoiseach Albert Reynolds at the EU summit in Edinburgh in December 1992, was one of the main attractions for Labour entering the coalition. During its two and a half years Labour managed to get a senior EU political office for the first time with the party's Dublin MEP and former Minister for Health Barry Desmond being appointed as Ireland's representative on the Court of Auditors. By the time the next EU referendum – the Amsterdam Treaty – came around in 1998 the party was almost totally united in favour of a 'Yes' vote. Michael D. Higgins, after his experience as a Cabinet minister between 1992 and 1997, was fully reconciled with his senior colleagues and content to support the 'Yes' campaign, as was Emmet Stagg, who had served as a junior minister during the same period.

By this stage negotiations on a merger between Labour and Democratic Left were already under way. The two parties had served in government together in the Rainbow Coalition of 1995–97 and that experience transformed the relationship between them. Like Higgins, leading members of the Democratic Left such as Proinsias De Rossa and Eamon Gilmore who had campaigned against all previous European treaties, advocated a 'Yes' vote this time. In party terms, the 'No' campaign in 1998 only involved Sinn Féin and the Greens. Despite the broad political consensus, and the fact that the referendum was held on the same day as the one on the Good Friday Agreement, the 'Yes' vote declined to 61.7 per cent and the 'No' vote increased to 38.3 per cent.

The merger between Labour and Democratic Left was completed in 1999 and for the next decade the party position on Europe was united and positively in favour of further integration. Ironically, the two EU treaties on which Labour and the former Democratic Left politicians campaigned for a 'Yes' vote in a unified manner, Nice and Lisbon, both ended up in defeat the first time around. Having been on the losing side in the 'No' campaign of 1972 Labour ended up on the losing side on the 'Yes' campaigns of 2001 and 2008. The party stuck with the 'Yes' position in the reruns of the Nice and Lisbon referendums and played an important role in getting the electorate to reverse their earlier decisions.

Eamon Gilmore was party leader by the time of the first Lisbon referendum in June of 2008 and his initial response to the 'No' vote echoed his reaction to the Danish 'No' to Maastricht the first time around. In the immediate aftermath of the Lisbon 'No' vote he insisted that the treaty was dead: 'It required 27 member states to ratify it and the Irish people have now decided in a referendum they do not want it ratified, therefore Ireland cannot ratify the Lisbon Treaty and therefore the Lisbon Treaty falls.' In another interview, he went on to point out that unlike the first Nice referendum the turnout had been good: 'I do not think there is any question of the Treaty being put a second time to the people.'[22]

In the following weeks he clarified his position saying that the same package as Lisbon One could not be put to the people again, but some of the pro-EU elements in the party worried that he might be reverting to his earlier suspicions about the European project. In the event Gilmore and Labour declared in favour of a 'Yes' vote in the second Lisbon referendum in October of 2009 and campaigned strongly in favour of it. Given the weakness of Brian Cowen's Fianna Fáil government at that stage, the support of Labour and Fine Gael was vital in winning the referendum for the 'Yes' side.

However, Gilmore's attitude to Europe became one of the surprise issues in the general election campaign of February 2011. Over the previous year the Labour leader had managed to win high approval ratings for his trenchant criticism of Brian Cowen in the Dáil. In the summer of 2010 Gilmore was getting a much higher satisfaction rating in opinion polls than any of the other party leaders and he was far ahead of Fine Gael leader Enda Kenny. At one stage Labour moved into first place ahead of Fine Gael in the polls and there was speculation in the media about a 'Gilmore Gale' that would make the party the biggest after the subsequent general election.

While Labour had slipped behind Fine Gael by the time the election was called at the beginning of February 2011, hopes were still high in Labour that the party could at least run their rivals a close second. The election was held against the background of the EU/IMF bailout of November 2010, which had stunned the country. The terms of the bailout, particularly the interest rate being charged on loans to Ireland by the European Central Bank, were strongly criticised by all of the opposition parties. On the third day of the campaign Gilmore told a press conference that the election was about whether the budget would be decided by the European Central Bank (ECB) in Frankfurt or by the democratically elected government of the Irish people. 'It's Frankfurt's way or Labour's way,' declared Gilmore who went on to describe the chairman of the ECB, Jean Claude Trichet, as 'a mere civil servant'.[23] The remarks enabled Gilmore's opponents to question his political judgement and his knowledge of how EU institutions work.

Nonetheless, the party had its best election result and, with thirty-seven Dáil seats, became the second party in the state for the first time. A coalition deal was agreed with Fine Gael and Gilmore became Minister for Foreign Affairs and Trade. Six months after the formation of the coalition and the deal with EU partners which led to considerably better terms on the bailout,

Gilmore said that his comments during the campaign had to be seen in context: 'I said that when I was talking about the renegotiation of the deal. The point I was making was that the Labour Party was committed to a renegotiation of the deal. What I was dealing with was a view that it couldn't be renegotiated. All I would say now is that we have renegotiated it. Very often in the course of an election campaign there is chapel gate language that is used to simplify what are at times very complex issues. But we have renegotiated the deal.'[24]

The euro crisis of 2011 and the bailouts for Ireland, Greece and Portugal led to a debate about the necessity for closer fiscal union in the EU and for constitutional or legal limits on budget deficits to prevent a similar crisis happening in the future. The challenge for the Labour Party and its leader will be to maintain Ireland's place in the EU while adapting to changing circumstances. With the party leader occupying the post of Tánaiste and Foreign Affairs, Labour will have an important role in determining Ireland's future relationship with our European partners.

13. Ireland's Journey to the Third Way: the hi-social model?

Jane Suiter

This chapter traces the Irish Labour Party's transition from a traditional, arguably illiberal, party to one in the mainstream of European social democracy. This was a journey that saw the party move from being socially conservative with values antagonistic to business to one where the value of entrepreneurial capitalism was welcomed and social democratic values emphasised. The journey is charted through changes in the party's economic policy stances and places these in a comparative context, tracing them from the traditional view of the state as the central provider of employment, to one where Labour today argues that it represents not just employees but the self-employed and employers, united under a common set of values. The focus is on changes in European social democratic thinking and particularly recent paradigms such as the Third Way. It argues that while the Labour Party did indeed tend to follow modernising forces elsewhere, it also attempted to find its own path through the challenges posed by neoliberalism. In the process it became a party that was far more business friendly while attempting to maintain a dialogue around civil society and equality.

In common with many Labour parties across Europe the Labour Party grew out of the rapidly mobilising labour movement, particularly following the 1913 lockout, with a primary objective to 'organise and unite the workers of Ireland in order to improve their status and conditions generally'. In other words, it was set up as the political wing of the trade union movement and many of its early members were trade unionists first and party members second.[1] Ireland was also unusual in Europe at that time for its low level of industrialisation, which was concentrated around Belfast.[2] As a result it is also notable and indeed unusual in a comparative context that many of its supporters in the first forty or so years were rural workers and farm labourers, rather than industrial working class. Hence, the Labour Party probably had less engagement with 'business' than many other socialist/social democratic parties, and all of its supporters did not necessarily regard business as 'the enemy'. But a greater challenge was the vastly different cleavages emerging in the new Irish state at that time. Far from divides between rich and poor, urban and rural and so on that were dominant across Europe, in Ireland the pursuit of sovereignty was a higher priority and the Labour Party stood back as the dominant split around sovereignty was formed.[3] One result was that, over the next forty years, the Labour Party was far from radical; in fact, it was almost 'incongruously conservative'[4] by European standards, shunning the word 'socialist' and believing even that liberalism was a dangerous creed. At the same time, European social democracy began at this time to diverge into a gradualist movement leaving the revolutionaries behind and becoming ever more mainstream.

At the end of the Second World War, the social democracies of northern and western Europe set the political agenda. Their tenets of the mixed economy and the welfare state provided an alternative to free market capitalism and the night watchman state.[5] In Britain, Norway, Sweden, France, Austria, Belgium and later West Germany and Italy, social democratic governments enjoyed long periods in office. In general, Marx was relegated to the bin and the emerging dominant economic paradigm was that Keynesian demand management and state investment would maintain full employment. Economic growth would fund state welfare programmes and thus equality was achievable; crucially this was not just perceived as equality of opportunity but a coincident equality of outcome. However, by the 1970s the new social democracies had hit the buffers of stagflation: a combination of inflation with low growth. By 1975 Prime Minister Jim Callaghan sounded its death knell in the UK, and under pressure from the IMF, announced that the era of Keynesian tax and spend economics was finished. The party was over. In Ireland, over the same period the Labour Party failed to expand, effectively held back by Fianna Fáil campaigning as a 'catch-all' party, portraying itself simultaneously as a populist, left-wing party derived from its first leader Éamon de Valera, as well as the pro-business policies of its next leader Seán Lemass.[6] As a result, membership of the parliamentary party did not shift significantly from a core of trade unionists while economic policy was focused almost exclusively on direct employment creation by the state. As leader Brendan Corish said in 1961: 'Where it is shown, and it has been shown recently, that private enterprise, whether foreign or in this country, fails to establish industry to absorb our unemployed, then we believe it is the responsibility of this State to extend the activities of the State bodies and semi-State industries in an effort to absorb the unemployed.'[7]

Almost from the beginning, the Labour Party was attracted to the professions and to the idea of broadening the base of its party membership and as early as 1930 the party planned to approach not only professionals but 'lawyers and professors' to join the ranks.[8] Yet it was 1965 before Dr John O'Connell was elected, and it was only in 1969–73 with the election of the 'new wave', as David Thornley, Conor Cruise O'Brien and Justin Keating were elected, that the dynamic changed perceptibly. The party began to have a wider focus, one that was in favour of redistribution of wealth and social equality, as well as one that espoused a broadly liberal social agenda.

For the first time in its history the Labour Party tilted towards radical economic policy and the 1969 conference, one marked by a mood of mass euphoria,[9] produced one of the party's first radical documents.[10] Then General Secretary Brendan Halligan developed proposals for a National Development Corporation (NDC), involving a partial takeover of the commercial banks and, in general, increased participation by the state in the economy.[11] In addition, companies (thought to be the nascent Cement Roadstone Holdings) in the buildings material industry were to be nationalised, as well as all building land and building societies, while the estates of large landowners would be vested in the community.[12] The proposals, needless to say, were not popular with the mercantile classes and caused immense problems with the centre-right Fine Gael party.[13]

Not only did the Labour Party have differences with mainstream business over the NDC proposals, the party was also anti-Europe and indeed campaigned against the first accession referendum. It had serious concerns that industries such as clothing and footwear, which were then reasonably successful on the east coast, would be affected by accession and it thus tended towards protectionism. However, the UK and Ireland's accession to membership of the European Economic Community in 1973 also played an important part in the gradually increasing influence of European Labour. The Europeanisation of Ireland also resulted in urbanising and modernising forces. This, of course, affected the Irish political trend in party detachment,[14] theoretically allowing the Labour Party to attempt to attract many voters previously frozen in their preferences over the older sovereignty cleavage. Meanwhile, across Europe the political spectrum continued shifting rightward with the new Right arguing against state intervention welfare programmes and high taxes, the Labour Party, like other 'labour' parties in the UK and France moved to 'progressive capitalism', as free-market principles became assumed as a constant. In Ireland, the Labour Party, which was in coalition government, granted private licences to mining[15] while simultaneously initiating European poverty programmes and introducing a short-lived wealth tax. Signs of further movement came during the second stage of the Finance Bill in 1978 when Ruairi Quinn made a commitment to the mixed economy model: 'The Labour Party has no argument in this context at this time in this House with the idea of a mixed economy ... When we – I mean the Labour Party and the labour movement – talk about the private sector we do not have some caricature of a large anonymous company concerned exclusively with how they are going to exploit their workers and invest their profits. That caricature is not true and does not exist.'[16]

By 1982, Michael Gallagher argues, the Labour Party enjoyed a solid electoral base, 'distinctive policies', 'loyal supporters', trade union backing, and a long track record of survival in unfavourable circumstances. He contended that 'for these reasons it will not disappear, but there are no signs either that it will grow dramatically, or throw off its third party status'.[17] In a bid to defeat this portrayal the party followed the UK Labour Party and began to modernise in earnest post-1987. It moved to expel its militants, marginalised troublesome deputies and ensured that the new leader Dick Spring was firmly in control.[18] This allowed it a steady rise in the opinion polls from 1988 onwards. The party also instigated a major policy review, the 'Spring Alternative'. The review quietly 'dumped' the anti-business rhetoric in a bid to make Labour more electable. Greg Sparks, an accountant and long-time activist, who later played a key role as an advisor to Spring, says, 'It was probably the first document issued to the parliamentary party worth reading ... There was now an acceptance that we could talk to business without being bought. That was new.'[19] Michael D. Higgins produced a counter document, but it had little impact on policy.

The Labour Party set about implementing much of the detail following its return to power in coalition with Fianna Fáil in 1992. In a key economic policy change the Department of Labour was abolished and a Department of Enterprise and Employment was created, an explicit tying together of the two narratives, with Quinn serving as the new minister. The word order was important: the party was demonstrating that it saw the need to encourage enterprise in order to produce jobs rather than the other way around.[20] Tax strategy also underwent a transformation to the extent that a tax strategy group proposed utilising the tax incentives for holiday homes. The symbiotic logic of merging private and public cooperation also made its appearance. For example, Quinn set up the Dublin Docklands Development Association in a bid to run the business and social aspects of development in tandem.

By the time Labour changed coalition partners mid-course to govern with Fine Gael it was confident in the economic sphere and succeeded in demanding the Finance Ministry, a first for Labour. A Labour minister was now in charge of the task of qualifying to join the single currency with the consequent focus on low inflation, low interest rates and a hard currency. Everything else was subject to that imperative. Quinn, as the new minister, was determined to prove that the Labour Party could not only handle the Department of Finance but could do it successfully and be prudent. He set up weekly breakfast meetings, not with the social partners, but with business figures and industrialists. Three years later, by the time of the next election in 1997, there was no difference between the Irish and the German spread on ten-year money, while a standardised 12.5 per cent corporation tax rate had been agreed despite some misgivings in the party.[21] Other misgivings arose over the length of a public sector pay pause and, given that Labour was still against the sale of state assets, to Quinn's perceived interest in selling state-owned TSB bank to NIB of Australia, but despite these tensions the party remained broadly united.

While the Labour Party had absorbed the lessons of lower corporate tax rates for business it failed to apply these to personal taxes and the government parties decided to fight the 1997 election on cuts to the relatively esoteric bands and allowances rather than tax rate cuts[22] and failed to return to power. However, across much of the rest of the world, social democrats were returning to power. Tony Blair's victory that same year followed Clinton's return to power a year earlier in 1996; the US President was a key inspiration in much of the Blairite changes. Within a few weeks of Labour's victory in the UK, Lionel Jospin came to power in France, winning control of the National Assembly in an election called by the Gaullist President Jacques Chirac. At this stage the Left were in power, either alone or as coalition leaders, in ten of the then fifteen EU member states.[23] Apart from Ireland, only in Germany and Spain were they in opposition; from the 1980s when Thatcher and Reagan had dominated economic discourse this was quite a turnaround.

Tony Blair had won the leadership of the British Labour Party in 1994 in a clear victory for the modernisers there. At the party conference the following year a banner reading 'New Labour New Britain' was unfurled. Through a process of constant repetition the adjective stuck. New Labour left behind almost all the old orthodoxies and became what Blair called the natural party for business. The new thinking was espoused in the Third Way, a policy proposal advanced by sociologist Anthony Giddens who was to prove very influential with Blair and other social democratic leaders. Giddens argued that the Third Way was an opportunity to transcend the ideologies of both the old Left and the new Right. He posited that the differences in narrative were unhelpful in addressing contemporary problems and that civil society, the government and the economy were interdependent.[24] This new European social democratic platform was a reiteration of the language of community and of citizenship, reciprocity and responsibility, justice and fairness.[25] Citizens and welfare were positioned within a superordinate economic discourse, people and communities became capital,[26] thus education became an investment in the future; equality was equality of access to education and opportunity. In many ways traditional left-wing or Labour concerns such as values about welfare and society were subordinated to the globalised economic discourse.[27]

Blair was an enthusiastic proponent. Addressing a meeting of the European Socialist Congress in Malmo, Sweden, he declared: 'Our task today is not to fight the old battles but to show that there is a third way, a way of marrying together an open, competitive and successful economy with a just, decent and humane society.' The Left, said Blair, had to modernise or die.[28] Labour used the Third Way to visualise its departure from the older narratives of owner and worker, implying a reconfiguration of the language of politics and a synthesis in economic thinking. Italian Prime Minster, Massimo D'Elema, summed it up: 'The Third Way suggests that it is possible to combine social solidarity with a dynamic economy, and this is a goal contemporary social democrats should strive for. To pursue it, we will need less national government, less central government, but greater governance over local processes.'[29] Or as Lionel Jospin, the Prime Minister of France, put it, there was a need to wrest the idea of modernity away from the dominance of new right thinking: 'The illusion of the neoliberals has been shed. Social democracy has found new leaders and has started to rebuild its political identity. The work is far from complete but I am confident about its outcome. Part of it is being carried out at a European level that is only logical, for socialism is a European idea, born in Europe and shaped by European thinkers.'[30]

In essence the central idea of the Third Way was a path between the market-led neoliberalism and the state-centred collectivism of the past. Thus the British Labour government would focus on equipping workers for globalisation rather than railing against it, on keeping taxes low to encourage business rather than spending on state-sponsored programmes, and on individual rather than collectivist wage bargaining. For many on the Left it was merely a continuation of neoliberal policies with a soft edge. However, there was also some retreat from market-led reform in the public sector and a softening of competition policy. The Third Way was also utilised by Bill Clinton in the US, and in some European countries where it generally was a code for continuing recognition of the importance of the global economy along with attention to the importance of social cohesion.[31] Despite criticism from many, the Third Way was not just about the inter-relationships between the state, the market and business but was also about social and cultural values, and civil society. It attempted to negotiate a break for the ideology of the Right along with recognition of the problem faced by social democratic governments across Europe.

The rapidly globalising economies the parties oversaw ensured their success was accompanied by a marked shift from the values of traditional social democracy. The shift towards the neoliberal paradigm was common to almost all but was perhaps most marked under Tony Blair and New Labour in Britain, although the social democrats in Sweden had stressed the importance of making the market for everyone since the 1930s. For many on the Left, globalisation merely acted as a convenient *post hoc* rationalisation for a logic of tax cutting which the Labour Party has already internalised[32] or, in other words, in some ways globalisation was useful in turning the old Labour into New Labour, making it possible to argue that the governments room for manoeuvre was limited and the demands of the international financial markets must be met. In general, however, New Labour's perspective was to see globalisation as a challenge and an opportunity rather than viewing it as a threat.

For the party, the focus on coming to power in 1997 was to prove that it could be trusted with the economy. It was keenly aware that management of the economy had often been a stick with which the Right beat the Left and, in addition, that its loss of powers in the 1979 election following the 'winter of discontent' was widely blamed on economic policy. One of its first steps was to place monetary policy with the Bank of England. New Labour also had two fiscal rules: the first, that over the economic cycle the government would borrow only to invest and not to fund current spending; and second, that net debt would, over the cycle, be held at a prudent level. For Blair, a close relationship with business was also important: 'People don't even question for a moment that the Democrats are a pro-business party. They shouldn't be asking that question about New Labour. New Labour is pro-business, pro-enterprise and we believe that there is nothing inconsistent between that and a just and decent society.'[33]

In Germany, social democratic leader Gerhard Schröder, who came to power in 1998, also stressed the importance of what he called the '*Die Neue Mitte*' or central way. Blair and Schröder published a joint manifesto focused on complementing 'the essential function of markets', declaring: 'We support a market economy, not a market society.'[34] Quite how these could be neatly separated was not spelled out. They also pledged to build support and 'seek discussion with political leaders in other European countries who wish to take forward with us modernising ideas for social democracy in their respective national contexts'.

In Ireland the picture was less clear-cut. There had never been a dominant Left/Right cleavage in Irish society and, therefore, the large political parties had, over time, swung both Left and Right, depending on the dominant ideology of the day and on pragmatism.[35] As a result it was as likely that Bertie Ahern's Fianna Fáil would attempt at least to utilise some of the rhetoric around the Third Way as it was that the Labour Party would do so. Indeed, Fianna Fáil's brief flirtation with community and socialism may have been motivated by this.[36] Eamon Gilmore also appears to be more of a social idealist than a true Blairite. Addressing a Labour meeting in 2008 he set out a coherent vision of what the Labour Party is: 'There is a need for us, in particular, to expand the meaning of the term "Labour" in the way we speak and are spoken of. We must go beyond old images of a downtrodden proletariat and smokestack industries – beyond the idea of Labour as an interest group representing a particular form of paid manual employment. Yes, those are our origins, and we are proud of them. But the context of Labour today relates to work in a much wider sense. Labour today applies to those who work for themselves, as well as those who work for employers … Labour is not a description of work – or simply a label for a political movement. Labour is a set of values …'[37]

But it is also worth noting that he did not rail against globalisation and, similar to New Labour, rather sought to espouse the idea of an 'ethical, civilised and sustainable globalisation' and this is still to be achieved on the 'basis of a vision of a small, open, entrepreneurial economy in a global marketplace'. In many ways, the Labour Party was internalising the central vision of the Third Way, yet it clearly wished to disown the term and to associate its economic policies with entrepreneurialism rather than business in general and with rather more emphasis on values than was generally evident in the Blairite philosophy.

The new language also impacted on how the problem of unemployment was perceived. In general, Keynesians, and most social democrats, conceive of unemployment as being largely involuntary, in other words if there is work available people will choose to work. In the UK this view was questioned under New Labour and advisors argued that the long-term unemployed are semi-detached from the labour market and can be either too demoralised or too stigmatised to seek work or to take it up should they get an offer. Enticing these people back to searching for work would decrease unemployment, increase tax receipts, reduce social welfare payments and could also be extended to other groups of workers such as lone parents. As a result New Labour introduced a raft of policies from the New Deal targeted at younger long-term unemployed people, to the working family tax credit and withdrawal of lone-parent payments to 'make work pay'. For many on the Left, this was evidence that Blair was likely to go down the US labour market route with few protections.[38] In contrast, during its time in government in the 1990s, the Labour Party had reservations about going this route and much of the benefits system remained relatively unreformed. At the same time, unemployment reduced significantly and indeed reached what many believed was the natural rate. Although then Minister for Social Welfare Proinsias De Rossa, at the time a Democratic Left politician, was more focused on rooting out fraud than perhaps any previous minister in his position.

There is a further crucial difference between New Labour policy and Labour Party policy in relation to business. In the UK the debate over corporatism took place in the 1970s and 1980s with many in the UK Labour Party seeing it as an appropriate way to run the Keynesian welfare state. However, the party's defeat in 1992 was partly attributed to its links to 'organised labour'. New Labour felt the need to distance itself from old Labour: in 1995 the party leadership deleted Clause 4 from the party's constitution while the union's block vote at the conference was lowered. Blair said he would govern for the whole nation and not an interest group within it.[39] On gaining power, Blair insisted that there would be no return to 'beer and sandwiches' at Number 10 Downing Street.[40] Addressing the TUC Annual Congress in September 1999 he insisted: 'You run the unions. We run the government. We will never confuse the two again.' This renunciation by New Labour of old Labour's corporatism meant there was to be little coordinated wage bargaining. The situation was, of course, very different in Ireland. A further unusual feature was that whereas across Europe most socialist or social democratic parties monopolised relations with trade unions, or at worst had to compete with a communist party doing so, the Labour Party faced rivalry with Fianna Fáil on this front. Many party activists were suspicious that the average rank-and-file trade unionist was more likely to vote for Fianna Fáil and suspected that many trade unionists were happier with the dominant party in government and were not unhappy about the Labour Party being in opposition. Under Fianna Fáil, social partnership, the Irish version of corporatism, was also still the primary model for policy making. Labour in government did not seek to separate itself from the unions, even when social partnership failed along with the boom economy and although leader Eamon Gilmore has explicitly tied union donations to corporate donations and said the system would be reformed.[41] In general, New Labour under Blair radically transformed social democracy, rejecting the rights–claiming culture of social democracy, as well as Keynesian economics, nationalisation, planning and egalitarian tax and spending policies. In its place it put free trade, flexible labour markets, sound money and the spirit of entrepreneurial capitalism.[42] For the Left this meant that Blair had sold his soul and indeed the soul of the Labour Party. For the Irish it provided a route map, one which the party tried to follow while avoiding some of the more obvious potholes. It also made the changes without the battles that were waged in the UK, for example, over Clause 4. As Pat Rabbitte said in 2006:[43]

> Despite my belief in renewal, I am not a fan of the term 'the Third Way'. It seems to imply that there are no longer any differences between left and right. In fairness to the proponents of the 'third way' that is not what they think of themselves as doing, but they don't always get that message across.
>
> I believe there are clear distinctions between left and right. I believe that there are deep dividing lines in politics ...
>
> Firstly, we must build a sustainable, prosperous and enterprising economy, which sees equality as a competitive strength, not inequality as a necessary incentive. We can never lose sight of the importance of economic stability. One of Ruairi's lasting legacies to Irish life is the stability that comes with membership of the Eurozone, and his contribution to building the Celtic Tiger. What the Right fails to recognise is that you can have stability and still address social needs. It

has been the failing of this Government that it has not translated the success of our economy into a successful society ...

In reality, we must seek to combine the dynamism and innovation of a hi-tech enterprise economy, with the high standards and protections of the European social model. We must blend the best of Boston and Berlin – what we might call the hi-social model. Ireland is well placed to achieve this goal.

In a similar vein to Gilmore, Rabbitte is here again explicitly tying together the values of social democracy while espousing the perceived benefits of neoliberal economic policies. He is also attempting to link the hi-tech sector and perhaps particularly the newer global internet firms settling in Dublin, the hi-social model, as he calls it. It is still a vision that regards the role of the state as mediating the conflicting interests but that fundamentally puts the needs of the economy first.

There are differences in emphasis among the party. In 2009, for example, Joan Burton, then finance spokesperson set out her vision for renewed state involvement in the financial sector, without the emphasis on the importance of sound money.[44] A close reading implies that Burton may have been calling for a reining back of the emphasis on neoliberal economics: 'Ireland needs a third way, that is, a mixed economy. This is inevitable with the collapse of the banking industry and I will discuss the blame for that presently. However, given the collapse of our banking and financial industries in the past five months, there should be a bigger role for the State in financial and banking affairs. That is inevitable and there is no point in the right-wing people in Fianna Fáil gnashing their teeth.'[45]

Since Labour returned to power in 2011, the party is treading a very difficult line trying to promote something akin to Rabbitte's hi-social model. On the one hand the measures agreed with the IMF/EU in relation to the bailout are almost uniformly neoliberal in nature. Labour ministers have granted private sector exploration licences, agreed the IMF austerity measures and introduced measures to encourage the young to work while there is also a focus on the hi-tech policy of attracting international internet businesses. But it is also committed to equality and to attempting to ensure that the poorest in society are not targeted. Maintaining some of the moral and civic values of social democracy in a period of austerity is a significant challenge. Labour's future as a social democratic party post-austerity may depend on its success in this regard.

During this time the challenges emanating from globalisation also came into sharper focus. It is worth noting that globalisation is an essentially contested concept: for some it is a malign force that requires organised resistance; for others it is merely an accelerated form of internationalism. There are many definitions but one that is widely accepted is that globalisation may be understood as a continuing and a dynamic process which reduces the significance of national boundaries (and hence the autonomy of nation states as economic policy actors) as impediments to the free movement of capital, goods, services and to a lesser extent labour. This is a serious challenge for all social democracies but particularly so in Ireland, one of the most globalised economies in the world. It is worth noting that rarely have the problems associated with globalisation been directly confronted by any new social democratic politicians in Ireland or Europe. Unfettered globalisation is accepted but there is little discussion of who should hold the reins of power once sovereignty is acceded, a point made quite forcibly in the autumn of 2011 when 'the markets' forced the resignation of two democratically elected European political leaders, Greek Prime Minister George Papandreou and Italian Prime Minister Silvio Berlusconi.

In conclusion, we can see that while the Labour Party grew out of the European-wide mass trade union movement at the beginning of the twentieth century, for its early years it was, like the Irish revolutionaries of the time, the most conservative of groups. As a result it was largely immune to the modernising influences of its sister European social democratic parties until the 1960s when the party became a recognisable socialist/ social democratic party. In the 1980s the party underwent a second wave of modernisation and at that point it enthusiastically embraced change, modernising rapidly. However, perhaps because it was out of power during the heyday of the Third Way, it never fully embraced this new paradigm, rather it continued with a policy of corporatism, of keeping the trade unions close while simultaneously hailing the benefits of the market economy and espousing the importance of values. In other words, the Labour Party went its own way, on the one hand accepting the diktats of the market economy including imposed austerity, while at the same time trying to maintain and promote its values. It is not the easiest of fits.

14. Labour and the Liberal Agenda

Ivana Bacik

THE PERCEPTION IS that the Labour Party in Ireland has had a long-standing connection with the cause of 'liberal' reform. In this context, liberal reform is understood to mean reform of the law to bring about progressive social change on a range of issues, notably legalisation of divorce; of contraception; abolition of the status of illegitimacy for children born outside marriage; rights for women; gay rights; and rights for those from ethnic or religious minorities. Labour is often described (sometimes in a disparaging sense) as the party of the 'liberal agenda' – usually meaning the party of an urban, middle-class, liberal vote.

This perception, however, is far from accurate. A review of the history of the party shows that its association with liberal reforms is relatively recent and that policies adopted in favour of liberal change have often followed hard-fought internal battles, both within the party membership and more often within the parliamentary Labour Party (the PLP). Internal tensions on social policy issues, of course, exist in many left-wing parties across Europe and beyond. However, in Ireland there is the added complication for Labour members of the strong and enduring influence within Irish politics and society of the Roman Catholic Church. The party has had a difficult relationship with the Church over the years and therein lies the source of many internal conflicts over liberal reform campaigns. In her review of the first fifty years of the Irish Labour Party, Niamh Puirséil emphasises the need to understand the important role of the Catholic Church in Labour's history, saying:

> The [Catholic] Church rarely mobilised against Labour, but only because Labour was assiduous in ensuring that it was never given

cause to do so. The degree of self-censorship was enormous in both policy and language: Labour's amendment of the Workers' Republic constitution; its silence over the Spanish civil war; and its failure to support social reforms such as non-means-tested social welfare benefits or health reforms which would have, in the eyes of the Church in Ireland, been contrary to Catholic social teaching.[1]

Labour had, as Michael Holmes suggests, made a 'tentative move to the left' in 1936, with the introduction of 'a new party constitution which called for the creation of a workers' republic. Under pressure from the Church, that phrase was soon recanted.'[2] Again in 1950, more Church pressure was brought to bear on the party, with the proposal by the Clann na Poblachta TD and Minister for Health, Noël Browne, of the 'Mother and Child Scheme', a scheme proposing free healthcare for mothers and children. The Catholic Church hierarchy infamously opposed the scheme and intervened politically to bring about its defeat. John Horgan, in his detailed account of the way in which the scheme was derailed by the Church, writes that Labour TDs 'abandoned' Noël Browne over the scheme; there was a marked divergence of views within the parliamentary party, with many TDs wishing to vote for the scheme following a Trades Union Congress call for its support, but the Chair of the PLP 'successfully countered the vote in favour of the Scheme'.[3] This sort of 'self-censorship' certainly contributed to the fact that, as Michael Gallagher writes, Labour even in the late 1950s was 'almost incongruously conservative by European standards; it shunned the word "socialist" and seemed to regard even "liberalism" as a dangerous creed'.[4]

In 1960, however, Brendan Corish had become Labour leader, and during the decade that followed there was a 'flurry of policy-making' within the party, as it moved steadily to the Left.[5] A number of 'high-profile intellectuals' joined the party, notably David Thornley and Justin Keating; in 1966 it openly declared itself to be socialist, and in 1967 became affiliated to the Socialist International.[6] A series of significant policy documents was published in 1969, including a document on health, education and social welfare policy, which was followed by the establishment of a women's advisory council within the party; and the publication of a policy document on women in 1971. The advisory council faced significant hostility towards its activities from elements within the party leadership and indeed was threatened with abolition by the party's Administrative Council (AC); but a group of committed activists kept it going and in 1975 it developed into the Labour Women's National Council (now Labour Women), an active and highly influential organisation within the party that has consistently called upon the PLP to adopt liberal stances on social issues over the years.

During this period, and subsequently, the development of liberal social policies within the party was far from straightforward. There were, and remain, powerful voices within Labour's membership, and within the PLP, supporting a more conservative stance on social issues. Stephen Collins has written that in the 1970s the parliamentary party 'was split between rural and urban TDs, between liberals and conservatives and between nationalists and anti-nationalists'.[7] During this time, he noted: 'Most of the urban TDs – anti-Republicans like Conor Cruise O'Brien, Barry Desmond, Frank Cluskey and Michael O'Leary – were also divided from their rural colleagues on liberal agenda issues.'[8] Similarly, in 1986, Horgan described rural deputies, in particular, as having a notably conservative influence upon the development of party policy.[9]

Indeed, on issues relating to sexual morality, Horgan suggested: 'Although Labour has generally – given the foot-dragging of its rural deputies – contributed modestly to the development of these policy areas, its initiatives have not been achieved without difficulty, internal as well as external.'[10] This difficulty was strongly evident, for example, during the bitter debate at the party conference in Galway in 1971 on the contraception issue; feelings at the meeting ran so high that delegates were literally spitting at each other. The opposition to contraception within the party was so vocal that, although the majority of Labour members at the conference supported legalisation, the bill introduced by Noël Browne and John O'Connell on contraception in 1972 was published as a private members' bill; and three Labour TDs voted against it (Dan Spring, Stevie Coughlan and Michael Pat Murphy).

The national campaign to legalise contraception had been kick-started by the foundation in 1970 of the Irish Women's Liberation Movement (IWLM). On 22 May 1971, members of the IWLM and supporters travelled from Dublin to Belfast and back on a 'Contraceptive Train', importing condoms illegally in a public act of defiance. This direct-action tactic prompted huge controversy, but the legalisation of contraception became a core demand for a range of individuals and organisations. Notably, Mary Robinson, then a senator, introduced an unsuccessful contraceptive bill in the Seanad in 1971; and feminists rallied to support the *McGee* case in 1973, which established the right of married couples to import contraceptives for their own use.

Within Labour, the Labour Women's National Council (LWNC) actively supported the contraception legalisation campaign, and indeed has since its foundation campaigned within the party for the adoption of stronger policies on women's rights. By the time the LWNC was formed, Labour had entered government with Fine Gael in 1973. This coalition remained in place for four years, with Liam Cosgrave as Taoiseach and Labour leader Brendan Corish as Tánaiste. During this time, a number of progressive changes were made by the coalition; notably the abolition of the 'marriage bar', which had prohibited women from continuing to work in the civil service, local authorities and health boards after marriage, through the Civil Service (Employment of Married Women) Act 1973. In 1973, the 'unmarried mother's allowance' was also introduced, easing considerably the difficult social and economic position of single mothers. This followed the establishment of Cherish, the single parents' organisation, in 1972, with then Senator Mary Robinson as its first president.

The year 1973 may be seen as a watershed for the development of equality law in Ireland generally. Irish entry into the EEC (European Economic Community) that year was a significant catalyst for change for women. The people had voted to join the EEC in a referendum held under the previous government in June 1972, and membership obliged the state to enact equality and maternity protection laws. For example, the Anti-Discrimination (Pay) Act 1974 and the Employment Equality Act 1977, both introduced by Labour TD Michael O'Leary as Minister for Labour, were initiated due to the necessity to comply with EC directives on equal pay and discrimination in employment, respectively.

However, the most notable social policy failure of the coalition was on contraception. In July 1974, on the initiative of the Labour members of government, a bill was introduced to permit the sale of contraception to married persons only. Mary Robinson commented that this highly restrictive legislation would 'to some extent make us the laughing stock of Europe'.[11] However, despite its highly restrictive provisions, the bill was opposed by the Catholic Church, and was sensationally defeated in the Dáil when Taoiseach Liam Cosgrave and six Fine Gael deputies voted against their own government's measure.

Similarly restrictive contraception legislation was eventually passed in 1979 under the Fianna Fáil government which took office in 1977, led by Taoiseach Charles J. Haughey who infamously described his bill as an 'Irish solution to an Irish problem' – it allowed married couples access to contraception upon prescription; enough contraceptive use to keep some campaigners happy, but not to offend the Catholic doctrine that sex should only take place within marriage.

Ailbhe Smyth has described the years between 1974 and 1977, which coincided with the term of office of the Fine Gael–Labour coalition, as marking a period of high energy and radical action within the feminist movement in Ireland. Between 1977 and 1983, she suggests that a consolidation of the movement took place, with the establishment of the women's right to choose campaign, and of rape crisis centres and groups offering support to women who had suffered violence in the home.[12]

The years between 1983 and 1990, however, Smyth sees as marking a succession of notorious political defeats for the women's movement. Labour was in power with Fine Gael between 1981 and 1982, and again from November 1982 to 1987, yet few gains were made for the 'liberal agenda' or for women's rights during those years. Some further liberalisation of contraceptive law occurred, with the 1985 legislative reform introduced by the Fine Gael–Labour coalition government, allowing a range of different outlets to sell condoms to anyone over the age of eighteen without a prescription. But only in 1992 was the sale of condoms finally deregulated, so that they may now be sold over the counter and in condom machines without any minimum age restriction.

These were highly volatile years politically, marked by a series of difficult elections. During this period, one defeat with significant lasting effect for Irish society was the 1983 referendum, which passed the Eighth Amendment to the Constitution (Article 40.3.3), giving the foetus an equal right to life with the pregnant woman. The campaign preceding this referendum starkly highlighted the tensions between conservative and liberal movements within Labour.

In 1979, the Women's Right to Choose group demanded the legalisation of abortion. Following the launch of this campaign, Linda Connolly writes that:

> The counter right then made itself visible and increasingly mobilised … by diverting the abortion debate into the legal/constitutional arena – an area which required extensive resources and expertise. Tactically, it aimed to block the women's movement from providing its services by actively campaigning for a constitutional referendum on the 'right to life of the unborn' …[13]

The anti-abortion campaign, which saw a referendum as necessary to prevent the Supreme Court from developing a right to abortion based on privacy rights (as the US Supreme Court had done in the 1973 case of *Roe v. Wade*), successfully played one political party against another to win promises from the government to hold a referendum.

The Garret FitzGerald-led Fine Gael–Labour coalition fell on 27 January 1982, and the incoming Charles Haughey-led Fianna Fáil government promised to hold the anti-abortion referendum. Labour Party chairperson Michael D. Higgins, Senator Mary Robinson and others in the party made known their opposition to this idea early on, and the LWNC was also strongly opposed to any such referendum. However, the PLP, which discussed the question in June 1982, was divided. Seven of the fifteen TDs elected in February 1982 had signed the so-called 'pro-life' pledge sent to all candidates before the election. Three of them, including Dick Spring, later changed their minds, but as John Horgan wrote 'this left a hard core of four who were prepared to support a constitutional amendment'.[14]

Dick Spring, who had succeeded Michael O'Leary as Labour leader, then became Tánaiste in a new coalition led by Garret FitzGerald following another election on 25 November 1982. This 'bizarre sequence of events' resulted in the Eighth Amendment (as it became known) being put to the people on 7 September 1983 by the new government – a Fine Gael–Labour government, many of whose members were strongly opposed to the referendum and indeed campaigned against it; the membership of the Labour Committee Against the Amendment included Mary Robinson, Barry Desmond and Ruairi Quinn.[15]

The bitter and angry referendum campaign has been described as a 'second partitioning of Ireland'.[16] Despite the serious divisions within the government, the referendum was ultimately passed by 67 per cent to 33 per cent on a low turnout of 54.6 per cent.

Another pressing issue for liberal reformers in the 1980s was the need to legalise divorce. Again, there were divisions within Labour over this. Horgan writes that the PLP dragged its feet for years on developing a divorce policy, causing Mary Robinson such great frustration that she published her own bill on divorce.[17] Her work on the issue, and the pressure brought by others within the party, eventually persuaded the coalition government to put a divorce referendum to the people on 25 June 1986. This was defeated by 63 per cent to 36 per cent, after a campaign marked by little or no preparation by the government for the aggressive tactics of the anti-divorce lobby. As Ray Kavanagh wrote, this lobby, by raising the 'unlikely spectre of middle-aged married men deserting their loyal and hardworking wives in droves', 'shamelessly exploited' the 'vulnerability and dependent status of many women'. He notes the infamous but influential statement by Alice Glenn, then a Fine Gael TD, that 'women voting for divorce would be like turkeys voting for Christmas'.[18]

The 1980s are thus widely seen as a period of political conservatism in Irish society and, of course, also a time of economic recession, with high unemployment and large numbers emigrating; and with little progressive change initiated by any government. However, this had begun to change by the late 1980s and indeed the 1990s represent a very different political landscape. In particular, it is widely considered that a significant turning point occurred in November 1990 with the election of Mary Robinson, the former Senator and Labour-nominated candidate, as President, after a lively and upbeat political campaign in which she saw off the Fianna Fáil candidate, Brian Lenihan, who had been expected to win comfortably. Robinson's impressive track record as a campaigner on liberal issues like contraception and gay rights had been seen by many as an obstacle to her success; her election can be seen as marking a real turning point in public opinion on such issues.

Another such turning point took place less than two years later, in February 1992, when it emerged that the state had sought to prevent a fourteen-year old pregnant rape victim from leaving Ireland with her parents to obtain an abortion. The Attorney General, Harry Whelehan, was granted an injunction by the High Court in what became known as the 'X case'. Judge Costello had interpreted the words of Article 40.3.3 to mean that the state would be obliged to prevent any pregnant girl or woman from travelling abroad if the purpose of the journey was to terminate her pregnancy. With this case, the nightmare scenario predicted by those who had campaigned against the 1983 amendment came to pass, and a pregnant child had effectively been imprisoned in her own country. Political uproar ensued, with popular outrage at the notion that this young girl might be prevented from travelling abroad for an abortion, and thus forced to proceed with an unwanted pregnancy against her own wishes and those of her parents.

In the face of mounting public pressure, the Fianna Fáil government offered to pay the legal costs of an appeal by the girl's parents to the Supreme Court. The appeal was heard within a matter of weeks, and the Supreme Court reversed the earlier decision, allowing the girl to travel. The Court found that because the girl was suicidal, the continuation of the pregnancy would have threatened her right to life – thus, the two rights were in direct conflict, and in such situations, the Court ruled the right to life of the girl should prevail. However, despite the decision in X's favour, the corollary of the court's test was that where a woman was not facing a threat to her life, then not only would it be illegal for her to have an abortion in Ireland, but she could also be prevented from travelling abroad to avail of legal abortion elsewhere.

When this effect of the judgment became clear, a massive campaign was launched by the pro-choice movement. As a result, the outgoing Fianna Fáil government put three amendments to the Constitution before the people on 25 November 1992, on the same date as the general election. The aim of the first (known as the 'substantive issue' amendment) was to rule out suicide as grounds for a lawful abortion, while allowing abortion on grounds of physical risk to the life of the pregnant woman. The second amendment guaranteed the freedom to travel abroad, and the third allowed for the provision of information on services lawfully available in other states. The 'substantive issue' amendment was rejected by the people; but the travel and information referenda were passed on the same date, in keeping with the 'no, yes, yes' position taken by those on the liberal side. Labour had taken a clear stance in support of this position, as Kennelly and Ward have written, 'pushed considerably by its National Women's Council'. The recently formed Democratic Left party also campaigned on the liberal side.[19]

Dick Spring, the Labour leader, then became Tánaiste, with Albert Reynolds as Taoiseach in the new Fianna Fáil–Labour government. After the dramatic fall of that coalition in 1994, following controversy over the failure to extradite the convicted child abuser Fr Brendan Smyth, a new government was formed without an election. Spring remained as Tánaiste in the 'Rainbow Coalition' with Fine Gael and Democratic Left. In 1993, the government established for the first time, at the instigation of the Labour Party, a Department of Equality and Law Reform, the aim of which was to oversee legal change in the area of equality. Indeed, Labour in opposition in the preceding years had actively promoted an equality agenda, as Quinn writes, 'not just on the general issue of freedom of information and ethics in government legislation, but also on the decriminalisation of homosexuality'.

Labour TD Mervyn Taylor was appointed as minister in the new department, and during the five years he was minister he 'enacted seventeen acts in family law reform, as well as two major pieces of equality legislation'.[20] One progressive family law change that Taylor sought to make was defeated, with the striking down in January 1994 by the Supreme Court of legislation that would have given automatic co-ownership rights in the family home to dependent spouses[21].

The most radical piece of family law reform, however, came on 24

November 1995, when a second referendum to permit divorce was put to the people, again at Labour's instigation. This was finally passed, albeit by the slimmest of majorities (50.28 per cent for to 49.72 per cent against, a majority of just over 9,000 voters). This time, as Quinn writes,[22] careful preparation was carried out to ensure that the different legal complexities around property division that had scuppered the 1986 referendum were resolved in advance of the vote. Moreover, the wording of the amendment provided that couples could not divorce unless they had lived apart for at least four out of the previous five years (Article 41.3.2) – no 'quickie divorces' permitted. In the same year, the government introduced the Regulation of Information (Services Outside the State for Termination of Pregnancies) Act, 1995, providing for the conditions under which information on abortion could be legally provided – although its provisions were criticised by the pro-choice campaign as being unduly restrictive for doctors and counsellors. More progressive laws passed in the 1990s while Labour was in government included 'laws liberalising the sale of contraceptives, and more far-reaching equality legislation, developed by the new Department and introduced to replace the Equal Pay and Employment Equality Acts of the 1970s'.[23] These equality laws were declared unconstitutional by the Supreme Court, but re-enacted by the subsequent Government in 1998 and 2000.

Other initiatives taken by Labour in government during the 1990s included significant changes in education policy. When she became Minister for Education in 1993, Labour Party TD Niamh Bhreathnach attempted to reduce the control of religious denominations over the education system through legislative reform of the composition of boards of management of schools. However, her moves towards a more secular system were strongly resisted by what Andy Pollak, religious affairs correspondent of *The Irish Times*, described as an 'unprecedented alliance' of the main Christian Churches together with the Muslim community. Although the Education Act that Minister Bhreathnach introduced brought about major reforms to the education system, it preserves the concept of 'patronage' upon which the denominational structures of the primary school network nationally are based.

Following the defeat of the Rainbow Coalition in the election of 1997, Fianna Fáil returned to power and continued to govern over three successive terms, with a series of smaller parties, until the general election of February 2011. Over those years, Labour in opposition, under the leadership successively of Ruairi Quinn, Pat Rabbitte and Eamon Gilmore, developed more radical social policies on a range of issues. In particular, at the party conference in Cork in September 2001, the LWNC succeeded in persuading a majority of members to vote in favour of pro-choice policy. In a further referendum on abortion that followed, held on 6 March 2002, Labour played a significant role in mobilising voters to defeat the amendment. If passed, its effect would have been to reverse the decision in the X case, by ruling out suicide risk as a ground for abortion; effectively a rerun of the 'substantive issue' referendum defeated in November 1992. Following extensive campaigning by Labour, the Irish Family Planning Association, and a combination of different groups under the common name 'ANV' (Alliance for a No Vote), the referendum was ultimately defeated, albeit on a tiny majority – just as with the 1995 divorce referendum. Turnout was just 43 per cent of the electorate, of which 49.6 per cent voted yes while 50.4 per cent voted no.

Unfortunately, while the defeat of the referendum was important symbolically, demonstrating that even the combined power of the Catholic Church, the anti-abortion movement and the Fianna Fáil party could not win over changing public opinion on this issue, defeat did not represent any real progress for the pro-choice movement; it simply stopped the clock turning backwards. The difference it made to the reality of crisis pregnancy for Irish women was negligible. Since then, thousands of women have continued to travel abroad for abortion, yet no legislation has been introduced to provide for the criteria for the carrying-out of lawful X-case abortions.

On a different social policy issue, but again one in which pregnancy-related matters played a strong role, a constitutional referendum was held in June 2004 by the Fianna Fáil-led government to amend Article 2 of the Constitution. The purpose of this was to deny automatic citizenship rights to those children born in Ireland to so-called 'non-national' parents. The amendment was justified by the government on the basis that the Masters of the maternity hospitals had complained that too many 'non-national' mothers were giving birth in their hospitals. Labour again took a courageous stance and mobilised against this referendum, during what was also a European and local election campaign; but by playing on people's fears about immigration in an insidious way, the government won the vote by a substantial majority (79 per cent for to 21 per cent against).

During the years in opposition, Labour also developed progressive policy on women's participation in politics following an internal report of a commission on women's participation in 2005, which recommended among other things the adoption of a gender quota model to ensure the selection of more women candidates. Labour in opposition also developed progressive policies on gay rights; Labour's Brendan Howlin introduced the first private members' bill in the Dáil to legalise civil partnerships for gay couples in 2006 (the Civil Unions bill), following a similar private members' bill introduced by Senator David Norris in 2004, but some years before the Fianna Fáil–Green Party government finally passed civil partnership legislation in 2010. During the debates on the government legislation, Labour TDs and senators supported the bill but spoke of the need to go further and recognise gay marriage – a campaign still ongoing.

Social policy issues, however, were generally relegated to second place during the first decade of the twenty-first century in Ireland; the first ten years of the new millennium were dominated by a national economic boom, which finally collapsed in 2008 with massive banking failures, a dramatic property crash and an ensuing recession. With the economy still appearing to prosper in 2007, the general election of June that year had been won again by Fianna Fáil, who had led the previous two governments; but from 2007–11 they required the support of the Green Party and others.

In the general election of February 2011, finally, the Fianna Fáil-led government was defeated, having justifiably carried the blame for the banking and financial collapse; and for the resultant transfer of economic sovereignty to the International Monetary Fund, the EU and the European Central Bank in November 2010. The programme for government of the incoming Fine Gael–Labour coalition, published in March 2011, is understandably dominated by economic policy considerations, but it also contains various important commitments on social policy issues. In particular, it commits to introducing legislation requiring political parties to select more women candidates (now introduced as the Electoral (Amendment) (Political Funding) Bill 2011. It also envisages a constitutional amendment to delete outdated references to 'women in the home' from the Constitution. Disappointingly, there is no commitment to legislate to provide for the circumstances in which abortion may be carried out in accordance with the X-case test, but an expert group to examine the issue has been established following the December 2010 decision of the European Court of Human Rights in a case taken by three women (*A, B and C v. Ireland*), in which Irish abortion law was ruled to be in breach of the European Convention on Human Rights.

On education policy, there is likely to be significant change under the new government, and potentially a move away from the denominational basis of the primary school system, with the appointment as Minister for

Education of Labour TD Ruairi Quinn. Shortly after his appointment, the minister gave recognition to Educate Together, the multi-denominational school movement, as a patron for secondary schools. In the primary sector, a National Forum on Patronage and Pluralism has been established to examine how best to ensure that parental choice as to religion may be respected within the educational system.

As this brief review of the role of the Labour Party in achieving liberal reform in Ireland has shown, Labour has not had a consistently progressive record on social issues. In the early years of the party's existence, the influence of the Catholic Church caused the party to adopt conservative positions generally. Even since then, at key times during the party's history, serious internal divisions over social policy issues have caused immense tensions and, more importantly, have caused delays and setbacks in achieving real change during the periods when the party has been in government. The tensions identified in earlier decades remain evident within the party's Oireachtas members, the PLP, but during the fourteen years in opposition from 1997 to 2011, the party has developed a more distinctly radical social agenda than at any time previously. Whether that agenda can or will be implemented within the lifetime of the current coalition government remains to be seen.

15. The Second Century of Labour

Eamon Gilmore

In marking our first 100 years, the Labour Party has an opportunity not just to reflect on our origins and development, and to assess our record of accomplishment, but also to engage in serious debate about our future purpose and direction. Reflecting on the past and looking to the future should go hand in hand.

I want our centenary to be a moment for appreciation of what has gone before and real reflection about the future. How better to ground that discussion than by producing a book looking at the history of the party through a series of different lenses? As the idea for this project developed, it quickly became evident that a book about the Labour Party would succeed only if the project itself was undertaken independently of the party. The debate about our future must be open, frank and honest, both about what we have achieved and what we should seek to achieve in the future. I believe this volume and its several contributors have been true to that ethic.

Hence, my contribution comes at the end of this volume and is focused not on the past, but on the future.

I feel immensely privileged to lead the Labour Party. I am deeply conscious that I walk in the footsteps both of great historic figures such as James Connolly and Tom Johnson, and of colleagues such as Dick Spring, Ruairi Quinn and Pat Rabbitte, whose contributions to the cause of Labour and the cause of Ireland are rightly and widely admired. I am deeply proud of the party, of its role in shaping Ireland's story during the twentieth century, and of the thousands of members who are part of it, and who give unstinting public service through the party.

Some of the contributions in this book deliver decidedly mixed verdicts on Labour, particularly in its early years. Certainly it is true that the party did not take the same path or have the same electoral successes as similar parties in the UK, or Sweden, or even Russia. Ours is a very different story. In looking back at the path we have taken, some critical moments stand out, such as the decision not to contest the 1918 election. It is also important, however, to weigh up the underlying social, economic and cultural factors that influenced or hindered the growth of the party in its early years. These included Ireland's limited industrialisation, the hostility of the dominant Church, and the overriding dominance of the national question. All of these made it more difficult for Labour to establish itself. Indeed, it is striking that, as Rónán O'Brien points out, the party we know now, grew up as one of three potential Labour parties that existed at the time of our foundation. This also helps to explain why, for much of our existence, Labour did not manage to grasp the mantle of being a truly national party – the natural vehicle for expression of the aspirations of a critical mass of working people. Whereas social democrats in the UK and Sweden were able to make this leap, in Ireland it was Fianna Fáil who, for significant periods, filled this role.

While it is true that Labour did not build up the electoral hegemony of our colleagues in Sweden, or establish ourselves as a party that would naturally lead a government as in the UK, those are not the only measures of Labour's impact on Irish society. In the last thirty years in particular, Ireland has been transformed into a far more open, tolerant and liberal society, through a series of political changes that were often led by Labour. Labour in those years did not always have to be in government to have an impact. Many of the campaigns that led to change in Ireland were peopled by party members. Labour was a major driver of reform through our campaigning as well as through our parliamentary activities and our role in government.

One of the most important lessons of this book, therefore, is that we must be clear in defining our own metrics of success. We will always seek to learn from the experiences of other countries, but we should not be defined by them.

Labour enters its second century in a stronger position than at any time in our history. We have the largest political representation that we have ever had at all levels of government – the greatest number of councillors, Dáil deputies, senators and MEPs. In the crowning achievement of our most successful ever year (and in what I readily admit was the happiest moment of my political life), our candidate, Michael D. Higgins, was elected President of Ireland. In the general election of 2011, we finally made the historic breakthrough of becoming the second largest party in the Dáil, and we go into 2012 as part of a strong and successful government.

Becoming the second largest party in the state is an important achievement, but it should not be the summit of our ambition. We still have work to do, if we are to establish ourselves fully as a national party, and as a natural party of government. My ambition is that Labour should become the largest party in the state, and lead a government; that Labour would be seen by people across Ireland, from all regions and from all backgrounds, as being their natural political home – the party that best expresses their political values and aspirations and which, in government, will build the kind of Ireland they want for their children.

To some that ambition may seem unrealistic. So be it. When I first suggested that Labour should make Irish politics a three-horse race, competing on equal terms with Fianna Fáil and Fine Gael, that idea was greeted with more than a little scepticism. Today it is a goal that we have already surpassed. Our challenge is to build on that electoral success, to build the party further, both organisationally and in terms of its standing among the Irish people.

What must also be clear, however, is that our goals as a party are not just defined in terms of electoral success. In fact, our aims and our reason for being are about the kind of Ireland that our children will inherit. One might argue that this puts us in a particularly difficult position, as a progressive party in government at a time of crisis, when progress is extremely difficult to achieve. I take the opposite view. Certainly, it is true that resources are heavily constrained. Yet it is from periods of crisis that new directions are set. Labour must be in government to fix the immediate problems facing Ireland and to shape the future direction of our country.

In 2011 when the new government was formed, Ireland was facing an unprecedented crisis in our economy. There was a jobs crisis, a banking crisis and a fiscal crisis. There was also a reputational crisis, in that the perception of Ireland abroad had reached an unprecedented low. In those circumstances, it was Labour's clear duty, both to the country and to those who elected us, to participate in a national government that would find solutions to these problems, to put employment creation at the heart of the strategy for recovery and to seek renegotiation of the EU/IMF deal.

We continue to work our way through these problems, with some success. That is the great task that we have taken on at a time of crisis, but it is also an opportunity. It was from the slowly grinding failure of the 1950s that Whitaker and Lemass were able to construct a new direction, characterised by economic, social and political openness, a direction that defined Ireland for the generation that followed. Now we, who are confronted by an even greater challenge, have the chance to shape the direction for the next chapter in our history.

We have to do that without the comfort of pre-packed intellectual templates. There is no model for how to fix an economic problem such as the one Ireland is now experiencing. We cannot simply reach out to the traditional social democratic toolkit for solutions, particularly since social democracy itself is going through a period of critical self-examination. More than ever, we have to look behind old policy manuals, to the core values on which social democracy has always been based.

The people who founded the Labour Party came from thatched cottages and tenements. Connolly, Johnson and O'Casey knew what it was to be poor. They grew to adulthood in a world being transformed by the technological revolution of the industrial age, and in a time of empire. Within this system of global capitalism, they found themselves defined, not by who they were, but by the circumstances of their class and birth. Both by instinct and by intellectual conviction, they believed that the system within which they lived could be changed. They believed in building a fairer world, where who you were mattered more than who your parents were, where everyone would be entitled to a decent standard of living that would banish poverty and disease, where education would be available to everyone, and where old age could be approached without the fear of destitution. Above all, they believed that solidarity was both a means to achieving this better world and a characteristic of it. They were naturally and instinctively internationalist, believing that people like them in other countries shared their goal of replacing the class-ridden, unequal and unfair system in which they lived. And they had courage in spades – the courage to stand up to those who wielded vastly greater power than they, to look them in the eye, and to demand a fairer deal.

Today, of course, times have changed. We live now in a country that is not a predominantly agricultural cog in an imperial machine, but a small, open and technologically advanced economy in a global trading system. We do not confront the extremes of poverty and disadvantage that could be seen on the streets of any Irish town in 1912. We have made advances in education, housing, healthcare and social protection that would have astounded the people who founded the party. Yet, some things remain the same. We continue to live in a world defined by technological change, in a global trading system where the distribution of economic power is far from fair, and far from equal. We continue to believe in the liberating power of education as a fundamental force for fairness in our society. We continue to believe that, contrary to the ideological individualism that has dominated world affairs for a generation, solidarity is both a characteristic of a civilised society and a means of building it. And we remain committed to the ideal that we can and should make common cause with those in other countries who share our progressive values.

We live at a time of tremendous change. The system of unfettered global capitalism that brought the world to the edge of another great depression has been fundamentally discredited. It is by no means clear what will replace it. It seems reasonable to expect that the power of global finance will be reined in, in some manner, and that the advanced economies in particular will seek greater control over the economic forces that threatened to overwhelm us all. Yet, the very idea of this kind of regulation remains contested, and the Left has yet to coalesce fully around a coherent set of ideas about what that kind of regulation might look like. Indeed, it is a striking fact that in Europe, the immediate electoral experience of the left during the crisis created by the ideology of the right has been extremely negative. Socialist and social democratic parties have been losing ground, not gaining. Part of what Labour in Ireland has to do is to play our role in refreshing and renewing the European Left, and to work with our sister parties to define the means by which we will do what it is that the term 'social democracy' means – applying democratic principles in the social and economic sphere.

Today, the immediate challenge is job creation. The greatest source of injustice in Ireland is the reality that too many people are unemployed, or are forced to leave because they cannot find work. The cause of this problem and, indeed, of the crisis in the public finances, is the catastrophic loss of output in the Irish economy. Between 2008 and 2010, the total value of goods and services produced in the Irish economy fell by 12 per cent. That activity, and the jobs and income that have been lost, must be replaced, but replaced with a sustainable economic model, where once again Ireland creates goods and services of real value that allow us to pay our way in the world. That is no small challenge. It requires us to rescue the economy from its immediate crisis and, at the same time, wean it off its dependence on property. This, in turn, requires quite significant tactical decisions, such as the need for a Strategic Investment Strategy, focused on building up firms and infrastructure that support a high-value exporting economy. It requires a strategic reconsideration of our position in the global trading system, and a shift in our focus towards the new centres of gravity in the global trading system in the emerging economies.

As we build this economy, we must be clear also that the economy exists to serve people and not the other way around. We need more and better jobs that will support decent living standards and a fairer society. Far from being a drain on economic efficiency, fairness and a focus on decent living standards are inextricably linked to the kind of innovative, adaptable and outward-focused economy that we seek to create.

There is also a challenge for progressive politics to encapsulate for voters, in practical ways, what fairness looks like in the twenty-first century. Fairness is one of those concepts that can be universally accepted, while simultaneously being interpreted in radically different ways.

Yet, that fire which propelled Connolly, Johnson and O'Casey – a society where hard work and merit, rather than birth, determines your fate – is still, I would argue, the kernel of what the majority instinctively call fairness.

The barriers to fairness facing the founding generation of the party were crystal clear. In the days of universal education, a relatively comprehensive social protection architecture and, in theory, universal access to hospital care, they can be less so. For some, fairness will begin and end with the question of redistribution. But while progressive taxation is necessary to fund the services that allow our people to live full and dignified lives, it is the means by which we reach our objective, not the end.

I believe that fairness is about liberating people. Not liberating people from the fetters of the state, as some would have it, but liberating them from arbitrary obstacles like background or class or income to reach their full potential. The question we have to ask ourselves is, what are the modern-day obstacles to a society based on merit?

One way of drilling down into this is to ask why universal provision – say, of education – does not lead to universal outcomes. We know instinctively that a child who arrives in school with only a handful of words, or an empty stomach, is already disadvantaged when it comes to benefiting from universal, taxpayer-funded education. So if fairness is not an inevitable by-product of universalism, we need to ask ourselves how we can spend our money to produce genuine equality of opportunity. One way is to look more closely at life chances from a very early age – and to focus on supporting children whose circumstances currently put them too far behind the starting line.

Universal healthcare is another key objective of progressive politics and, almost without exception, has been the legacy of social democratic governments in Europe in the post-war period. However, these systems were built at a time when citizens' relationship with the state was different – and more accepting of conformity – than it is today. The Labour–Fine Gael government formed in March 2011 is the first to have, as its objective, a single-tier health system based on universal health insurance. The challenge for us in achieving that objective will be to find ways of meeting, within the framework of universal provision, today's citizens' expectations of individual choice.

Indeed, the changes that have taken place in people's lifestyles, in family life, and in how we consume goods and services, mean that this expectation of individual choice and aspiration cannot be ignored in the reform of other public services.

The 100th anniversary of the foundation of our party is not just the end of one century – it is the beginning of another. We begin the second century of Labour in a stronger position than ever before. We can take pride in our past, in what we have achieved and in the role we played in shaping modern Ireland. Yet, our work is still not done. At this time of crisis in the history of our country, our first priority is to rescue the economy, and create employment and opportunities for our people. But other great battles also lie ahead, to build the Ireland that our children deserve.

Notes

Chapter 1. **A Various and Contentious Country: Ireland in 1912** by William Murphy

1. R. F. Foster, *W. B. Yeats: A Life. Volume 1* (Oxford, 1997), p. 494; Diarmaid Ferriter, *The Transformation of Ireland 1900–2000* (London, 2004), p. 97.

2. Emmet O'Connor, *A Labour History of Ireland 1824–1960* (Dublin, 1992), p. 82; Arthur Mitchell, *Labour in Irish Politics, 1890–1930* (Dublin, 1974), p. 35.

3. Eugene McNulty, *The Ulster Literary Theatre and the Northern Revival* (Cork, 2008), pp. 186–207; Laura E. Lyons, 'Of Orangemen and Green Theatres: The Ulster Literary Theatre's Regional Nationalism', Stephen Watt, Eileen Morgan, and Shakir Mustafa (eds), *A Century of Irish Drama: Widening the Stage* (Bloomington, 2000), pp. 43–5.

4. *Cork Examiner*, 19 February 1912; Paul Bew, *Ideology and the Irish Question: Ulster Unionism and Irish Nationalism 1912–1916* (Oxford, 1994), p. 71.

5. Bew, *op. cit.*; Alan O'Day, *Irish Home Rule 1867–1921* (Manchester, 1998); Alvin Jackson, *Home Rule: An Irish History 1800–2000* (London, 2003); Michael Wheatley, *Nationalism and the Irish Party: Provincial Ireland 1910–1916* (Oxford, 2005).

6. Timothy Bowman, *Carson's Army: The Ulster Volunteer Force, 1910–1922* (Manchester, 2007), pp. 18–24.

7. O'Day, *op. cit.*, pp. 251–3.

8. *Irish Catholic Directory* (1913), p. 515; *Irish Independent*, 9 March 1912.

9. *The Irish Times*, 2 July 1912; Bew, *op. cit.*, p. 56; A. C. Hepburn, *Catholic Belfast and Nationalist Ireland in the Era of Joe Devlin 1871–1934* (Oxford, 2008), p. 142.

10. Patrick Maume, *The Long Gestation: Irish Nationalist Life 1891–1918* (Dublin, 1999), pp. 134–5; Wheatley, *op. cit.*, p. 168.

11. Neal Garnham, *Association Football and Society in Pre-partition Ireland* (Belfast, 2004), pp. 125–7.

12. Mary E. Daly, *The First Department: A History of the Department of Agriculture* (Dublin, 2002), p. 50.

13. Matthew Kelly, '"Parnell's Old Brigade": the Redmondite-Fenian nexus in the 1890s', *Irish Historical Studies, xxxiii, 130* (2002), pp. 209–232; James McConnel, '"Fenians at Westminster": the Edwardian Irish Parliamentary Party and the legacy of the New Departure', *Irish Historical Studies, xxxiv, 133* (2004), pp. 42–64.

14. Wheatley, *op. cit.*, p. 256–7.

15. William Murphy, 'Narratives of Confinement: Fenians, Prisons and Writing, 1867–1916', Fearghal McGarry and James McConnel (eds), *The Black Hand of Republicanism: Fenianism in Modern Ireland* (Dublin, 2009), pp. 169–70.

16. M. J. Kelly, *The Fenian Ideal and Irish Nationalism* (Woodbridge, 2006), pp. 200–4.

17. Marnie Hay, *Bulmer Hobson and the Nationalist Movement in Twentieth-Century Ireland* (Manchester, 2009), p. 103.

18. Michael Laffan, *The Resurrection of Ireland: The Sinn Féin Party 1916–1923* (Cambridge, 1999), pp. 21–32.

19. *Irish Independent*, 16 January 1912.

20. *Irish Worker*, 20 and 27 January 1912; Mitchell, *op. cit.*, p. 29; Emmet Larkin, *James Larkin: Irish Labour Leader 1876–1947* (London, 1965), pp. 102–3.

21. *Irish Worker*, 20 January 1912.

22. Marie O'Neill, 'Sarah Cecilia Harrison: Artist and City Councillor', *Dublin Historical Record, 42:2* (1989), pp. 69–71.

23. Mary E. Daly, *Dublin – The Deposed Capital: A Social and Economic History 1860–1914* (Cork, 1984), pp. 63–4, 103–16.

24. Leeann Lane, *Rosamond Jacob: Third Person Singular* (Dublin, 2010), pp. 55–7, 83–4.

25. Martin Pugh, *The Pankhursts* (London, 2002); June Purvis, *Emmeline Pankhurst: A Biography* (London, 2002).

26. Prisoner Record Sheets in File A, Box 1, and File C, Box 1, in Suffragette Files in GPB, NAI.

27. Rosemary Cullen Owens, *Smashing Times: A History of the Irish Women's Suffrage Movement 1889–1922* (Dublin, 1984), pp. 50–3.

28. Cullen Owens, *op. cit.*, pp. 57–8.

29. William Murphy, 'Suffragettes and the Transformation of Political Imprisonment in Ireland, 1912–1914', Louise Ryan and Margaret Ward (eds), *Irish Women and the Vote: Becoming Citizens* (Dublin, 2007), pp. 114–35

30. Francis Sheehy-Skeffington to Hanna Sheehy-Skeffington, 28 July 1912, in Ms 40,463/3, Sheehy-Skeffington Papers, National Library of Ireland (NLI).

31. Penny Holloway and Terry Cradden, 'The Irish Trade Union Congress and Working Women, 1894–1914', *Saothar*, 23 (1998), p. 55.

32. *Irish Independent*, 30 May 1912; Donal Nevin, *James Connolly: A Full Life* (Dublin,

2005), p. 400; Frances Clarke, 'Mary Galway', James McGuire and James Quinn (eds), *Dictionary of Irish Biography, 4* (Cambridge, 2009), pp. 17–8.

33. *Irish Independent*, 29 May 1912; Maria Luddy, 'Working Women, Trade Unionism and Politics in Ireland 1830–1945', Fintan Lane and Donal Ó Drisceoil (eds), *Politics and the Irish Working Class, 1830–1945* (Basingstoke, 2005), p. 51.

34. Larkin, *op. cit.*, pp. 106–13.

35. *Irish Ecclesiastical Record*, xxxi (1912), p. 15.

36. *Irish Catholic Directory* (1913), pp. 510–11.

37. Canon P. A. Sheehan, *Miriam Lucas* (Dublin, 1912); Ruth Fleischmann, *Catholic Nationalism in the Irish Revival: A Study of Canon Sheehan 1852–1913* (London, 1997), pp. 122–7.

38. *Irish Independent*, 10 October 1912; Maurice Curtis, *The Splendid Cause: The Catholic Action Movement in Irish in the Twentieth Century* (Dublin, 2009), pp. 37–49.

39. Curtis, *op. cit.*, pp. 26–37; Peter Martin, *Censorship in the Two Irelands 1922–1939* (Dublin, 2006), pp. 5–6.

40. *Irish Independent*, 5 January 1912.

41. *Ibid.*, 19 February and 19 April 1912.

42. *Ibid.*, 2 July 1912.

43. *Catholic Bulletin*, II:2 (February 1912).

44. Richard Ellmann, *James Joyce* (Oxford, 1959), p. 339.

45. Brendan Grimes, *Irish Carnegie Libraries: A Catalogue and Architectural History* (Dublin, 1998), pp. 25–30 and 260–1.

46. Marc Zimmermann, *The History of Dublin Cinemas* (Dublin, 2007), pp. 136–7 and 181–2.

47. Kevin Rockett, Luke Gibbons and John Hill (eds), *Cinema and Ireland* (Syracuse, 1988), p. 6; Diarmaid Ferriter, *op. cit.*, p. 103.

48. William Nolan (ed.), *The History of Dublin GAA, I* (Dublin, 2005), p. 97.

49. Mark Duncan, 'The Camera and the Gael: The Early Photography of the GAA, 1884–1914', Mike Cronin, William Murphy and Paul Rouse (eds), *The Gaelic Athletic Association 1884–2009* (Dublin, 2009), p. 103.

50. Garnham, *Association Football and Society in Pre-partition Ireland*, p. 105.

51. Cormac Ó Grada, *Ireland: A New Economic History 1780–1939* (Oxford, 1994), p. 213.

52. W. E. Vaughan and A. J. Fitzpatrick, *Irish Historical Statistics: Population 1821–1971* (Dublin, 1978), pp. 260–3.

53. Vaughan and Fitzpatrick, *op. cit.*, pp. 36–7.

54. Ó Grada, *Ireland: A New Economic History 1780–1939*, p. 295.

55. Vaughan and Fitzpatrick, *op. cit.*, pp. 28–9, 32–6, 40–1.

56. Eamon O'Flaherty, *Irish Historic Towns Atlas No. 21: Limerick* (Dublin, 2010), p. 10.

57. Ó Grada, *Ireland: A New Economic History 1780–1939*, p. 241.

58. Daly, *op. cit.*, p. 295.

59. *Ibid.*, p. 243.

60. Greta Jones, *'Captain of all these men of death': The History of Tuberculosis in Nineteenth and Twentieth Century Ireland* (Amsterdam, 2001), pp. 101 and 104.

61. Jones, *op. cit.*, pp. 110–3.

62. Cormac Ó Grada, '"The Greatest Blessing of All": The Old Age Pension in Ireland', *Past & Present, 175:1* (2002), pp. 124–61; Mel Cousins, 'The Creation of Association: The National Insurance Act, 1911 and Approved Societies in Ireland', Jennifer Kelly and R.V. Comerford (eds), *Associational Culture in Ireland and Abroad* (Dublin, 2010), pp. 155–64.

63. Ó Grada, 'The Greatest Blessing of All', pp. 126–8.

64. Cousins, 'The Creation of Association', pp. 156–9.

65. *Irish Independent*, 9 December 1912. Burke was later elected a TD for Clare between 1937 and 1951. See Lawrence William White, 'Thomas Burke', James McGuire and James Quinn (eds), *Dictionary of Irish Biography, 2* (Cambridge, 2009), pp. 61–2. Catherine Cox, 'The Medical Marketplace and Medical Tradition in Nineteenth Century Ireland', Ronnie Moore and Stuart McClean (eds), *Folk Healing And Health Care Practices In Britain and Ireland: Stethoscopes, Wands and Crystals* (Oxford, 2010), pp 55-79.

66. Ferriter, *op. cit.*, p. 63.

67. Fergus Campbell, *Land and Revolution: Nationalist Politics in the West of Ireland 1891–1921* (Oxford, 2005), p. 91.

68. Campbell, *op. cit.*, pp. 85–123 and 226–85.

69. Conor Kostick, *Revolution in Ireland: Popular Militancy 1917–1923* (Cork, 2009), pp. 118–24.

70. David Fitzpatrick, 'The Disappearance of the Irish Agricultural Labourer, 1841–1912', *Irish Economic and Social History, vii* (1980), p. 81.

71. Enda McKay, 'The Housing of the Rural Labourer, 1883–1916', *Saothar, 17* (1992), pp. 33–7.

72. *Irish Independent*, 27 and 31 August 1912.

73. L. P. Curtis, Jr, 'Ireland in 1914', *A New History of Ireland, VI: Ireland Under the Union 1870–1912* (Oxford, 1989), p. 188.

74. James Joyce, *Dubliners* (London, 1992), p. 225.

Chapter 2. **A Divided House – The Irish Trades Union Congress and the origins of the Irish Labour Party** by Rónán O'Brien

1. *Irish Trades Union Congress Report (ITUC Report)*, 1912.

2. *Ibid.*, 1912.

3. Brian *Farrell*, '*Labour* and *Political Revolution*', Donal Nevin (ed.), *Trade Union Century* (Dublin, 1994), pp. 42–54.

4. *ITUC Report*, 1894.

5. *Ibid.*, 1898.

6. *Ibid.*, 1900.

7. *Ibid.*, 1902.

8. *Ibid.*, 1903.

9. *Ibid.*, 1904.

10. *Ibid.*, 1904.

11. *Forward,* 1 July 1911.

12. Quoted in Mitchell, *Labour in Irish Politics* (Dublin, 1973), p. 19.

13. The GAA were afforded similar representation!

14. *ITUC Report*, 1896.

15. *Ibid.*, 1903.

16. John W. Boyle, *The Irish Labor Movement in the Nineteenth Century* (Washington, 1989), p. 236.

17. F. S. L. Lyons, *Ireland Since the Famine* (London, 1971), p. 275.

18. Quoted in Boyle, *op. cit.*, p. 240.

19. Boyle, *op. cit.*, p. 242.

20. *Ibid.*, p. 239.

21. Captain D. D Sheehan, *Ireland Since Parnell* (Dublin, 1921), p. 101. Sheehan was a supporter of William O'Brien's All for Ireland League, a former President of the Irish Land and Labour Association and an attendee at the Cork Congress of 1902.

22. *ITUC Report*, 1907.

23. *Ibid.*, 1910.

24. *Ibid.*, 1912.

25. *Ibid.*, 1912.

26. O'Brien is perhaps the most underwritten figure in Labour history. A confidant of Connolly and later a Labour TD, he was responsible for rebuilding the ITGWU in the aftermath of the Easter Rising. His place in the Labour story

may be influenced by the animosity between himself and Jim Larkin following Larkin's return from the United States.

27. Michael Gallagher, *The Irish Labour Party in Transition, 1957–82* (Manchester, 1982), p. 3.

28. Barry Desmond, *No Workers' Republic: Reflections on Labour and Ireland* 1913–1967 (Dublin, 2009), p. 18.

29. See B. M. Walker (ed.), *Parliamentary Election Results in Ireland, 1801–1922* (Dublin, 1978), p. 165.

30. See *The Irish Times*, 12 November 1902.

31. Mitchell, op. cit., p. 38.

32. *Ibid.*, p. 39.

33. *Ibid.*, p. 38.

34. Thomas Morrissey, *William O'Brien 1881–1968* (Dublin, 2007), pp. 259–60.

35. *ITUC Report*, 1910.

36. Quoted in Morrissey, op. cit., pp. 253–4.

37. *Report of ILP & ITUC Debate on Special Commission*, 28/2/1930-1/3/1930, p. 5.

38. Niamh Puirséil, *The Irish Labour Party, 1922–73*, (Dublin, 2007), p. 3.

39. *Ibid.*, p. 7.

40. Cited in Mitchell, *op. cit.*, p. 16.

Chapter 3 **In the Shadow of the National Question** by Michael Laffan

1. *Hansard (House of Commons Daily Debates)*, 5s, 36, 1408, 11 Apr. 1912; *The Irish Times*, 12 April 1912.

2. *Irish Trades Union Congress ... Report,* 1912, pp. 12–19.

3. *Irish Independent*, 4 May 1912.

4. Donal Nevin (ed.), *Between Comrades: James Connolly, Letters and Correspondence, 1889–1916* (Dublin, 2007), pp. 478–9.

5. Emmet Larkin, *James Larkin: Irish Labour Leader, 1876–1947* (London, 1965), pp. 102–3.

6. Nevin, *op. cit.*, pp. 481, 489.

7. Nevin, *op. cit.*, pp. 481–2.

8. Emmet O'Connor, *A Labour History of Ireland, 1824–1960* (Dublin, 1992), p. 68.

9. *Irish Independent*, 16 January 1913.

10. Dillon to T. P. O'Connor, 15 October 1913, Trinity College Dublin, MS 6740, 206; *Freeman's Journal*, 3 November 1913.

11. James McConnel, 'The Irish parliamentary party, industrial relations and the

1913 Lockout', *Saothar*, 28 (2003), p. 31.

12. *The Irish Times*, 24 January 1914; Arthur Mitchell, *Labour in Irish Politics* (Dublin, 1973), p. 53.

13. W. P. Partridge, *Irish Independent*, 20 January 1914.

14. *Irish Trades Union Congress (with which has been incorporated the Irish Labour Party) ... Report*, 1914, p. 3.

15. *Irish Independent*, 16 January 1915.

16. *Freeman's Journal*, 9 June 1915.

17. *Irish Independent*, 14 June 1915.

18. Michael Gallagher, 'Socialism and the nationalist tradition in Ireland, 1798–1918', *Eire-Ireland*, 12, 2 (1977), p. 94.

19. *Irish Trades Union Congress and Labour Party ... Report*, 1916, pp. 21–23.

20. Emmet O'Connor, 'Labour and Politics 1830–1945: Colonisation and Mental Colonisation', Fintan Lane and Donal Ó Drisceoil (eds), *Politics and the Irish Working Class, 1830–1945* (Basingstoke, 2005), p. 34.

21. Circular, 20 September 1918, NLI, MS 17,249.

22. *Freeman's Journal*, 18 September 1918; 'Sinn Féin Notes', *Sligo Champion*, 12 October 1918.

23. O'Brien, diary, 23 September 1918, NLI, MS 17,505 (11).

24. *Irish Labour Party and Trade Union Congress, Report of a Special Conference ...* 1918, pp. 103, 108, 114.

25. *The Irish Times*, 22 January 1919.

26. 'Draft of Democratic Programme' NLI, MS 17,124.

27. *Irish Labour Party and Trade Union Congress ... Report*, 1920, p. 9; Conor McCabe, 'The Irish Labour Party and the 1920 local elections', *Saothar*, 35 (2010), p. 18.

28. *Watchword of Labour*, 19 June 1920, p. 2; 4 December 1920, p. 3.

29. *Irish Independent*, 9 May 1921.

30. *Irish Labour Party and Trade Union Congress ... Report*, 1921, pp. 19, 82.

31. Patrick Lynch, 'The Social Revolution that never was', Desmond Williams (ed.), *The Irish Struggle, 1916–1926* (London, 1966), p. 49.

32. *The Voice of Labour*, 17 December 1921, p. 4.

33. National Executive, statement, 12 April 1922, NLI, MS 17,139.

34. *The Voice of Labour*, 21 January 1922, p. 4; 4 February 1922, p. 4.

35. *Irish Labour Party and Trade Union Congress ... Report*, 1922, pp. 62, 71, 77, 79. On opposition to contesting the election see Niamh Puirséil, *The Irish Labour Party, 1922–73* (Dublin, 2007), p. 10.

36. *The Voice of Labour*, 27 May 1922, p. 1.

37. *Freeman's Journal*, 12 June 1922.

38. See Michael Laffan, *The Resurrection of Ireland: the Sinn Féin Party, 1916–1923* (Cambridge, 1999), pp. 403–4.

39. Bill Kissane, *The Politics of the Irish Civil War* (Oxford, 2005), pp. 147–8.

Chapter 4. **Labour and Dáil Éireann, 1922–32** by Ciara Meehan

1. I am grateful to Dr Niamh Cullen for her comments on this chapter.

2. *Dáil Debates*, vol. 3, cols. 411–2, 10 January 1922.

3. *The Irish Times*, 12 June 1922.

4. *The Irish Times*, 6 June 1922.

5. *The Irish Times*, 2 June 1922.

6. Michael Laffan, *The Resurrection of Ireland: the Sinn Féin Party, 1916–1923* (Cambridge, 1999), p. 394.

7. Laffan, *op. cit.*, p. 389.

8. J. Anthony Gaughan, 'Thomas Johnson', *Dictionary of Irish Biography* (Cambridge, 2009).

9. Gilbert Lynch, quoted in Niamh Puirséil, *The Irish Labour Party, 1922–73*, (Dublin 2007), p. 19.

10. Laffan, *op. cit.*, p. 259.

11. 9 September 1922, Diary 46, U271/A/46, de Róiste Papers, Cork City & County Archives (CCCA).

12. *Dáil Debates*, vol. 1, cols. 696–7 and 700, 25 September 1922.

13. *Dáil Debates*, vol. 4, col. 1457, 25 July 1923.

14. *Dáil Debates*, vol. 4, cols. 1591–2, 30 July 1923.

15. *Dáil Debates*, vol. 3, cols. 1136–8, 18 May 1923.

16. Quoted in J. J. Lee, *Ireland 1912–1985: Politics and Society* (Cambridge, 1989), p. 95.

17. Richard Sinnott, *Irish Voters Decide: Voting Behaviour in Elections and Referendums Since 1918* (Manchester, 1995), p. 97.

18. Larkin had left Ireland in 1914, disillusioned by the events of the previous year's strike and lockout.

19. Puirséil, *op. cit.*, pp. 16–7.

20. *Ibid.*, p. 19.

21. *Clonmel Chronicle*, 11 May 1927.

22. *The Irish Times*, 9 June 1927.

23. Kevin O'Higgins to Frank MacDermot, 18 May 1927, 1065/1/1, MacDermot papers, NAI.

24. See Ciara Meehan, *The Cosgrave Party: a History of Cumann na nGaedheal 1923–33* (Dublin, 2010), pp. 73–80.

25. *Thirty-third annual report of Irish Labour Party and Trade Union Congress* (Dublin, 1927), p. 41.

26. *Ibid.*, p. 43.

27. Report with notes on meeting with President Cosgrave after the assassination of O'Higgins, 12 July 1927, MS 17,162, Johnson Papers, NLI.

28. *Thirty-third annual report of Irish Labour Party and Trade Union Congress*, p. 44.

29. *The Irishman*, 16 July 1927.

30. See, for example, *Donegal Democrat*, 16 July; *Roscommon Messenger*, 30 July; and *Northern Standard*, 12 August 1927.

31. *The Irish Times*, 1 August 1927.

32. *Northern Standard*, 12 August 1927.

33. Quoted in William O'Brien observations on the 1927 political crisis and Enniskerry affair, MS 15,704 (7), O'Brien papers, NLI.

34. Memorandum on present political situation, August 1927, MS 17168, Johnson Papers, NLI.

35. *Thirty-fourth annual report of Irish Labour Party and Trade Union Congress* (Dublin, 1928), p. 25.

36. *Dáil Debates*, vol. 20, col. 1670, 16 August 1927.

37. Interview with T. J. O'Connell, quoted in Arthur Mitchell, *Labour in Irish Politics, 1890–1930: the Irish Labour Movement in an Age of Revolution* (Dublin, 1974), p. 261.

38. *Thirty-fourth annual report of Irish Labour Party and Trade Union Congress* (Dublin, 1928), p. 25.

39. Observations on the 1927 political crisis and Enniskerry affair, MS 15,704 (7), O'Brien papers, NLI; *Thirty-fourth annual report of Irish Labour Party and Trade Union Congress*, p. 25.

40. Diary, 1, 6, 8 and 12 August 1927, MS 15706 (7), O'Brien papers, NLI.

41. Minutes of the parliamentary party, 12 August 1927, P176/442, Fianna Fáil papers, University College Dublin Archives (UCDA).

42. Observations on the 1927 political crisis and Enniskerry affair, MS 15704 (7), O'Brien papers, NLI.

43. William Redmond to Thomas Johnson, 12 August 1927, MS 17,165, Johnson papers, NLI.

44. *Ibid.*, 17 August 1927, MS 17,165, Johnson papers, NLI.

45. *Dáil Debates*. vol. 20, col. 1676, 16 August 1927.

46. *Dáil Debates.* vol. 20, col. 1686, 16 August 1927.

47. *Dáil Debates*, vol. 20, cols. 1700 and 1724, 16 August 1927.

48. Mitchell, *op. cit.*, p. 265.

49. *Evening Herald*, 26 August 1927.

50. *Limerick Leader*, 27 August 1927.

51. *Thirty-fourth annual report of Irish Labour Party and Trade Union Congress*, p. 26.

52. The full poem from which this line is taken was found in a ballot box and was reproduced in the *Kildare Observer*, 24 September 1927. It concluded with the line, 'But the Cosgrave bunch will never fail / Up Cosgrave! Cumann na nGaedheal!'

53. *Thirty-fourth annual report of Irish Labour Party and Trade Union Congress*, p. 65.

54. Puirséil, *The Irish Labour Party, 1922–73*, p. 30.

55. *Dáil Debates*, vol. 21, col. 378, 26 October 1927.

56. *Dáil Debates*, vol. 21, col. 437, 26 October 1927.

57. *Dáil Debates*, vol. 21, col. 676, 2 November 1927.

58. Ciara Meehan, *op. cit.*, p. 233.

59. *Kildare Observer*, 5 December 1931.

60. Cumann na nGaedheal, *Fighting Points for Speakers and Workers: General Election 1932* (Dublin, 1932), p. 61.

61. *The Irish Press*, 4 January 1932.

62. Labour election statement, reproduced in Warner Moss, *Political Parties in the Irish Free State* (New York, 1933), pp. 209–16.

63. Michael Gallagher, *Political Parties in the Republic of Ireland* (Dublin, 1985), p. 74.

64. *Dáil Debates*, vol. 4, col. 2003, 9 August 1923.

Chapter 5. **Forging a Better World: Socialists and International Politics in the Early Twentieth Century** by William Mulligan

1. Adrian Gregory, *The Last Great War: British Society and the First World War* (Cambridge, 2008), pp. 11–12.

2. Nicholas Stargardt, *The German Idea of Militarism. Radical and Socialist Critics, 1866–1914* (Cambridge, 1994), pp. 32–34.

3. 'L'odeur de ce charnier', La Dépêche de Toulouse, 25 November 1912, in Jean-Pierre Rioux (ed.), *Jean Jaurès: Rallumer tous les soleils* (Paris, 2006), p. 878.

4. David Nevin, *James Connolly: A Full Life* (Dublin, 2005), p. 507.

5. Theresa Moriarty, 'Work, workers, and wages: industrial controls and Irish trade unionism in the First World War', in Adrian Gregory and Senia Paseta (eds), *Ireland and the Great War. A war to unite us all?* (Manchester, 2002), pp. 76–83.

6. John Horne, 'The Comité d'Action (CGT-Parti socialiste) and the origins of wartime labor reformism', Patrick Fridenson (ed.), *The French Home Front, 1914–1918* (Providence, 1992), p. 253.

7. Ethel Snowden to Independent Labour Party, 1 September 1917, in National Library of Scotland, Acc. 5241/6, Papers of the Edinburgh Central Association of the ILP.

8. 'Appeal of the Dutch delegation to the Socialists of all countries, 30 April 1917, http://labourhistory.net/stockholm1917/documents/p4a.php (accessed 25 May 2011).

9. *American Labor's Position in Peace and War*, 12 March 1917.

10. See, for example, the pamphlet addressed by the Odessa Soviet to 'Genossen, Deutsche, Oesterreichische, Bulgarische, Türkische Krieger', SPD Archive, Friedrich Ebert Stiftung Bonn, Hörsing Papers, Mappe 11, Kriegsdienst, 1916–1918.

11. Geoff Eley, *Forging Democracy. The History of the Left in Europe, 1850–2000* (Oxford, 2002), pp. 123–276.

12. Evan Mawdsley, *The Russian Civil War* (Boston, 1987), pp. 285–7.

13. Peter Jackson, 'French security policy and a British "continental commitment" after the First World War: a reassessment', *English Historical Review*, 519 (April 2011), pp. 348–9, 365–7.

14. See Albert Thomas, *Dix ans d'Organisation Internationale de Travail* (Geneva, 1931) for a fulsome account of the ILO's successes.

15. 'Une manifestation en favuer de la paix', *Journal des debats politiques et littéraires*, 26 May 1929, p. 2.

16. See press cuttings in SPD Archive, Friedrich-Ebert Stiftung, Bonn, NL Carl Severing, Mappe 147.

17. Gilbert Hantry, 'Shop Stewards at Renault', in Fridenson (ed.), *French Home Front*, pp. 224–8.

18. 'Schreie eines Aufgewachten', SPD Archive, Friedrich-Ebert Stiftung, NL Osterrorth, Mappe 13.

Chapter 6. 'If it's socialism you want, join some other party': Labour and the Left by Niamh Puirséil

1. John Horgan, *Labour: The Price of Power* (Dublin, 1986), p. 1.

2. Joe Deasy quoted in Brian Kenny, *Joe Deasy: A Life on the Left* (Dublin, 2009), p. 36. Deasy began his political career in the Labour Party in the 1940s before becoming active in the Irish Workers' League and its successors. He left the Communist Party of Ireland in 1975 and subsequently rejoined Labour, where he has remained to this day.

3. Noël Browne, *Against the Tide* (Dublin, 1986), p. 180. Jim Larkin Junior (1904–1969) was popularly known as Young Jim to distinguish him from his father Jim Larkin Senior (1874–1947), popularly known as Big Jim.

4. Browne, *op. cit.*, pp. 179–80.

5. David Thornley, 'The development of the Irish Labour Movement', *Christus Rex* 1970 (this is based on a paper presented to the Tuairim group in 1963).

6. *Ibid.*, p. 222.

7. Richard English, *Radicals and the Republic: Socialist Republicanism in the Irish Free State 1925–37* (Oxford, 1994), p. 188.

8. Donal Ó Drisceoil, *Peadar O'Donnell* (Cork, 2001), p. 23. See also Emmet O'Connor, *Syndicalism in Ireland 1917–23* (Cork, 1988), p. 148.

9. Cathal O'Shannon was especially vocal on the matter.

10. See Niamh Puirséil, *The Irish Labour Party, 1922–73* (Dublin, 2007), p. 14.

11. Including one delivered personally by Lile O'Donel who told Tom Johnson that he would be shot 'if anything happened to Peadar' [O'Donnell, whom she would soon marry], Ó Drisceoil, *op. cit.*, p. 32.

12. Emmet O'Connor, *James Larkin* (Cork, 2002), p. 53.

13. *Ibid.*, p. 70.

14. *Ibid.*, pp. 88, 96.

15. *Ibid.*, p. 97.

16. Puirséil, *op. cit.*, pp. 53–6.

17. Labour Party, *Fourth annual report,* p. 70.

18. Puirséil, *op. cit.*, p. 69.

19. On the Workers' Republic controversy see Fearghal McGarry, '"Catholics First, Politicians Afterwards": The Labour Party and the Workers' Republic, 1936–39', *Saothar,* 25 (2000), pp. 57–66; J. H. Whyte, *Church and State in Modern Ireland* (Dublin, 1980), pp. 81–86; Puirséil, *op. cit.,* pp. 54–73 *passim*.

20. Andrée Sheehy Skeffington, *Skeff: A life of Owen Sheehy Skeffington 1909–1970* (Dublin, 1991), p. 107.

21. Uinseann MacEoin, *Survivors* (Dublin, 1980), p. 213.

22. See Puirséil *op. cit.,* pp. 83–94 *passim*; Ciaran Crossey and James Monaghan, 'The Origins of Trotskyism in Ireland', *Revolutionary History* 6:2/3 (Summer 1996), pp. 4–57.

23. Emmet O'Connor, *Reds and the Green: Ireland, Russia and the Communist Internationals 1919–43* (Dublin, 2004), p. 231.

24. John de Courcy Ireland, 'As I Remember Big Jim', Donal Nevin (ed.) *Lion of the Fold* (Dublin, 1998), pp. 451–2.

25. The advice of A. C. Overend KC was that Larkin could not be expelled for actions he took when he was not a member of the party. See Puirséil, *op. cit.*, pp. 91–107 *passim*.

26. *Ibid.*

27. Brian Inglis, *West Briton* (London, 1962), p. 108.

28. See Niamh Puirséil 'Catholic Stakhanovites? Religion and the Irish Labour Party', Francis Devine, Fintan Lane and Niamh Puirséil (eds) *Essays in Irish Labour History: A Festschrift for Elizabeth and John Boyle* (Dublin, 2008), p. 188.

29. See Puirséil, *op. cit.*, p. 113.

30. *Review*, April 1945.

31. *The Irish People,* 28 February 1948.

32. Young Jim Larkin to John de Courcy Ireland, 28 July 1946. UCDA P291/365.

33. 'Communism in Ireland' confidential Department of Justice memorandum, 31 December 1947. UCDA P67/548(i).

34. Barry Desmond, *Finally and in Conclusion: A Political Memoir* (Dublin, 2000), p. 32.

35. Puirséil, *op. cit.*, p. 185.

36. Quoted in John O'Connell, *Dr. John: Crusading Doctor and Politician* (Dublin, 1989), p. 87.

37. Puirséil, *op. cit.*, p. 199.

38. See Goodwillie 'Lesser Marxist Movements in Ireland: a Bibliography, 1934–84', *Saothar*, 11 (1986), pp. 116–123; *Gralton*, August/September 1983; see also *Hibernia*, February 1972, *Magill*, 2 October 1977.

39. *The Irish Times*, 17 June 1969.

40. *Irish Independent*, 29 June 1969.

41. In fairness, politicians are not a group known for humility, but the 1969 cohort were especially confident. See Puirséil, *op. cit.*, p. 274.

42. On Labour and the coalition question, see Michael Gallagher, *Irish Labour Party in transition, 1957–82* (Manchester, 1982), pp. 154–96.

43. See Horgan, *op. cit.*, p. 34.

44. Gallagher, *op. cit.*, p. 166. It was also the case that the Just Society element in Fine Gael was trying to woo Labour into accepting coalition at a time where Fianna Fáil was looking increasingly arrogant.

45. Dermot Boucher quoted in Gallagher, *op. cit.*, p. 180.

46. Gallagher, *op. cit.*, p. 184.

47. Puirséil, *Irish Labour Party,* p. 284.

48. The LCLL actually canvassed (unsuccessfully) against Labour when it stood on a joint National Coalition platform with Fine Gael.

49. *Magill,* 2 December 1977.

50. See Michael Gallagher, *Political Parties in the Republic of Ireland* (Dublin, 1985), pp. 118–9.

51. Labour had three new leaders in a five-year period: Brendan Corish had resigned as leader after the election and, following the tightest of votes, Frank Cluskey became party leader and appointed Michael O'Leary, whom he had beaten by a single vote, as deputy leader. Cluskey lost his seat in 1981 and was replaced by O'Leary who subsequently defected to Fine Gael in 1982 to be replaced by Dick Spring.

52. Horgan, *op. cit.*, pp. 48–9; Stephen Collins, *Spring and the Labour Party* (Dublin, 1993), p. 91.

53. For an account of Labour Left see Paul Dillon, 'Explaining the emergence, political impact and decline of Labour Left, 1983–1992' MA thesis, UCD, 2007.

54. *The Irish Times,* 13 March 1989.

55. Although the Workers' Party won only two seats in November 1982, its vote had gone up and, as Ruairi Quinn noted, 'in Dublin, their strength was in direct proportion to our weakness'. Ruairi Quinn, *Straight Left: A Journey in Politics* (Dublin, 2006), p. 171

56. *The Irish Times*, 24 October 1982.

57. Ray Kavanagh, *Spring, Summer and Fall: The Rise and Fall of the Labour Party 1986–1999* (Dublin, 2001), p. 1.

58. See Michael Gallagher, 'The outcome', Michael Laver, Peter Mair and Richard Sinnott (eds), *How Ireland Voted 1987* (Dublin, 1987), p. 78.

59. *Ibid.*

60. Fergus Finlay, *Snakes and Ladders,* (Dublin, 1998), pp. 51–61; See also Kavanagh, *Spring,* p. 44; Dillon, 'Explaining … Labour Left' pp. 24–8; Collins, *Spring,* pp. 162–7. The Labour Left faction continued until 1992 but it had long lost any real influence among Labour members and began to look outside for alliances on the left. See Dillon, 'Labour Left' pp. 27–30. This reached perhaps its logical conclusion when Mervyn Taylor left Labour in 1992 with the intention of joining Democratic Left. When his constituency organisation refused to go in to the new party with him, however, he changed his mind and asked to come back.

61. Finlay, *op. cit.*, p. 159.

62. At the 1992 election, DL took four seats where the Workers' Party had taken seven seats in 1989. More worryingly for the party, its vote fell by half in Dublin which was its stronghold. Parenthetically, Pat Rabbitte had wanted to join Labour rather than establish a new party but was in a minority of his colleagues. See Kevin Rafter, *Democratic Left: The Life and Death of an Irish Political Party* (Dublin, 2011), p. 93.

63. Joe Higgins of the Socialist Party (previously Militant) took a seat in 1997 and 2002 but failed to keep it in 2007. Sinn Féin, which portrays itself as a party to the left of Labour, took five seats in 2002 and four in 2007.

64. A total of sixty seats, which is 50 per cent more than the previous high point in 1992.

65. Roisín Shorthall on the RTÉ television programme, *This Week*, quoted in *Sunday Tribune,* February 2011.

66. Tom Garvin, *The Evolution of Irish Nationalist Politics* (Dublin, 1981), p. 149.

Chapter 7. **Labour and the Pursuit of Power** by Paul Daly

1. Eamon Gilmore, 'Labour can be proud of role in modernising Ireland', speech to mark the ninetieth anniversary of the Democratic Programme, Liberty Hall, Dublin. http://www.labour.ie/press/listing/123229246077121.html (accessed 7 February 2012).

2. Arthur Mitchell, *Labour in Irish Politics*, (Dublin, 1974), p. 94.

3. *Ibid.*, p. 97.

4. Barry Desmond, *No Workers' Republic! Reflections on Labour and Ireland 1913–1967* (Dublin, 2009), p. 44.

5. Mitchell, *op. cit.*, p. 126.

6. *The Voice of Labour,* 24 June 1922.

7. Mitchell, *op. cit.*, p. 224.

8. Richard Dunphy, *The Making of Fianna Fáil Power in Ireland,* (Dublin, 1995), p. 82.

9. Niamh Puirséil, *The Irish Labour Party, 1922–73* (Dublin, 2007), p. 20.

10. Dunphy, *op. cit.*, p. 133.

11. For a full account of contacts between Labour and Fianna Fáil that summer see Puirséil, *op. cit.*, pp. 23–4.

12. Dáil Éireann Debates, 16 August 1927.

13. Dáil Éireann Debates, 16 August 1927.

14. Puirséil, *op. cit.*, p. 36.

15. Peter Mair, *The Changing Irish Party System* (London, 1987), p. 9.

16. John Horgan, *Labour: The Price of Power* (Dublin, 1986), p. 30.

17. Dáil Éireann Debates, 2 July 1969.

18. Dáil Éireann Debates, 2 July 1969.

19. Horgan, *op. cit.*, p. 25.

20. Horgan, *op. cit.*, p. 180.

21. Peter Mair, 'Fianna Fáil, Labour and the Irish Party System', in Michael Gallagher

and Michael Laver (eds), '*How Ireland Voted 1992* (Dublin, 1992), p. 171.

22. RTÉ Millward Brown Lansdowne Exit Poll (General Election 2011).

Chapter 8. **'No good Catholic can be a true Socialist': The Labour Party and the Catholic Church, 1922–52** by Diarmaid Ferriter

1. *The Irish Times*, 17 March 2011.

2. Ruairi Quinn, *Straight Left: A Journey in Politics* (Dublin, 2005), pp. 35–51.

3. Diarmaid Ferriter, *The Transformation of Ireland: 1900–2000* (London, 2004), p. 751.

4. Arthur Mitchell, *Labour in Irish Politics 1890–1930: The Irish Labour Movement in an age of Revolution* (Dublin, 1974), pp. 25–47.

5. Peter Murray, 'Electoral Politics and the Dublin Working Class before the First World War', *Saothar*, 6, 1980, pp. 8–25.

6. James Newsinger, 'As Catholic as the Pope: James Connolly and the Roman Catholic Church in Ireland', *Saothar*, 11, 1986, pp. 7–19.

7. Michael Laffan, '"Labour Must Wait": Ireland's Conservative Revolution', Patrick Corish (ed.), *Radicals, Rebels and Establishments* (Belfast, 1985), pp. 202–12.

8. Niamh Puirséil, *The Irish Labour Party, 1922–73* (Dublin, 2007), pp. 8–12.

9. Seán Hutton, 'Labour in post-independent Ireland', Seán Hutton and Paul Stewart (eds), *Ireland's Histories: Aspects of State, Society and Ideology* (London, 1991), pp. 48–68.

10. Mitchell, *op. cit.*, p. 188.

11. *Ibid.*, p. 227.

12. Sean Hutton, *op. cit.*, p. 68; *Irish Labour Party and Trade Union Congress Report* (Dublin, 1928), p. 26.

13. Fearghal McGarry, '"Catholics First and Politicians afterwards": The Labour Party and the Worker's Republic 1936–39', *Saothar*, 25, 2000, pp. 57–67.

14. Puirséil, *op. cit.,* p. 61.

15. *The Irish Times*, 16 May 1931.

16. *Irish Labour Party, 4th Annual Report*, (Dublin, 1934), p. 119.

17. *Irish Labour Party, 6th Annual Report*, (Dublin, 1936), p. 133.

18. *The Standard*, 18 June 1929.

19. McGarry, 'Catholics First', pp. 57–67.

20. Entry on Michael Keyes by Diarmaid Ferriter in James McGuire and James Quinn (eds), *Dictionary of Irish Biography: From the Earliest Times to the year 2002* (Cambridge, 2009) Vol. 5, p. 168.

21. John H. Whyte, *Church and State in Modern Ireland, 1923–79* (Dublin, 1980), pp. 92–3.

22. McGarry, *op. cit.*, pp. 57–67.

23. *Ibid.*

24. Puirséil, *op. cit.*, pp. 72–3 and McGarry, *op. cit.*, pp. 57–67.

25. Whyte, *op. cit.*, p. 84.

26. Don O'Leary, *Vocationalism and Social Catholicism in twentieth century Ireland: The search for a Christian social order* (Dublin, 2000), pp. 77–96.

27. *Sunday Business Post*, 29 April 2007.

28. Barry Desmond, *No Worker's Republic! Reflections on Labour and Ireland 1913–67*, (Dublin, 2009), p. 151.

29. John Kenna, *James Everett: Trade Unionist to Government Minister* (Wicklow, 2011), pp. 27–9.

30. Desmond, *op. cit.*, p. 184.

31. *Ibid.*, pp. 190–9.

32. *Ibid.*, p. 148.

33. Angela Bolster, *The Knights of Saint Columbanus* (Dublin, 1979), p. 98.

34. *Ibid.*, pp. 98–103.

35. David McCullagh, *Makeshift Majority: the first inter-party government 1948–51* (Dublin, 1998), p. 190.

36. Entry on William Norton by Lawrence William White in McGuire and Quinn (eds), *Dictionary of Irish Biography*, Vol. 6 pp. 958–962.

37. Ruth Barrington, *Health Medicine and Politics in Ireland 1900–1970* (Dublin, 1987), pp. 201–2; Puirséil, *op. cit.*, p. 155.

38. John Cooney, *John Charles McQuaid: Ruler of Catholic Ireland* (Dublin, 1999), p. 268.

39. Barrington, *op. cit.*, pp. 201–2; Puirséil, *op. cit.*, p. 158.

40. Puirséil, *op. cit.*, pp. 155–8.

41. *Dáil Debates*, Vol. CXXV, pp. 951–953, Desmond, *op. cit.*, p. 233; Michael Gallagher, *The Irish Labour Party in Transition, 1957–82* (Manchester, 1982), p. 57.

42. Kenna, *op. cit.*, p. 39.

43. Diarmaid Ferriter, *Judging Dev: A Reassessment of the Life and Legacy of Eamon de Valera* (Dublin, 2007), pp. 231–2.

44. McGarry, *op. cit.*, pp. 57–67.

45. Bernard Canning, *The Bishops of Ireland, 1870–1987* (Donegal, 1987), p. 62.

Chapter 9. **'A particular view of what was possible': Labour in Government** by David McCullagh

1. Quoted in Niamh Puirséil, *The Irish Labour Party, 1922–73* (Dublin, 2007), p. 304.

2. The 1951 result is slightly confusing, because Labour contested the previous election as two parties, Labour and National Labour, which won fourteen and five seats respectively. The reunited party won just sixteen seats in 1951.

3. David McCullagh, *The Reluctant Taoiseach* (Dublin, 2010), p. 64.

4. Ronan Fanning, *The Irish Department of Finance, 1922–58* (Dublin, 1978), p. 237.

5. The TD was Richard Anthony. *Dáil Debates*, Vol. 40, Col. 1831, 28 September 1933. Quoted in Niamh Puirséil, *op. cit.*, p. 40.

6. UCD Archives Department (UCDA), P7/D/116, Mulcahy to Costello, 17 July 1967.

7. John A. Costello to his son, Declan Costello, 29 February 1948. Quoted in McCullagh, *The Reluctant Taoiseach*, p. 162.

8. McCullagh, *A Makeshift Majority* (Dublin, 1998), p. 37.

9. United States National Archives (USNA), RG 84, Dublin Security Segregated Records, 1936–49, Box 12, 550.4, Chapin to Washington, 21 September 1948.

10. Notes on conference, 16 January 1949. UCDA, P35/c/184

11. *The Irish Times*, 15 February 1950.

12. *The Irish Times*, 24 February 1950.

13. Ronan Fanning, *The Irish Department of Finance, 1922–58* (Dublin, 1978), p. 449.

14. *This Week*, RTÉ Radio, 27 April 1969.

15. *The Leader*, 25 October 1952.

16. McCullagh, *A Makeshift Majority*, p. 70.

17. Dublin Diocesan Archives, AB8/B/XVIII, Box 5, Mother and Child Scheme, 1951, report to Standing Committee of the Hierarchy, 3 April 1951.

18. McCullagh, *A Makeshift Majority*, p. 252.

19. UCDA, P7/D/116, Mulcahy to Costello, 29 April 1967.

20. McCullagh, *The Reluctant Taoiseach*, p. 283.

21. T. F. O'Higgins, *A Double Life* (Dublin, 1996), pp. 163–4.

22. *The Leader*, 14 May 1955.

23. *The Irish Press*, 27 September 1956.

24. UCDA, P190/779, Norton to Sweetman, 20 August 1956.

25. UCDA, P190/717, Norton to Sweetman, 4 September 1956.

26. National Archives of Ireland (NAI), S 2850 B, Murray note, 14 March 1955.

27. British National Archives (TNA), DO 35/5290, Fortnightly report, 30 October 1954.

28. TNA, DO 35/5207, record of meeting, 8 November 1954.

29. TNA, DO 35/5208, record of conversation, 15 December 1954.

30. USNA, RG 84, Dublin Security Segregated Records, Box 23, 350, Taft to Secretary of State, 17 December 1956.

31. UCDA, Costello Papers, P190/837, Costello to Thomas Kehoe, 11 October 1956. Of course, without Labour support he would not have been Taoiseach in the first place!

32. Puirséil, *op. cit.*, p. 203.

33. John Horgan, *Labour: The Price of Power* (Dublin, 1986), p. 36.

34. TNA, CAB 133/464.

35. Liam Cosgrave speech at launch of *A Makeshift Majority* by David McCullagh, 25 November 1998.

36. NAI, 2006/133/317, 3 September 1974.

37. Horgan, *op. cit.*, p. 155.

38. NAI, 2006/133/321 subcommittee minutes, 1 September 1976 and 2 September 1976.

39. Ruairi Quinn, *Straight Left: A Life in Politics* (Dublin, 2005), pp. 114–5.

40. Horgan, *op. cit.*, p. 150.

41. See NAI, 2007/116/8.

42. NAI, 2006/133/335, Corish to Cosgrave, 12 June 1975.

43. Interview with Richie Ryan, December 2004.

44. *Ibid.*, December 2007.

45. Quinn, *op. cit.*, p. 166.

46. Quoted in Stephen O'Byrnes, *Hiding Behind a Face: Fine Gael under FitzGerald*, (Dublin, 1986), p. 180.

47. O'Byrnes, *op. cit.*, pp. 125–6.

48. *Ibid.*, p. 218.

49. Fergus Finlay, *Snakes and Ladders* (Dublin, 1998), p. 3.

50. Quoted in O'Byrnes, *op. cit.*, p. 222.

51. Barry Desmond, *Finally and in Conclusion* (Dublin, 2000), p. 210.

52. Finlay, *op. cit.*, p. 13.

53. O'Byrnes, *op. cit.*, p. 235.

54. Finlay, *op. cit.*, p. 12.

55. *Ibid.*, p. 29.

56. Gemma Hussey, *At the Cutting Edge: Cabinet Diaries* (Dublin, 1990), pp. 7–8.

57. Quinn, *op. cit.*, p. 238.

58. Finlay, *op. cit.*, p. 15.

59. Hussey, *op. cit.*, p. 60.

60. O'Byrnes, *op. cit.*, p. 242.

61. Finlay, *op. cit.*, p. 34.

62. Desmond, *op. cit.*, p. 319.

63. Hussey, *op. cit.*, p. 197.

64. Quinn, *op. cit.*, p. 230.

65. Finlay, *op. cit.*, p. 22.

66. Hussey, *op. cit.*, p. 59.

67. See Finlay, *op. cit.*, p. 25; Quinn, *op. cit.*, pp. 204–5; Hussey, *op. cit.*, p. 74.

68. O'Byrnes, *op. cit.*, pp. 244–5.

69. Finlay, *op. cit.*, p. 25.s

70. Desmond, *op. cit.*, p. 203.

71. Hussey, *op. cit.*, p. 226.

72. *Ibid.*, p. 235.

73. Seán Duignan, *One Spin on the Merry-go-round*, (Dublin, 1995), p. 63.

74. Desmond, *op. cit.*, p. 217.

75. Duignan, *op. cit.*, pp. 72–3.

76. Quinn, *op. cit.*, pp. 290–1.

77. Duignan, *op. cit.*, p. 84.

78. *Ibid.*, p. 86.

79. Hussey, *op. cit.*, p. 12; author's conversation with Seán Barrett.

80. Quinn, *op. cit.*, p. 297.

81. *Ibid.*, p. 300.

82. Duignan, *op. cit.*, p. 89.

83. Finlay, *op. cit.*, pp. 154–5.

84. Quoted in Quinn, *op. cit.*, p. 294.

85. Finlay, *op. cit.*, p. 169.

86. Duignan, *op. cit.*, pp. 88–9.

87. Finlay, *op. cit.*, p. 170.

88. Quinn, *op. cit.*, p. 314.

89. Duignan, *op. cit.*, p. 86.

90. Bertie Ahern, *Bertie Ahern: The Autobiography* (London, 2009), pp. 150–1.

91. Duignan, *op. cit.*, p. 91.

92. Finlay, *op. cit.*, p. 171.

93. Ahern, *op. cit.*, p.153.

94. Quoted in Duignan, *op. cit.*, p. 91.

95. Albert Reynolds, *Albert Reynolds: My Autobiography* (Dublin, 2010), p. 226.

96. Duignan, *op. cit.*, p. 92.

97. Finlay, *op. cit.*, p. 215.

98. *Ibid.*, p. 216.

99. Ahern, *op. cit.*, p. 154.

100. Finlay, *op. cit.*, p. 235.

101. Duignan, *op. cit.*, p. 131.

102. Finlay, *op. cit.*, p. 265.

103. Duignan, *op. cit.*, p. 133.

104. Quinn, *op. cit.*, p. 322.

105. Finlay, *op. cit.*, p. 277.

106. Quinn, *op. cit.*, p. 323.

107. *Ibid.*, pp. 362–3.

108. Finlay, *op. cit.*, p. 307.

109. Quinn, *op. cit.*, p. 366.

110. *This Week*, RTÉ Radio, 11 February 1973.

Chapter 10. **Labour and the media: The promise of socialism, negative campaigning and** *The Irish Times* by Kevin Rafter

1. *The Irish Times,* 28 May 1969.

2. *Ibid.*

3. Michael Gallagher, *The Irish Labour Party in Transition, 1957–82* (Manchester, 1982), p. 54.

4. *Ibid.*, pp. 86–91.

5. *The Irish Times,* 23 May 1969.

6. *The Irish Times,* 4 June 1969.

7. *Irish Independent*, 19 February 1990. Article by Brendan Halligan: 'On Brendan Corish: the man who transformed Labour.'

8. Brendan Halligan (ed.), *The Complete Text of 'The New Republic' address by Brendan Corish T.D., leader of the Labour Party* (Dublin, 1968).

9. Gallagher, *op. cit.*, p. 56.

10. Diarmaid Ferriter, *The Transformation of Ireland 1900–2000* (London, 2004), p. 559.

11. Gallagher, *op. cit.*, p. 53.

12. Garret FitzGerald, 'Presentation to the Brendan Corish Seminar', Halligan, B. (ed.) *The Brendan Corish Seminar Proceedings, 11 March 2006* (Dublin, 2006), p. 11.

13. Roy Foster, *Modern Ireland 1600–1972* (London, 1989), p. 596.

14. Gallagher, *op. cit.*, p. 55.

15. *The Irish Times*, 19 February 1990.

16. *Irish Independent*, 19 February 1990. Article by Brendan Halligan: 'On Brendan Corish: the man who transformed Labour.'

17. Brendan Halligan, 'Presentation to the Brendan Corish Seminar', Halligan, B. (ed.) *op. cit.*, p. 20.

18. Niamh Puirséil, *The Irish Labour Party, 1922–73* (Dublin, 2007), p. 254.

19. *The Irish Times*, 19 February 1990.

20. *The Irish Times*, 23 May 1969.

21. Foster, *op. cit.*, p. 576.

22. J. J. Lee, *Ireland 1912–1985* (Cambridge, 1989), p. 410.

23. Dermot Keogh, *Jack Lynch: A Biography* (Dublin, 2009), p. 154.

24. Gallagher, *op. cit.*, pp. 82–3.

25. John Horgan, 'Presentation to the Brendan Corish Seminar', Halligan, B. (ed.) *op. cit.*, p. 48.

26. *The Irish Times*, 16 October 1967. The article by Donal Foley was entitled 'Socialism in the Seventies According to Corish.'

27. Michael Mills, 'Presentation to the Brendan Corish Seminar', Halligan, B. (ed.) *op. cit.*, p. 14.

28. Keogh, *op. cit.*, p. 153.

29. *The Irish Times*, 4 June 1969.

30. *The Irish Times*, 4 June 1969.

31. J. J. Lee, *op. cit.*, p. 327.

32. J. Fanagan (ed.), *Belling the Cats: Selected speeches and articles of John Kelly* (Dublin, 1992, p. 166.

33. *The Irish Times*, 12 June 1969.

34. Chubb, Basil, *The Government and Politics of Ireland* (Dublin, 1992), p. 129).

35. Brian Farrell, 'The Mass Media and the 1977 Campaign', Penniman, H. R. (ed.) *Ireland at the Polls: The Dáil Elections of 1977* (Washington, 1978), p. 102.

36. *Ibid.*, p. 128.

37. Michael Mills, 'Presentation to the Brendan Corish Seminar', Halligan, B. (ed.) *op. cit.*, p. 13.

38. Gallagher, *op. cit.*, pp. 92–3.

39. Brian Maye, *Fine Gael 1923–1987* (Dublin, 1993), p. 126.

40. Mark O'Brien, *The Irish Times: A History* (Dublin, 2008), p. 185.

41. Geraldine Kennedy, 'Appreciation', A. Whittaker (ed.), *Bright, Brilliant Days: Douglas Gageby and* The Irish Times (Dublin, 2006), p. 227.

42. Farrell, *op. cit.*, p. 99.

43. James Downey, *In My Own Times: Inside Irish Politics and Society* (Dublin, 2009), p. 104.

44. Bruce Arnold, 'Behind his cultivated stance', A. Whittaker (ed.), *op. cit.*, p. 73.

45. Downey, *op. cit.*, p. 97.

46. *The Irish Times*, 22 May 1969.

47. *The Irish Times*, 7 June 1969.

48. *The Irish Times*, 13 June 1969.

49. E. H. Courtney, 'Letter to the Editor', *The Irish Times*, 10 June 1969.

50. T. P. O'Mahony, *Jack Lynch: A Biography* (Dublin, 1991), p. 105.

51. *The Irish Times*, 29 May 1969.

52. *The Irish Times*, 31 May 1969.

53. *The Irish Times*, 4 June 1969.

54. *The Irish Times*, 12 June 1969.

55. *The Irish Times*, 10 June 1969.

56. *The Irish Times*, 13 June 1969.

57. *The Irish Times*, 14 June 1969.

58. *The Irish Times*, 10 June 1969.

59. Annemarie Walter and Rens Vliegenthart, 'Negative Campaigning across Different Communication Channels: Different Ball Games', *International Journal of Press Politics*, 15(4): (2010), pp. 441–61.

60. *The Irish Times*, 17 June 1969.

61. *The Irish Times*, 17 June 1969.

62. *The Irish Times*, 16 May 1969.

63. Gallagher, *op. cit.*, p. 58.

64. *The Irish Times*, 26 May 1969.

65. Lee, *op. cit.*, p. 410.

66. *The Irish Times*, 21 June 1969.

67. Horgan, *Labour: The Price of Power*, (Dublin, 1986), p. 8.

Chapter 11. **Labour and the Making of Irish Foreign Policy, 1973–77** by Eunan O'Halpin

1. Catherine O'Donnell, *Fianna Fáil, Irish Republicanism and the Northern Ireland Troubles, 1968–2005* (Ireland, 2007), pp. 21–42.

2. The National Archives, London (TNA), FCO33/12000, Annual Review for 1969, 23 January 1970.

3. TNA, FCO33/1595, Annual Review for 1970, 8 January 1971.

4. Noël Browne, *Against the Tide: An Autobiography* (Dublin, 1986), pp. 251–3, offers a powerful if unflattering portrait of Thornley. John Horgan, *Noël Browne: Passionate Outsider* (Dublin, 2000), p. 238.

5. TNA, FCO33/1202, report from British embassy, Dublin, 6 June 1970. Horgan, *op. cit.*, p. 244.

6. TNA, FCO33/1202, report from British embassy, Dublin, 17 December 1970.

7. Churchill College Cambridge Archives, British Diplomatic Oral History Project, interview with Sir Oliver Wright, 18 September 1996.

8. David McKittrick, Seamus Kelters, Brian Feeney and Chris Thornton, *Lost Lives: the stories of the men, women and children who died as a result of the Northern Ireland Troubles* (Edinburgh, 1999; 2nd ed., 2001), p. 1494.

9. Barry Desmond, *Finally and in Conclusion* (Dublin, 2000), p. 58. In *At the Cutting Edge: Cabinet Diaries 1982–1987* (Dublin, 1990), p. 7, the former Fine Gael minister Gemma Hussey ascribed the Labour leader Dick Spring's somewhat sombre persona largely to his continual difficulties keeping his party in order.

10. Tara Keenan Thomson, *Irish Women and Street Politics 1956–1973* (Dublin, 2010), pp. 179–82.

11. Brendan Halligan, 'What difference did it make? Setting the scene', in Rory O'Donnell (ed.), *Europe: The Irish Experience* (Dublin, 2000), pp. 24–8; Gary Murphy, *Economic Realignment and the Politics of EEC Entry: Ireland, 1948–1972* (Dublin, 2003), p. 251.

12. Emmet O'Connor, *Reds and the Green: Ireland, Russia and the Communist Internationals 1919–43* (Dublin, 2004), p. 232.

13. TNA, KV2/3359, MI5 minute dated 21 August 1947, and KV2/3360, MI5 transcript of bugged conversation between Greaves and Palme Dutt in CPGB headquarters, 22 February 1955. Greaves' approach towards Irish questions is concisely analysed by Matt Treacy, *The IRA 1956–69: Rethinking the Republic* (Manchester, 2011), pp. 73–7.

14. Treacy, *op. cit.*, p. 108.

15. Brian Hanley & Scott Millar, *The Lost Revolution: The Official IRA and the Workers' Party* (London, 2010), p. 141.

16. On this see particularly R. W. Johnston, *Century of Endeavour: A Biographical & Autobiographical View of the Twentieth Century in Ireland* (Dublin, 2003; 2nd ed., 2005), pp. 167–259. At pp. 155–6 see his criticisms of the Irish Workers League (a *nom de guerre* of the Communist Party of Ireland) in 1956–57. Treacy, *op. cit.*, pp. 122–3.

17. At a Centre for Contemporary Irish History research seminar, Trinity College Dublin, 3 December 2003. On the evolution of Labour Party attitudes towards the EU, see Karen Gilland, 'Shades of Green: Euroscepticism in Irish political parties', Aleks Szczerbiak and Paul Taggart (eds), *Opposing Europe? The Comparative Party Politics of Euroscepticism: Vol. 1 Case Studies and Country Surveys* (Oxford, 2008), pp. 120–1.

18. Desmond, *op. cit.*, pp. 76–7.

19. NARA, CREST, CIA RDP79T00865A001200170002-2, 'Western European Canada International Organisations', 23 June 1975. This at least was his reputation when I joined what had been his department as a junior civil servant in September 1977.

20. Desmond, *op. cit.*, p. 78; Garret FitzGerald, *All in a Life: An Autobiography* (London, 1991), pp. 296–7.

21. NARA, CREST, CIA RDP85T00353R0001001 20004-9, undated, 11 December 1974.

22. Kissinger to President Ford, 2 September 1975, Gerald R. Ford Presidential Library, Presidential Country File for Europe and Canada, Box 7, folder Ireland (1).

23. Desmond, *op. cit.*, p. 78.

24. Hanley and Millar, *op. cit.*, pp. 519–45.

25. NARA, Nixon National Security Council records, Country Files Europe Box 694, memorandum to Flanagan (White House commercial aviation specialist) conveying President Nixon's decision, 7 May 1971.

26. NARA, RG59, Box 2384, Folder Pol Ire-US 10-8-70, Dublin embassy report, 30 November 1971; RG59 150 73 16 Box 1, Folder AV4 Dublin Landing Rights 1969, Ambassador Moore to Washington, 4 April 1973, and unsigned State Department annotation, 4 January 1972.

27. TNA, PREM15/1046, text of Heath to Lynch, 1 March 1972; FitzGerald, *op. cit.*, pp. 603–4; NARA, RG59, Box 2384, Folder Pol IRE-USSR 1-13-1972, meeting with Irish ambassador, 9 October 1972.

28. NARA, CREST, CIA RDP79T00975A0253001200001-7, 'Central Intelligence

Bulletin', 1 October 1973; interview with the late Dermot Nally who, in 1973, was assistant secretary to the government.

29. NARA, State Department D740065-0316, United States embassy report, 26 March 1974, http://aad.archives.gov/aad/series-list.jsp?cat=WR43 (accessed 3 November 2011).

30. TNA, FCO87/187, Foreign Office to British Embassy, Dublin, 9 March 1973.

31. London School of Economics, Merlyn Rees papers 1/4, journal entry, 2 June 1974.

32. NARA, CREST, CIA RDP79-01209A000400010001-4, Weekly Intelligence Digest, 12 August 1974.

33. Anthony Craig, *Crisis of Confidence: Anglo-Irish relations in the early Troubles* (Dublin, 2010), pp. 175–86; London School of Economics, Merlyn Rees papers 1/4, journal entry 28 July 1974.

34. London School of Economics, Merlyn Rees papers 1/4, journal entry 1 September 1974.

35. NARA, State Department D740300-0030, United States embassy report, 21 October 1976, http://aad.archives.gov/aad/series-list.jsp?cat=WR43 (accessed 3 November 2011).

36. NARA, State Department D750140-1152, United States embassy report, 22 April 1975.

37. FitzGerald, *op. cit.*, pp. 266–7.

38. NARA, State Department D750169-0399, United States embassy report, 14 May 1975, http://aad.archives.gov/aad/series-list.jsp?cat=WR43 (accessed 3 November 2011).

39. NARA, RG57, United States embassy report, 24 November 1976, http://aad.archives.gov/aad/series-list.jsp?cat=WR43 (accessed 3 November 2011).

40. TNA, CJ4/1895, Northern Ireland Office briefing note, 19 January. 1977.

41. NARA, State Department D760343-1421, United States embassy report, 10 September 1976, http://aad.archives.gov/aad/series-list.jsp?cat=WR43 (accessed 3 November 2011).

42. Nicholas Henderson, *Mandarin: The Diaries of an Ambassador 1969–1982* (London, 1994), p. 294, entry for 23 September 1979.

43. Ronald Reagan Presidential Library, European & Soviet Directorate, NSC (Thatcher Visit – December 84 [3] Box 90902; telephone interview with Dermot Nally, 22 October 2009, and interview with Lord Armstrong, London, 3 December 2009.

44. The support of the Irish Research Council for the Humanities and Social Sciences is gratefully acknowledged.

Chapter 12. **Labour and Europe: From No to Yes** by Stephen Collins

1. Tom Garvin, *News from a New Republic* (Dublin, 2010), pp. 14, 32.
2. Michael Gallagher, *The Labour Party in Transition* (Manchester, 1982), p. 50.
3. Brendan Halligan, interview with author, June 2011.
4. Brendan Halligan, interview with author, June 2011.
5. *Dáil Debates*, 23 June 1970.
6. Gallagher, *op. cit.*, p. 110.
7. *The Irish Times*, 1 March 1971.
8. Barry Desmond, *Finally and in Conclusion* (Dublin, 2000), p. 76.
9. *Dáil Debates*, 21 March 1972.
10. *Dáil Debates*, 22 March 1972.
11. Desmond, *op. cit.*, p. 74.
12. Conor Cruise O'Brien, *States of Ireland* (London, 1972), p. 273.
13. Gallagher, *op. cit.*, p. 115
14. Desmond, *op. cit.*, p. 77.
15. Garret FitzGerald, *All In A Life: An Autobiography* (Dublin, 1991), pp. 296–7.
16. Desmond, *op. cit.*, p. 78.
17. FitzGerald, *op. cit.*, p. 600.
18. *The Irish Times*, 14 May 1987.
19. *The Irish Times*, 20 May 1992.
20. *The Irish Times*, 26 May 1992.
21. *The Irish Times*, 6 June 1992.
22. *The Irish Times*, 17 June 2008.
23. *The Irish Times*, 4 February 2011.
24. *The Irish Times*, 5 September 2011.

Chapter 13. **Ireland's Journey to the Third Way: the hi-social model?** by Jane Suiter

1. Niamh Puirséil, *The Irish Labour Party, 1922–73* (Dublin, 2007), p. 6.
2. David Farrell, 'Ireland: a party system transformed?', David Broughton and Mark Donovan (eds), *Changing Party Systems in Western Europe* (London, 1999), p. 33.
3. Tom Garvin, *The Evolution of Irish Nationalist Politics*, (Dublin, 1981), pp. 1–6.
4. Michael Gallagher, *The Irish Labour Party in Transition 1957–1982* (Manchester, 1982), p. 253.

5. Stephen Driver and Luke Martell, *New Labour: Politics after Thatcherism* (Cambridge, 1998), p. 8.

6. Peter Mair and Michael Marsh, 'Political parties in electoral markets in post-war Ireland', Peter Mair, Wolfgang Müller and Fritz Plasser (eds), *Political Parties and Electoral Change: Party Responses to Electoral Markets* (London, 2004), p. 238.

7. *Dáil Debates*, 11 October 1961.

8. Puirséil, *op. cit.*, p. 12.

9. Gallagher, *op. cit.*, p. 78.

10. Labour Party Outline Policy (Dublin Irish Labour Party, 1969).

11. Gallagher, *op. cit.*, p. 199.

12. Gallagher, *op. cit.*, p. 81.

13. Fergus Finlay, *Snakes and Ladders* (Dublin, 1998), p. 23.

14. Mair and Marsh, *op. cit.*, pp. 240–1.

15. *Sunday Independent,* 3 January 2010.

16. *Dáil Debates, Vol. 306 No. 6,* 11 May 1978.

17. Gallagher, *op. cit.*, p. 264.

18. Finlay, *op. cit*, p. 61; Ray Kavanagh, *Spring, Summer and Fall: The Rise and Fall of the Labour Party* (Dublin, 2001), pp. 58–9.

19. Greg Sparks, interview with author, January 2011.

20. Ruairi Quinn, interview with author, January 2011.

21. Kavanagh, *op. cit.,* p. 187.

22. Kavanagh, *op. cit.,* p. 188.

23. Driver and Martell, *op. cit.,* p. 7.

24. Anthony Giddens, *The Third Way and its Critics* (Cambridge, 2000), p. 5.

25. Janet Newman, *Modernising Governance: New Labour, Policy and Society* (London, 2001), p. 41.

26. Giddens, *op. cit.*, p. 52.

27. Newman, *op. cit.*, p. 42.

28. Tony Blair and Gerhard Schröder, *Europe The Third Way*/Die Neue Mitte (1999), located at www.fcpp.org/publication.php/349.

29. Cited in Giddens, *op. cit.,* p. 5.

30. Newman, *op. cit.,* p. 41; Lionel Jospin, *Modern Socialism* (London, 1998), p. 5.

31. Newman, *op. cit.,* p. 2

32. C. Hay and M. Watson, '*Labour's Economic Policy: Studiously Courting* Competence', G. R. Taylor (ed.), *The Impact of New Labour* (London, 1999), p. 5.

33. *Financial Times*, 16 January 1997.

34. See https://netfiles.uiuc.edu/jchays/www/PS455/Readings/Schroeder-Blair-engl.pdf for the manifesto issued by Blair and Schröder setting out their views; and http://dissentmagazine.org/article/pdfs/Barkan-ThirdWay.pdf for a critique.

35. Kenneth Benoit & Michael Laver, 'Mapping the Irish Policy Space: Voter and Party Spaces in Preferential Elections', *Economic and Social Review* 36, 2, Summer/ Autumn (2005), pp. 83–108.

36. Rosie Meade, 'We hate it here, please let us stay! Irish social partnership and the community/voluntary sectors' conflicted experiences of recognition', *Critical Social Policy*, August 2005, Vol. 25, no. 3, pp. 349–73.

37. Eamon Gilmore addresses opening meeting of 21st-century Labour commission http://www.labour.ie/press/listing/1206782928575870.html

38. Grant Wyn, 'Globalisation, Big Business and the Blair Government', *CSGR Working Papers,* No 58/00, August 2000.

39. Driver and Martell, *op. cit.,* p. 41.

40. Andrew Glyn and Stewart Wood, 'Economic Policy under New Labour: How Social Democratic is the Blair Government?', *The Political Quarterly*, Vol. 72, Issue 1, January 2001, pp. 50–66.

41. *The Irish Times*, 7 April 2011.

42. Driver and Martell, *op. cit.,* p. 2.

43. http://labour.ie/press/listing/20060116174726.html

44. http://www.joanburton.ie/economy-jobs-finance/ireland-needs-a-clean-break-from-business-as-usual

45. http://www.joanburton.ie/economy-jobs-finance/ireland-needs-a-clean-break-from-business-as-usual

Chapter 14. **Labour and the Liberal Agenda** by Ivana Bacik

1. Niamh Puirséil, *The Irish Labour Party, 1922–73* (Dublin, 2007), p. 310.

2. Michael Holmes, 'The Irish Labour Party', Robert Ladrech and Philippe Marlière (eds), *Social Democratic Parties in the European Union: History, Organisation, Policies* (Basingstoke, 1999), p. 123.

3. John Horgan, *Noël Browne: Passionate Outsider* (Dublin, 2000), p. 129.

4. Michael Gallagher, *The Irish Labour Party in Transition 1957–82* (Dublin, 1982), p. 253.

5. John Horgan, *Labour: The Price of Power* (Dublin, 1986), p. 142.

6. Holmes, *op. cit.*, p. 124.

7. Stephen Collins, *Spring and the Labour Story* (Dublin, 1993), p. 39.

8. *Ibid.*, p. 45.

9. Horgan, *Labour*, p. 88.

10. *Ibid.*, p. 156.

11. Michael O'Sullivan, *Mary Robinson; The Life and Times of an Irish Liberal* (Dublin, 1993), p. 64.

12. Ailbhe Smyth, *Irish Women's Studies Reader* (Cork, 1993).

13. Linda Connolly, 'From Revolution to Devolution: Mapping the Contemporary Women's Movement in Ireland', Anne Byrne and Madeline Leonard (eds), *Women and Irish Society* (Belfast, 1997), p. 561.

14. John Horgan, *Mary Robinson – An Independent Voice* (Dublin, 1997), p. 103.

15. *Ibid.*, p. 104.

16. Tom Hesketh, *The Second Partitioning of Ireland* (Dublin, 1990).

17. Horgan, *Mary Robinson*, p. 106.

18. Ray Kavanagh, *Spring, Summer and Fall: The Rise and Fall of the Labour Party 1986–1999* (Dublin, 2001), p. 10.

19. Brendan Kennelly and Eilís Ward, 'The abortion referendums', Michael Gallagher and Michael Laver (eds), *How Ireland Voted 1992* (Dublin, 1993), p. 124.

20. Ruairi Quinn, *Straight Left: A Journey in Politics* (Dublin, 2005), pp. 334–5.

21. *Re Matrimonial Home bill* [1994] 1 IR 305.

22. *Ibid.*, pp. 335–6.

23. Ivana Bacik, *Kicking and Screaming: Dragging Ireland into the Twenty-first Century* (Dublin, 2004), p. 88.

BIBLIOGRAPHY

Chapter 1 **A Various and Contentious Country: Ireland in 1912** by William Murphy

Bew, Paul, *Ideology and the Irish Question: Ulster Unionism and Irish Nationalism 1912–1916* (Oxford, 1994)

Bowman, Timothy, *Carson's Army: The Ulster Volunteer Force, 1910–1922* (Manchester, 2007)

Campbell, Fergus, *Land and Revolution: Nationalist Politics in the West of Ireland 1891–1921* (Oxford, 2005)

Clarke, Frances, 'Mary Galway', James McGuire and James Quinn (eds), *Dictionary of Irish Biography, 4* (Cambridge, 2009)

Cousins, Mel, 'The Creation of Association: The National Insurance Act, 1911 and Approved Societies in Ireland', Jennifer Kelly and R.V. Comerford (eds), *Associational Culture in Ireland and Abroad* (Dublin, 2010)

Cullen Owens, Rosemary, *Smashing Times: A History of the Irish Women's Suffrage Movement 1889–1922* (Dublin, 1984)

Curtis, Jr, L. P., 'Ireland in 1914', *A New History of Ireland, VI: Ireland Under the Union 1870–1912* (Oxford, 1989)

Curtis, Maurice, *The Splendid Cause: The Catholic Action Movement in Irish in the Twentieth Century* (Dublin, 2009)

Daly, Mary E., *Dublin – The Deposed Capital: A Social and Economic History 1860–1914* (Cork, 1984)

Daly, Mary E., *The First Department: A History of the Department of Agriculture* (Dublin, 2002)

Duncan, Mark, 'The Camera and the Gael: The Early Photography of the GAA, 1884–1914', Mike Cronin, William Murphy and Paul Rouse (eds), *The Gaelic Athletic Association 1884–2009* (Dublin, 2009)

Ellmann, Richard, *James Joyce* (Oxford, 1959)

Ferriter, Diarmaid, *The Transformation of Ireland 1900–2000* (London, 2004)

Fitzpatrick, David, 'The Disappearance of the Irish Agricultural Labourer, 1841–1912', *Irish Economic and Social History, vii* (1980)

Fleischmann, Ruth, *Catholic Nationalism in the Irish Revival: A Study of Canon Sheehan 1852–1913* (London, 1997)

Foster, R. F., *W.B. Yeats: A Life. Volume 1* (Oxford, 1997)

Garnham, Neal, *Association Football and Society in Pre-partition Ireland* (Belfast, 2004)

Grimes, Brendan, *Irish Carnegie Libraries: A Catalogue and Architectural History* (Dublin, 1998)

Hay, Marnie, *Bulmer Hobson and the Nationalist Movement in Twentieth-Century Ireland* (Manchester, 2009)

Hepburn, A. C., *Catholic Belfast and Nationalist Ireland in the Era of Joe Devlin 1871–1934* (Oxford, 2008)

Holloway, Penny and Cradden, Terry, 'The Irish Trade Union Congress and Working Women, 1894–1914', *Saothar,* 23 (1998)

Jackson, Alvin, *Home Rule: An Irish History 1800–2000* (London, 2003)

Jones, Greta, *'Captain of all these men of death': The History of Tuberculosis in Nineteenth and Twentieth Century Ireland* (Amsterdam, 2001)

Kelly, Matthew, '"Parnell's Old Brigade": the Redmondite-Fenian nexus in the 1890s', *Irish Historical Studies, xxxiii, 130* (2002)

Kelly, M. J., *The Fenian Ideal and Irish Nationalism* (Woodbridge, 2006)

Kostick, Conor, *Revolution in Ireland: Popular Militancy 1917–1923* (Cork, 2009)

Laffan, Michael, *The Resurrection of Ireland: The Sinn Féin Party 1916–1923* (Cambridge, 1999)

Lane, Leeann, *Rosamond Jacob: Third Person Singular* (Dublin, 2010)

Larkin, Emmet, *James Larkin: Irish Labour Leader 1876–1947* (London, 1965)

Luddy, Maria, 'Working Women, Trade Unionism and Politics in Ireland 1830–1945', Fintan Lane and Donal Ó Drisceoil (eds), *Politics and the Irish Working Class, 1830–1945* (Basingstoke, 2005)

Lyons, Laura E., 'Of Orangemen and Green Theatres: The Ulster Literary Theatre's Regional Nationalism', Stephen Watt, Eileen Morgan, and Shakir Mustafa (eds), *A Century of Irish Drama: Widening the Stage* (Bloomington, 2000)

McConnel, James, '"Fenians at Westminster": the Edwardian Irish Parliamentary Party and the legacy of the New Departure', *Irish Historical Studies, xxxiv,* 133 (2004)

McKay, Enda, 'The Housing of the Rural Labourer, 1883–1916' in *Saothar,* 17 (1992)

McNulty, Eugene, *The Ulster Literary Theatre and the Northern Revival* (Cork, 2008)

Martin, Peter, *Censorship in the Two Irelands 1922–1939* (Dublin, 2006)

Maume, Patrick, *The Long Gestation: Irish Nationalist Life 1891–1918* (Dublin, 1999)

Mitchell, Arthur, *Labour in Irish Politics, 1890–1930* (Dublin, 1974)

Murphy, William, 'Suffragettes and the Transformation of Political Imprisonment in Ireland, 1912–1914', Louise Ryan and Margaret Ward (eds), *Irish Women and the Vote: Becoming Citizens* (Dublin, 2007)

Murphy, William, 'Narratives of Confinement: Fenians, Prisons and Writing, 1867–1916', Fearghal McGarry and James McConnel (eds), *The Black Hand of Republicanism: Fenianism in Modern Ireland* (Dublin, 2009)

Nevin, Donal, *James Connolly: 'A Full Life'* (Dublin, 2005)

Nolan, William (ed.), *The History of Dublin GAA, I* (Dublin, 2005)

O'Connor, Emmet, *A Labour History of Ireland 1824–1960* (Dublin, 1992)

O'Day, Alan, *Irish Home Rule 1867–1921* (Manchester, 1998)

O'Flaherty, Eamon, *Irish Historic Towns Atlas No. 21: Limerick* (Dublin, 2010)

Ó Grada, Cormac, *Ireland: A New Economic History 1780–1939* (Oxford, 1994)

Ó Grada, Cormac, '"The Greatest Blessing of All": The Old Age Pension in Ireland', *Past & Present, 175:1* (2002)

O'Neill, Marie, 'Sarah Cecilia Harrison: Artist and City Councillor', *Dublin Historical Record, 42:2* (1989)

Pugh, Martin, *The Pankhursts* (London, 2002)

Purvis, June, *Emmeline Pankhurst: A Biography* (London, 2002)

Rockett, Kevin, Luke Gibbons and John Hill (eds), *Cinema and Ireland* (Syracuse, 1988)

Vaughan, W. E., and Fitzpatrick, A. J., *Irish Historical Statistics: Population 1821–1971* (Dublin, 1978)

Wheatley, Michael, *Nationalism and the Irish Party: Provincial Ireland 1910–1916* (Oxford, 2005)

White, Lawrence William, 'Thomas Burke', James McGuire and James Quinn (eds), *Dictionary of Irish Biography, 2* (Cambridge, 2009)

Zimmermann, Marc, *The History of Dublin Cinemas* (Dublin, 2007)

Chapter 2. **A Divided House – the Irish Trades Union Congress and the Origins of the Irish Labour Party** by Rónán O'Brien

Boyle, J. W. (ed.), *Leaders and Workers* (Cork, 1978)

Boyle, J. W., *The Irish Labor Movement in the Nineteenth Century* (Washington, 1988)

Desmond, Barry, *No Workers' Republic: Reflections on Labour and Ireland 1913–1967* (Dublin, 2009)

Gallagher, Michael, *The Irish Labour Party in Transition 1957–82* (Dublin, 1982)

Gaughan, J. Anthony, *Thomas Johnson* (Dublin, 1980)

Kavanagh, Ray, *Labour from the Beginning* (Dublin, 1988)

Keogh, Dermot, *The Rise of the Irish Working Class* (Belfast, 1982)

King, Carla, *Michael Davitt* (Dublin, 2009)

Laffan, Michael, 'Labour Must Wait: Ireland's Conservative Revolution', P. J. Corish (ed.), *Radicals, Rebels & Establishments* (Belfast, 1985)

Lyons, F. S. L., *Ireland Since the Famine* (London, 1971)

Mitchell, Arthur, *Labour in Irish Politics* (New York, 1974)

Morrissey, Thomas J., *William O'Brien 1881–1968* (Dublin, 2007)

Nevin, Donal, *James Connolly: 'A Full Life'* (Dublin, 2006)

O'Day, Alan, *Irish Home Rule 1867–1921* (Manchester, 1988)

Puirséil, Niamh, *The Irish Labour Party, 1922–73* (Dublin, 2007)

Rumpf, E. & Hepburn, A. C., *Nationalism and Socialism in Twentieth Century Ireland* (New York, 1977)

Sheehan, Captain D. D., *Ireland Since Parnell* (London, 1921)

Walker, B. M. (ed.), *Parliamentary Election Results in Ireland, 1801–1922*, (Dublin, 1978)

Chapter 3. **In the Shadow of the National Question** by Michael Laffan

Gallagher, Michael, 'Socialism and the nationalist tradition in Ireland, 1798–1918', *Eire-Ireland*, 12, 2 (1977)

Gaughan, J. Anthony, *Thomas Johnson* (Dublin, 1980)

Kissane, Bill, *The Politics of the Irish Civil War* (Oxford, 2005)

Laffan, Michael, *The Resurrection of Ireland: The Sinn Féin Party, 1916–1923* (Cambridge, 1999)

Larkin, Emmet, *James Larkin: Irish Labour Leader, 1876–1947* (London, 1965)

Lane, Fintan and Ó Drisceoil, Donal (eds), *Politics and the Irish Working Class, 1830–1945* (Basingstoke, 2005)

McCabe, Conor, 'The Irish Labour Party and the 1920 local elections', *Saothar,* 35 (2010)

McConnel, James, 'The Irish parliamentary party, industrial relations, and the 1913 Lockout', *Saothar,* 28 (2003)

Mitchell, Arthur, *Labour in Irish Politics 1890–1930* (Dublin, 1973)

O'Connor, Emmet, *A Labour History of Ireland, 1824–1960* (Dublin, 1992)

Puirséil, Niamh, *The Irish Labour Party, 1922–1973* (Dublin, 2007)

Williams, Desmond (ed.), *The Irish Struggle, 1916–1926* (London, 1966)

Yeates, Padraig, *Lockout: Dublin 1913* (Dublin, 2000)

Chapter 4. **Labour and Dáil Éireann, 1922–1932** by Ciara Meehan

Gallagher, Michael, *Political Parties in the Republic of Ireland* (Dublin, 1985)

Gaughan, J. Anthony, *Thomas Johnson, 1872–1963: First Leader of the Labour Party in Dáil Éireann* (Dublin, 1980)

Laffan, Michael, *The Resurrection of Ireland: The Sinn Féin Party, 1916–1923* (Cambridge, 1999)

Lee, J. J., *Ireland 1912–1985: Politics and Society* (Cambridge, 1989)

Meehan, Ciara, *The Cosgrave Party: A History of Cumann na nGaedheal, 1923–33* (Dublin, 2010)

Mitchell, Arthur, *Labour in Irish Politics, 1890–1930: The Irish Labour Movement in an Age of Revolution* (Dublin, 1974)

Murphy, John A., *Ireland in the Twentieth Century* (Dublin, 1975)

Puirséil, Niamh, *The Irish Labour Party, 1922–73* (Dublin, 2007)

Sinnott, Richard, *Irish Voters Decide: Voting Behaviour in Elections and Referendums Since 1918* (Manchester, 1995)

Chapter 5. **Forging a Better World: Socialists and International Politics in the Early Twentieth Century** by William Mulligan

Eley, Geoff, *Forging Democracy. The History of the Left in Europe, 1850–2000* (Oxford, 2002)

Fridenson, Patrick (ed.), *The French Home Front, 1914–1918* (Providence, 1992)

Gregory, Adrian, *The Last Great War. British Society and the First World War* (Cambridge, 2008)

Gregory, Adrian, and Paseta, Senia (eds), *Ireland and the Great War. A War to Unite Us All?* (Manchester, 2002)

Jackson, Peter, 'French security policy and a British "continental commitment" after the First World War: a reassessment', *English Historical Review*, 126, 519 (2011)

Mawdsley, Evan, *The Russian Civil War* (Boston, 1987)

Nevin, David, *James Connolly. A Full Life* (Dublin, 2005)

Rioux, Jean-Pierre (ed.), *Jean Jaurès : Rallumer tous les soleils* (Paris, 2006)

Stargardt, Nicholas, *The German Idea of Militarism. Radical and Socialist Critics, 1866–1914* (Cambridge, 1994)

Thomas, Albert, *Dix ans d'Organisation Internationale de Travail* (Geneva, 1931)

Chapter 6. 'If it's socialism you want, join some other party': Labour and the Left by Niamh Puirséil

Browne, Noël, *Against the Tide* (Dublin, 1986)

Collins, Stephen, *Spring and the Labour Party* (Dublin, 1993)

Crossey, Ciaran and Monaghan, James, 'The Origins of Trotskyism in Ireland' *Revolutionary History* 6:2/3 (1996)

Desmond, Barry, *Finally and in Conclusion: A Political Memoir* (Dublin, 2000)

Dillon, Paul, 'Explaining the emergence, political impact and decline of the Labour Left, 1983–1992' (unpublished MA thesis, UCD, 2007)

English, Richard, *Radicals and the Republic: Socialist Republicanism in the Irish Free State 1925–37* (Oxford, 1994)

Finlay, Fergus, *Snakes and Ladders* (Dublin, 1998)

Gallagher, Michael, *The Irish Labour Party in Transition 1957–82* (Manchester, 1982)

Gallagher, Michael, *Political Parties in the Republic of Ireland* (Dublin, 1985)

Gallagher, Michael, 'The outcome', Michael Laver, Peter Mair and Richard Sinnott (eds), *How Ireland voted 1987* (Dublin, 1987)

Garvin, Tom, *The evolution of Irish Nationalist Politics* (Dublin, 1981)

Goodwillie, John, 'Lesser Marxist Movements in Ireland: a bibliography, 1934–84', *Saothar*, 11 (1986)

Horgan, John, *Labour: The Price of Power* (Dublin, 1986)

Inglis, Brian, *West Briton* (London, 1962)

Kavanagh, *Spring, Summer and Fall: the Rise and Fall of the Labour Party 1986–1999* (Dublin, 2001)

Kenny, Brian, *Joe Deasy: A Life on the Left* (Dublin, 1999)

Larkin, Emmet, 'Socialism and Catholicism in Ireland' *Church History* 33:4 (1964)

MacEoin, Uinseann, *Survivors* (Dublin, 1980)

McGarry, Fearghal, '"Catholics First, Politicians afterwards": The Labour Party and the Workers' Republic, 1936–9' *Saothar*, 25 (2000)

Nevin, Donal (ed.) *Lion of the Fold* (Dublin, 1998)

O'Connell, John, *Dr. John: Crusading Doctor and Politician* (Dublin, 1989)

O'Connor, Emmet, *Syndicalism in Ireland 1917–23* (Cork, 1988)

O'Connor, Emmet, *James Larkin* (Cork, 2002)

O'Connor, Emmet, *The Reds and the Green: Ireland, Russia and the Communist Internationals 1919–43* (Dublin, 2004)

Ó Drisceoil, Donal, *Peadar O'Donnell* (Cork, 2001)

Puirséil, Niamh, *The Irish Labour Party, 1922–73* (Dublin, 2007)

Puirséil, Niamh, 'Catholic Stakhanovites? Religion and the Irish Labour Party', Francis Devine, Fintan Lane and Niamh Puirséil (eds), *Essays in Irish Labour History* (Dublin, 2009)

Quinn, Ruairí, *Straight Left: A Journey in Politics* (Dublin, 2006)

Rafter, Kevin, *Democratic Left: The Life and Death of an Irish Political Party* (Dublin, 2011)

Sheehy Skeffington, Andrée, *Skeff: A Life of Owen Sheehy Skeffington 1909–70* (Dublin, 1991)

Thornley, David, 'The Development of the Irish Labour Movement' *Christus Rex* 1970

Whyte, J. H., *Church and State in Modern Ireland 1923–79* (Dublin, 1980)

Chapter 7. **Labour and the Pursuit of Power** by Paul Daly

Desmond, Barry, *No Workers' Republic! Reflections on Labour and Ireland 1913–1967* (Dublin, 2009)

Dunphy, Richard, *The Making of Fianna Fáil Power in Ireland* (Dublin, 1995)

Horgan, John, *Labour: The Price of Power* (Dublin, 1986)

Mitchell, Arthur, *Labour in Irish Politics* (Dublin, 1974)

Mair, Peter, *The Changing Irish Party System* (London, 1987)

Mair, Peter, 'Fianna Fáil, Labour and the Irish Party System', Michael Gallagher and Michael Laver (eds), *How Ireland Voted 1992* (Dublin, 1992)

Puirséil, Niamh, *The Irish Labour Party, 1922–73* (Dublin, 2007)

RTÉ Millward Brown Lansdowne Exit Poll (General Election 2011)

Chapter 8. **'No good Catholic can be a true Socialist': The Labour Party and the Catholic Church, 1922–52** by Diarmaid Ferriter

Barrington, Ruth, *Health Medicine and Politics in Ireland 1900–1970* (Dublin, 1987)

Cooney, John, *John Charles McQuaid: Ruler of Catholic Ireland* (Dublin, 1999)

Bolster, Angela, *The Knights of Saint Columbanus* (Dublin, 1979)

Canning, Bernard, *The Bishops of Ireland, 1870–1987* (Donegal, 1987)

Desmond, Barry, *No Worker's Republic! Reflections on Labour and Ireland 1913–67* (Dublin, 2009)

Ferriter, Diarmaid, *The Transformation of Ireland: 1900–2000* (London, 2004)

Ferriter, Diarmaid, *Judging Dev: A Reassessment of the Life and Legacy of Éamon de Valera* (Dublin, 2007)

Gallagher, Michael, *The Irish Labour Party in Transition, 1957–82* (Manchester, 1982)

Hutton, Seán, 'Labour in post-independent Ireland', Seán Hutton and Paul Stewart (eds), *Ireland's Histories: Aspects of State, Society and Ideology* (London, 1991)

Kenna, John, *James Everett: Trade Unionist to Government Minister* (Wicklow, 2011)

Laffan, Michael, '"Labour Must Wait": Ireland's Conservative Revolution', Patrick Corish (ed.), *Radicals, Rebels and Establishments* (Belfast, 1985)

McCullagh, David, *Makeshift Majority: The First Inter-party Government 1948–51* (Dublin, 1998)

McGarry, Fearghal, '"Catholics First and Politicians afterwards": The Labour Party and the Worker's Republic 1936–39', *Saothar*, 25 (2000)

McGuire, James and Quinn, James (eds), *Dictionary of Irish Biography: From the Earliest Times to the year 2002* (Cambridge, 2009)

Mitchell, Arthur, *Labour in Irish Politics: The Irish Labour Movement in an Age of Revolution* (Dublin, 1974)

Murray, Peter, 'Electoral Politics and the Dublin Working Class before the First World War', *Saothar,* 6 (1980)

Newsinger, James, 'As Catholic as the Pope: James Connolly and the Roman Catholic Church in Ireland', *Saothar*, 11 (1986)

O'Leary, Don, *Vocationalism and Social Catholicism in Twentieth Century Ireland: The search for a Christian social order* (Dublin, 2000)

Puirséil, Niamh, *The Irish Labour Party, 1922–73* (Dublin, 2007)

Quinn, Ruairi, *Straight Left: A Journey in Politics* (Dublin, 2005)

Whyte, John H., *Church and State in Modern Ireland, 1923–79* (Dublin, 1980)

Chapter 9. **'A particular view of what was possible': Labour in Government** by David McCullagh

Ahern, Bertie, *Bertie Ahern: The Autobiography* (London, 2009)

Desmond, Barry, *Finally and in Conclusion* (Dublin, 2000)

Duignan, Seán, *One Spin on the Merry-go-round,* (Dublin, 1995)

Fanning, Ronan, *The Irish Department of Finance, 1922–58* (Dublin, 1978)

Finlay, Fergus, *Snakes and Ladders* (Dublin, 1998)

Horgan, John, *Labour: The Price of Power* (Dublin, 1986)

Hussey, Gemma, *At the Cutting Edge: Cabinet Diaries* (Dublin, 1990)

McCullagh, David, *A Makeshift Majority* (Dublin, 1998)

McCullagh, David, *The Reluctant Taoiseach* (Dublin, 2010)

O'Byrnes, Stephen, *Hiding Behind a Face: Fine Gael under FitzGerald,* (Dublin, 1986)

O'Higgins, T. F., *A Double Life* (Dublin, 1996)

Puirséil, Niamh, *The Irish Labour Party, 1922–73* (Dublin, 2007)

Quinn, Ruairi, *Straight Left: A Life in Politics* (Dublin, 2005)

Reynolds, Albert, *Albert Reynolds: My Autobiography* (Dublin, 2010)

Chapter 10. **The promise of Socialism, Negative Campaigning and** *The Irish Times* by Kevin Rafter

Arnold, Bruce, 'Behind his cultivated stance', Andrew Whittaker (ed.), *Bright, Brilliant Days: Douglas Gageby and* The Irish Times (Dublin, 2006)

Chubb, Basil, *The Government and Politics of Ireland* (Dublin, 1992)

Downey, James, *In My Own Time: Inside Irish Politics and Society* (Dublin, 2009)

Fanagan, J. (ed.), *Belling the Cats: Selected Speeches and Articles of John Kelly* (Dublin, 1992)

Farrell, Brian, 'The Mass Media and the 1977 Campaign', H. R. Penniman (ed.), *Ireland at the Polls: The Dáil Elections of 1977* (Washington, 1978)

Ferriter, Diarmaid, *The Transformation of Ireland 1900–2000* (London, 2004)

FitzGerald, Garret, 'Presentation to the Brendan Corish Seminar', Brendan Halligan (ed.), *The Brendan Corish Seminar Proceedings, 11 March 2006* (Dublin, 2006)

Foster, Roy, *Modern Ireland 1600–1972* (London, 1989)

Halligan, Brendan (ed.), *The Complete Text of 'The New Republic' address by Brendan Corish T.D., Leader of the Labour Party* (Dublin, 1968)

Halligan, Brendan (ed.), *The Brendan Corish Seminar Proceedings, 11 March 2006* (Dublin, 2006)

Halligan, Brendan, 'Presentation to the Brendan Corish Seminar', Brendan Halligan (ed.), *The Brendan Corish Seminar Proceedings, 11 March 2006* (Dublin, 2006)

Horgan, John, *Labour: The Price of Power* (Dublin, 1986)

Horgan, John, 'Presentation to the Brendan Corish Seminar', Brendan Halligan (ed.), *The Brendan Corish Seminar Proceedings, 11 March 2006* (Dublin, 2006)

Kennedy, Geraldine, 'Appreciation', Andrew Whittaker (ed.), *Bright, Brilliant Days: Douglas Gageby and* The Irish Times (Dublin, 2006)

Keogh, Dermot, *Jack Lynch: A Biography* (Dublin, 2009)

Lee, J. J. *Ireland 1912–1985* (Cambridge, 1989)

Gallagher, Michael, *The Irish Labour Party in Transition, 1957–82* (Manchester, 1982)

Maye, Brian, *Fine Gael 1923–1987* (Dublin, 1993)

Mills, Michael, 'Presentation to the Brendan Corish Seminar', Brendan Halligan (ed.), *The Brendan Corish Seminar Proceedings, 11 March 2006* (Dublin, 2006)

O'Brien, Conor Cruise, *Memoir: My Life and Themes* (London, 1998)

O'Brien, Mark, *The Irish Times: A History* (Dublin, 2008)

O'Mahony, T. P., *Jack Lynch: A Biography* (Dublin, 1991)

Puirséil, Niamh, *The Irish Labour Party, 1922–73* (Dublin, 2007)

Walter, Annemarie and Vliegenthart, Rens, 'Negative Campaigning across Different Communication Channels: Different Ball Games', *International Journal of Press Politics*, 15(4): (2010)

Whittaker, Andrew (ed.), *Bright, Brilliant Days: Douglas Gageby and* The Irish Times (Dublin, 2006)

Chapter 11. **Labour and the Making of Irish Foreign Policy, 1973–77** by Eunan O'Halpin

Browne, Noël, *Against the Tide: An Autobiography* (Dublin, 1986)

Craig, Anthony, *Crisis of Confidence: Anglo-Irish relations in the early Troubles* (Dublin, 2010)

Desmond, Barry, *Finally and in Conclusion* (Dublin, 2000)

FitzGerald, Garret, *All in a Life: An Autobiography* (London, 1991)

Hanley, Brian and Millar, Scott, *The Lost Revolution: The Official IRA and the Workers' Party* (London, 2010)

Henderson, Nicholas, *Mandarin: The Diaries of an Ambassador 1969–1982* (London, 1994)

Horgan, John, *Noël Browne: Passionate Outsider* (Dublin, 2000)

Hussey, Gemma, *At the Cutting Edge: Cabinet Diaries 1982–198* (Dublin, 1990)

Johnston, R.W., *Century of Endeavour: A Biographical & Autobiographical View of the Twentieth Century in Ireland* (Dublin, 2003; 2nd ed., 2005)

Keenan Thomson, Tara, *Irish Women and Street Politics, 1956–1973* (Dublin, 2010)

McKittrick, David, et al., *Lost Lives: The stories of the men, women and children who died as a result of the Northern Ireland Troubles* (Edinburgh, 1999; 2nd ed., 2001)

Murphy, Gary, *Economic Realignment and the Politics of EEC Entry: Ireland, 1948–1972* (Dublin, 2003)

O'Connor, Emmet, *Reds and the Green: Ireland, Russia and the Communist Internationals 1919–43* (Dublin, 2004)

O'Donnell, Catherine, *Fianna Fáil, Irish Republicanism and the Northern Ireland Troubles, 1968–2005* (Dublin, 2007)

O'Donnell, Rory (ed.), *Europe: The Irish Experience* (Dublin, 2000)

Puirséil, Niamh, *The Irish Labour Party, 1922–73* (Dublin, 2003)

Szczerbiak, Aleks, and Taggart, Paul (eds), *Opposing Europe? The Comparative Party Politics of Euroscepticism: Vol. 1 Case Studies* (Oxford, 2008)

Treacy, Matt, *The IRA 1956–1969: Rethinking the Republic* (Manchester, 2011)

Chapter 12. **Labour and Europe: From No to Yes** by Stephen Collins

Collins, Stephen, *Spring and the Labour Story* (Dublin, 1993)

Desmond, Barry, *Finally and in Conclusion* (Dublin, 2000)

FitzGerald, Garret, *All In A Life: An Autobiography* (Dublin, 1991)

Gallagher, Michael, *The Labour Party in Transition* (Manchester, 1982)

Horgan, John, *Labour: The Price of Power* (Dublin, 1986)

Garvin, Tom, *News from a New Republic* (Dublin, 2010)

O'Brien, Conor Cruise, *States of Ireland* (London, 1972)

O'Leary, Cornelius, *Irish Elections 1918–1977* (Dublin 1979)

Chapter 13. **Ireland's Journey to the Third Way: the hi-social model?** by Jane Suiter

Benoit, Kenneth and Laver, Michael, 'Mapping the Irish Policy Space: Voter and Party Spaces in Preferential Elections', *Economic and Social Review* 36, 2, Summer/Autumn (2005)

Blair, Tony and Schröder, Gerhard, *Europe The Third Way*/Die Neue Mitte (1999), located at www.fcpp.org/publication.php/349

Collins, Liam and Keating, Justin, 'A "new wave" hero who got tangled in a political disaster' (*Sunday Independent,* 3 January 2010)

Corish, Brendan, *Dáil Debates* Vol. 192 No 52-53, 11 October 1961

Driver, Stephen and Martell, Luke, *New Labour: Politics after Thatcherism* (Cambridge, 1998)

Farrell, David, 'Ireland: a party system transformed?', David Broughton and Mark Donovan (eds), *Changing Party Systems in Western Europe* (London, 1999)

Finlay, Fergus, *Snakes and Ladders* (Dublin, 1998)

Gallagher, Michael, *The Irish Labour Party in Transition 1957–1982* (Manchester, 1982)

Garvin, Tom, *The Evolution of Irish Nationalist Politics*, (Dublin, 1981)

Giddens, Anthony, *The Third Way and its Critics* (Cambridge, 2000)

Glyn, Andrew and Wood, Stewart, 'Economic Policy under New Labour: How Social Democratic is the Blair Government?', *The Political Quarterly,* Vol. 72, Issue 1, January 2001

Grant, Wyn, 'Globalisation, Big Business and the Blair Government' *CSGR Working Papers,* No 58/00 August 2000

Hay, Colin and Watson, Matthew, 'Labour's Economic Policy: Studiously Courting Competence', G. R. Taylor (ed.), *The Impact of New Labour* (London, 1999)

Jospin, Lionel, *Modern Socialism* (London, 1998)

Kavanagh, Ray, *Spring, Summer and Fall: The Rise and Fall of the Labour Party* (Dublin, 2001)

Mair, Peter and Marsh, Michael, 'Political parties in electoral markets in post-war Ireland', Peter Mair, Wolfgang Müller and Fritz Plasser (eds), *Political Parties and Electoral Change: Party Responses to Electoral Markets* (London, 2004)

Meade, Rosie, 'We hate it here, please let us stay! Irish social partnership and the community/voluntary sectors' conflicted experiences of recognition', *Critical Social*

Policy, August 2005, Vol. 25, no. 3

Newman, Janet, *Modernising Governance: New Labour, Policy and Society* (London, 2001)

O'Regan, Michael, 'Ban on corporate donations to include trade unions', (*The Irish Times,* 7 April 2011)

Puirséil, Niamh, *The Irish Labour Party, 1922–73* (Dublin, 2007)

Quinn, Ruari, *Dáil Debates, Vol. 306 No. 6, 11 May 1978*

Chapter 14. **Labour and the Liberal Agenda** by Ivana Bacik

Bacik, Ivana, *Kicking and Screaming: Dragging Ireland into the Twenty-first Century* (Dublin, 2004)

Collins, Stephen, *Spring and the Labour Story* (Dublin, 1993)

Connolly, Linda, 'From Revolution to Devolution: Mapping the Contemporary Women's

Movement in Ireland', Anne Byrne and Madeline Leonard (eds), *Women and Irish Society* (Belfast, 1997)

Desmond, Barry, *Finally and in Conclusion: A Political Memoir* (Dublin, 2001)

Gallagher, Michael, *The Irish Labour Party in Transition 1957–82* (Dublin, 1982)

Hesketh, Tom, *The Second Partitioning of Ireland* (Dublin, 1990)

Holmes, Michael, 'The Irish Labour Party', Robert Ladrech and Philippe Marlière (eds), *Social Democratic Parties in the European Union: History, Organisation, Policies* (Basingstoke, 1999)

Horgan, John, *Labour: The Price of Power* (Dublin, 1986)

Horgan, John, *Mary Robinson: An Independent Voice* (Dublin, 1997)

Horgan, John, *Noël Browne: Passionate Outsider* (Dublin, 2000)

Kavanagh, Ray, *Spring, Summer and Fall: The Rise and Fall of the Labour Party 1986–1999* (Dublin, 2001)

Kennelly, Brendan and Ward, Eilís, 'The abortion referendums', in Michael Gallagher and Michael Laver (eds), *How Ireland Voted 1992* (Dublin, 1993)

O'Sullivan, Michael, *Mary Robinson: The Life and Times of an Irish Liberal* (Dublin, 1993)

Puirséil, Niamh, *The Irish Labour Party, 1922–73* (Dublin, 2007)

Quinn, Ruairi, *Straight Left: A Journey in Politics* (Dublin, 2005)

Smyth, Ailbhe, *Irish Women's Studies Reader* (Cork, 1993)

CONTRIBUTOR BIOGRAPHIES

William Murphy is a lecturer in Irish Studies at the Mater Dei Institute of Education, Dublin City University. He has written extensively on the political, social and cultural history of late nineteenth-century and twentieth-century Ireland.

Rónán O'Brien joined the Labour Party in 1989 while studying history and politics at University College Dublin. He was Chef de Cabinet to Ruairi Quinn TD as leader of the Labour Party between 1997 and 2002. He has a particular interest in early twentieth-century Irish history and has contributed a number of articles on this era to 'An Irishman's Diary' in *The Irish Times*.

Michael Laffan studied in University College Dublin, Trinity Hall Cambridge and the Institute for European History in Mainz. He lectured briefly in the University of East Anglia, Norwich, before taking up what proved to be a long-term post in University College Dublin. He lectured there for over three decades, served in various positions, including that of head of the School of History and Archives, and retired in 2010. He has lectured widely in Ireland and across the globe. From 2010–12 he was president of the Irish Historical Society. He has published widely on modern Irish history. His publications include *The Partition of Ireland* (Dublin, 1983) and *The Resurrection of Ireland: the Sinn Féin Party, 1916–23* (Cambridge, 1999), he edited *The Burden of German History, 1919–1945* (London, 1988), and he is currently writing a biography of W. T. Cosgrave. When that is complete he hopes to return to his research on Irish political funerals.

Ciara Meehan is a lecturer in history at University College Dublin. She is the author of *The Cosgrave Party: A History of Cumann na nGaedheal, 1923–33* (Royal Irish Academy, 2010). She is currently working on a book that explores the transformation of Irish politics and society between 1964 and 1987 through the lens of Declan Costello's Just Society and Garret FitzGerald's Constitutional Crusade, to be published by Palgrave Macmillan in 2013.

William Mulligan lectures in modern European history at University College Dublin. He is the author of *The Origins of the First World War* (Cambridge, 2010) and *The Creation of the Modern German Army* (Oxford, 2005).

Niamh Puirséil has written widely on Irish political and labour history. She is author of *The Irish Labour Party, 1922–1973* (Dublin, 2007), the first full-length scholarly history of the party. She was previously joint editor of *Saothar*, the journal of the Irish Labour History Society, and co-edited (with Fintan Lane and Francis Devine) *Essays in Irish Labour History: A Festschrift for Elizabeth and John W. Boyle* (Dublin, 2008).

Paul Daly is a graduate of University College Dublin and holds a Masters degree in Political Communication from Dublin City University. He formerly worked in the Labour Party Press Office. In November 2008 his book *Creating Ireland* – a history of Irish parliamentary debates – was published. He currently manages his own communications consultancy in Dublin and lectures part-time in Dublin City University.

Diarmaid Ferriter is Professor of Modern Irish History at University College Dublin and has published extensively on twentieth-century Irish history. His books include the bestsellers *The Transformation of Ireland 1900–2000* (London, 2004) and *Judging Dev: A Reassessment of the Life and Legacy of Éamon de Valera* (Dublin, 2007). His latest book is *Occasions of Sin: Sex and Society in Modern Ireland* (London, 2009). He is a regular broadcaster on RTÉ television and radio.

David McCullagh has been reporting on politics for over twenty years, first for the *Evening Press* and then for RTÉ, where he has been a Political Correspondent since 2001. He has a PhD in Politics from University College Dublin, and is the author of *A Makeshift Majority*, a history of the first Inter-Party Government (Dublin, 1998), and *The Reluctant Taoiseach,* a biography of John A. Costello (Dublin, 2010). He researches and presents 'Behind Closed Doors', an annual television documentary on the release of state papers under the thirty-year rule.

Kevin Rafter is the author of several books on Irish politics including histories of Fine Gael, Democratic Left and Sinn Féin. He is also the editor of *Irish Journalism before Independence: More a Disease than a Profession* (Manchester, 2011). Having previously worked as a political correspondent he is currently a senior lecturer in political communication and journalism at Dublin City University.

Eunan O'Halpin is Professor of Contemporary Irish History at Trinity College Dublin. His most recent book is *Spying on Ireland: British Intelligence and Irish Neutrality during the Second World War* (Oxford, 2008). He is currently preparing books on the dead of the Irish revolution, and on Afghanistan and the Second World War.

Stephen Collins is the political editor of *The Irish Times*. He has been a political journalist for over twenty years and was formerly the political editor of the *Sunday Tribune* and *The Sunday Press*, having started work as a journalist with the Irish Press Group. He has written a number of books on Irish politics, the most recent being *People, Politics and Power: From O'Connell to Ahern* (Dublin, 2007). His other books include *Breaking the Mould: How the PDs changed Irish Politics* (Dublin, 2005), *The Power Game: Ireland under Fianna Fáil* (Dublin, 2001), *The Cosgrave Legacy* (Dublin, 1996) and *Spring and the Labour Story* (Dublin, 1993). He was educated at Oatlands College, Mount Merrion, County Dublin, and University College Dublin where he graduated with a BA in History and Politics, and an MA in Politics.

Jane Suiter is a lecturer in Government at University College Cork. She is the author of several works on Irish party politics, elections and manifestos and is a board member of the Irish Election Study. Jane was previously a journalist working for a range of organisations from *The Irish Times*, where she was Economics Editor, to the Financial Times Group.

Ivana Bacik is a Labour Party senator and is Deputy Leader of Seanad Éireann. She is also the Reid Professor of Criminal Law, Criminology and Penology at Trinity College Dublin. She is a Senior Lecturer and also a Fellow of Trinity College (elected in 2005), and a practising barrister.

Eamon Gilmore is Tánaiste and leader of the Labour Party.

INDEX

242